Postcommunist Welfare States

Postcommunist Welfare States

Reform Politics in Russia
and Eastern Europe

Linda J. Cook

Cornell University Press
Ithaca and London

First published 2007 by Cornell University Press

Printed in the United States of America

Library of Congress Cataloging-in-Publication Data
Cook, Linda J.
   Postcommunist welfare states : reform politics in Russia and Eastern Europe / Linda J. Cook.
      p. cm.
   Includes bibliographical references and index.
   ISBN 978–0–8041–4526–2 (cloth : alk. paper)
   1. Public welfare—Russia (Federation)   2. Public welfare—Europe, Eastern.   3. Welfare state—Russia (Federation)   4. Welfare state—Europe, Eastern.   5. Post-communism—Russia (Federation)   6. Post-communism—Europe, Eastern.   7. Russia (Federation)—Politics and government—1991–   8. Europe, Eastern—politics and government—1989–   I. Title.

   HV315.15.c66   2007
   361.6'50947—dc22

                                                                2007018956

Cornell University Press strives to use environmentally responsible suppliers and materials to the fullest extent possible in the publishing of its books. Such materials include vegetable-based, low-VOC inks and acid-free papers that are recycled, totally chlorine-free, or partly composed of nonwood fibers. For further information, visit our website at www.cornellpress.cornell.edu.

Cloth printing   10 9 8 7 6 5 4 3 2 1

To
My Father, Roland A. Cook
and
the Memory of My Mother,
Anna L. (Herlihy) Cook
for their wisdom, support, and encouragement
always

Contents

Figures and Tables

Figures

Tables

Acknowledgments

This book is a product of years of research and study, and there are many people whose help and support I would like to acknowledge. First, I thank the social scientists in Moscow who have devoted their careers to studying Russia's social sector and who gave generously of their expertise and time to explain a reality that was often obscured as much as revealed by documents and statistics. Much of what I have understood I owe to them. I thought it best not to identify interviewees individually, but I very much appreciate the knowledge and help of everyone who spoke with me over the course of the research, including those from the research community, and from the Russian government, the World Bank, and other organizations.

Many colleagues have contributed to this work. I especially want to thank Sarah Oates, Sarah Brooks, and Judyth Twigg for their generosity in providing research materials that would otherwise have been inaccessible. I also thank the following scholars for reading and commenting on various parts of the draft: Sarah Brooks, Michael Cain, Gerald Easter, Stephan Haggard, Robert Kaufman, Conor O'Dwyer, Mitchell Orenstein, Thomas Remington, Marilyn and Dietrich Rueschemeyer, Barney Schwalberg, Richard Snyder, Barbara Stallings, Janet Vaillant, Kurt Weyland, Jeanne Wilson, and two anonymous reviewers for Cornell University Press. I have tried to respond to their insightful comments and critiques, which have led to many improvements in the manuscript. The final product remains my responsibility entirely.

Several institutions supported the research for this book. Here I acknowledge especially my department at Brown University for providing leave time to work on the manuscript. A two-year working group on Globalization and the Welfare State, directed by Dietrich Rueschemeyer at Brown University's Watson Institute, provided a critical source of ideas and inspiration for the project. Crucial parts of the writing were accomplished during a year as a senior scholar at the Davis Center for Russian and Eurasian Studies at Harvard University, directed by Timothy Colton. The National Council for Eurasian and East European Studies and the International Research and Exchanges Board provided support for research time as well as numerous trips to Moscow and Washington, D.C. Parts of the research were presented at conferences or seminars at the Davis Center, the Watson Institute, the Mershon Center at Ohio State University, and the Wilson Center for Scholars in Washington, D.C. Several research assistants, who have since gone on to bigger and better things, provided invaluable help: Tanya Abrams, Sava Savov, Matthew Crosston, Catherine (Sam) Johnson, Andrew Matheny, Sean Yom, Anna Rasulova, and most especially Gavril Bilev, who prepared all the figures and without whose assistance I could not have finished the project.

Sincere thanks go to my editor at Cornell Press, Roger Haydon, whose interest in the project from the outset greatly encouraged me, to his extraordinary assistant, Sara Ferguson, and to Teresa Jesionowski, for her abundant help in the editing process. To my colleague and friend, Elena Vinogradova, who has been my host in Moscow and aided my work in countless ways throughout, I am deeply grateful.

As he has from the time we first met, my husband Dan encouraged me to "inch along" and has given his support generously in so many ways. My greatest pleasure while writing has been in seeing our son David grow from a child into a young man with great intelligence, integrity, and enthusiasm for life. Finally, the book is dedicated to my father and to the memory of my mother.

L.J.C.

Postcommunist Welfare States

Introduction

Welfare States and Postcommunist Transitions

The postcommunist transitions that altered the political and economic systems of the Soviet Union and Eastern Europe had dramatic effects on their welfare states. As these countries moved into market transformation and deep recession in the early 1990s, their inherited systems of broad, basic social provision became financially unsustainable and ineffective. Governments were caught between preexisting commitments to provide welfare for their populations and intense pressures to restructure their economies, cut social expenditures, and adopt more market-conforming welfare models. This book looks at how governments in Russia and four other postcommunist states responded to these conflicting pressures as their centrally planned economies collapsed and market economies began to emerge. It asks how welfare state change was negotiated through transitional recessions and subsequent economic recoveries, and it compares the outcomes for welfare state structures, expenditure levels, and provision of social services, insurance, and protections.

For postcommunist states and societies, a great deal was at stake. Communist-era social sectors were fully administered and financed by states, which had eliminated markets and alternative sources of social provision. State-funded social services such as health and education, although comparatively of low quality, were nearly universally available. Social insurance, subsidized housing, and myriad other benefits and transfer payments were provided to broad populations and privileged groups. Communist welfare states faced high demand, and they were chronically underfinanced.

The situation had worsened significantly during the 1980s as economic growth across the region slowed and welfare performance deteriorated. Moreover, these welfare states were embedded in full-employment economies based on the centralized state planning and resource allocation that formed part of the communist developmental model. The transformation to market economies and privatization of production cut away their core by ending full-employment guarantees and greatly reducing states' control over allocations. In addition, deep economic recessions affected postcommunist economies during the 1990s, calling for programs of fiscal stabilization and substantial cuts in welfare expenditures. At various points in the decade, economic recovery eased these financial pressures on governments, but for the most part the old welfare models were no longer viable.

At the same time that they faced strong economic and structural pressures to cut back on welfare, postcommunist governments confronted potentially high political costs for doing so. Here there were three major problems: populations were state-dependent, popular attachments to the welfare state were strong, and organized stakeholders favored its maintenance. Communist systems had allowed almost no accumulation of personal wealth, and most savings were eliminated by inflation in the early 1990s. Pensioners and other recipients of transfer payments depended on the state—most had no alternative sources of income. Moreover, postcommunist populations remained strongly attached to public provision, sharing a broad sense that the state was responsible for accustomed social services and entitlements. The governments in newly democratizing postcommunist states had to be concerned about a possible political backlash against welfare cuts that could threaten their power as well as the broader reform program. Third, communist-era welfare states had produced organized stakeholders, social-sector elites and welfare bureaucracies with vested interests in public administration and financing of social welfare. Powerful stakeholders could try to block reforms or press for compensation. While some parts of communist-era publics and social-sector elites had become critical of the old welfare system and supported reform efforts, many resisted changes.

Most fundamentally, popular welfare, or the fulfillment of "crucial needs," was at stake in the postcommunist transition.[1] If reformers responded to economic pressures by dismantling statist structures and cutting

---

[1]   This term is used in Robert R. Kaufman and Joan Nelson, eds., *Crucial Needs, Weak Incentives: Social Sector Reform, Democratization, and Globalization in Latin America* (Baltimore: Johns Hopkins University Press, 2004) to refer to health and education because of their centrality to societal well-being and development.

entitlement programs, they risked leaving large parts of their populations without access to basic services or income. If they tried to keep the inherited welfare state in place, existing beneficiaries might retain some protection but overall deterioration of welfare provision seemed inevitable. Services and benefits could become seriously underfinanced, leading to declines and arrears in social payments, corruption among poorly paid service providers in health and education, and exclusion of low-income groups from access. Moreover, there would be no resources available to address pressing new social needs such as transition-induced unemployment and poverty.

On the face of it, the best strategy was to restructure the inherited welfare state, to create a new system of social provision that reduced and re-allocated spending. Reforms could be designed to rationalize social-service delivery, transfer responsibilities for social insurance to markets, and cut broad entitlements while refocusing expenditures on the poor. Such a reform strategy was advocated by domestic and international social policy and financial elites. These reformers promoted changes based on a liberal paradigm of reduced subsidies and entitlements, means testing, and privatization, changes that moved responsibilities for welfare provision away from the state and to individuals and markets.[2] But this strategy was difficult and demanding. It required governments that were already under severe stress to design and build consensus around a reform agenda, to overcome constituents' and stakeholders' opposition, and to build and regulate complex new welfare institutions. In addition, the costs would have to be transferred to populations whose incomes were falling, and poorly designed reforms could disorganize social sectors and worsen the allocation of scarce welfare resources.

In the event, postcommunist governments relied on different mixes of three strategies: dismantling statist welfare structures, keeping them in place with declining resources, or restructuring them according to a liberal model. These mixes, and the resulting trajectories of welfare state change, depended primarily on two sets of factors.

1. First, and more important, on the balance of political power between supporters and opponents of liberal reform in governmental, state, and party structures.
2. Second, on the capacities of postcommunist states to extract revenue, maintain administrative control over social sectors, and implement new market-conforming welfare models.

---

[2]   By *liberal* here, I mean a model that emphasizes market provision and individual responsibility for welfare and that de-emphasizes public provision and state responsibility.

No postcommunist society escaped the serious worsening of welfare indicators or sustained increases in poverty and inequality that resulted from economic contraction and structural changes. But governments' differing responses to the pressures and constraints of the transition had profound effects on how their welfare states were reshaped and how social costs were distributed.

I look, then, at the efforts of liberalizing governments to cut and reshape old welfare states and at the efforts of societal beneficiaries and statist stakeholders to preserve them. This book focuses on several central questions: Were powerful executives and finance ministries in postcommunist states able to impose social costs, to reduce welfare expenditures and restructure social provision, in the interests of stabilization, fiscal austerity, and/or technocratic rationalization? Did the societal beneficiaries of communist welfare states, such as public-sector workers, pensioners, and women who depended on state protections for access to labor markets, gain representation and contest retrenchment and restructuring? Did state-bureaucratic stakeholders defend public financing and administration against privatizing efforts?

POLITICS AND TRAJECTORIES OF WELFARE STATE CHANGE

In emphasizing political factors to explain differing trajectories of change, I am situating my book within the comparative welfare state literature which argues that politics matters.[3] This literature by no means ignores the significance of economic factors, but it argues that economic and financial pressures do not translate directly into welfare outcomes. Rather, politics mediates the effects of economics on welfare, largely determining the shape of expenditure cuts, how they are turned into distributive outcomes, and whether they produce deep structural changes in welfare states. This literature argues that welfare programs and

[3] See, for example, Duane Swank, *Global Capital, Political Institutions, and Policy Change in Developed Welfare States* (Cambridge, UK: Cambridge University Press, 2002); Paul Pierson, *Dismantling the Welfare State: Reagan, Thatcher, and the Politics of Retrenchment* (Cambridge, UK: Cambridge University Press, 1994); Paul Pierson, ed., *The New Politics of the Welfare State* (Oxford: Oxford University Press, 2001); Evelyne Huber and John D. Stephens, *Development and Crisis of the Welfare State: Parties and Policies in Global Markets* (Chicago: University of Chicago Press, 2001). For extensions of the argument to Latin America and East Europe, see Miguel Glatzer and Dietrich Rueschemeyer, eds., *Globalization and the Future of the Welfare State* (Pittsburgh: University of Pittsburgh Press, 2005); Gøsta Esping-Andersen, ed., *Welfare States in Transition: National Adaptations in the Global Economy* (London: Sage Publications, 1996).

entitlements produce constituencies with vested interests in maintaining them. Where such constituencies have relatively strong representation and influence, they can limit change. Benefit recipients, trade unions, public-sector organizations, and women's groups use political alliances and electoral feedback to resist cuts and negotiate compensation. Conversely, where liberalizing governments have more power and face fewer political constraints or veto actors, change is facilitated. If welfare state constituencies are strongly represented and governmental power is constrained, retrenchment may be limited and liberalization largely averted even in the face of strong economic pressures. If welfare constituencies are weakly represented and liberalizing governments face few constraints, retrenchment and liberalization may proceed. In sum, economic and financial pressures may dictate the need to scale back welfare states, but the scope and consequences are subject to political bargaining.

If one considers economic pressures as the central cause of liberalization and retrenchment, the patterns of change across the postcommunist welfare states appear puzzling. In the Russian Federation, the central subject of this book, the government's liberalizing reform program was blocked for most of the 1990s despite a deep and ongoing recession and market transformations. After a brief, early effort at reform, inherited welfare programs and structures were kept in place amid stagnant welfare effort (welfare spending as a percentage of GDP). They failed to translate into a new system of social provision even as the old system suffered from chronic breakdowns and corruption. Liberal restructuring proceeded only at the end of the 1990s, when the economy had begun to recover.

The transitional democracies in Poland and Hungary, by contrast, increased welfare effort significantly in the depths of their recessions. And although their recessions were much briefer and shallower than Russia's, they liberalized sooner, reforming their welfare states gradually through the 1990s.

The authoritarian post-Soviet governments in Kazakhstan and Belarus had similar trajectories of economic contraction and recovery but moved their welfare states in opposite directions. The first implemented deep retrenchment and radical liberalization; the second maintained welfare effort and statist structures. In sum, although economic pressure was the major factor fueling welfare state reform, the various cases show no straightforward relationship between such pressures and either welfare effort or liberalizing structural change. Economic determinist arguments cannot explain patterns of welfare state change. (See table I.1).

TABLE I.1
Contrasting welfare state outcomes in the postcommunist transition

Case	Russian Federation	Poland, Hungary	Kazakhstan	Belarus
Outcome	Delayed liberalization Low welfare effort	Gradual liberalization Moderate welfare effort	Rapid liberalization Low welfare effort	No liberalization Moderate welfare effort

A focus on politics helps to explain the differences, both across time in Russia and across the cases. Postcommunist political institutions in some cases empowered liberalizing governments and in other cases antirestructuring political and state interests. To discover how reformist and anti-reformist interests actually affected welfare, I look at who influenced decisions to cut, preserve, or restructure programs and entitlements across major areas of inherited welfare states—health and education, pensions and social security, social assistance, and labor protections—from 1990 to 2004. The analysis shows how differences in political institutions and shifts in political coalitions shaped changes in welfare state structures and spending.

The politics matters literature has concentrated mainly, although not exclusively, on the industrial democracies. I extend and adapt this conceptual framework to Russia and four additional postcommunist cases—Poland, Hungary, Kazakhstan, and Belarus—arguing that different political configurations in these states help to explain the variations in their welfare state trajectories. My analysis recognizes that democratic feedback mechanisms are much weaker in the postcommunist context and that downward economic pressures on welfare have been far more severe than in the industrial democracies. It adds that the statist welfare inheritance—the presence within postcommunist polities of large, inherited social-sector bureaucracies that rely on public provision and expenditures—produces an additional set of stakeholders that is much stronger than any counterpart in older democratic welfare states. The influence of these state-bureaucratic interests must be added into the political balance.

The Postcommunist Cases

I focus first on the Russian Federation during three periods with distinct institutional and political configurations: the immediate posttransition period of executive hegemony, a period of incipient democratization in the mid- to late 1990s, and a period of democratic decay and semi-authoritarianism beginning in 1999. The first period produced radical but poor-quality liberalization. During the second, the balance between liberalizing and anti-liberal state actors and legislative coalitions resulted in a disabling deadlock over welfare state change. In the third, political shifts enabled liberalization even as economic conditions improved and fiscal pressures eased. Societal interests mattered more than is generally assumed in Russia's welfare politics, especially in the mid-1990s. However, social-sector elites and statist welfare bureaucracies increasingly dominated negotiations over restructuring. The semi-authoritarian regime that emerged at the end of the decade produced a distinctive mediation process that provided political access and compensation mainly for elite and statist welfare interests. Broader societal constituencies were largely closed out, although popular opposition did constrain attempts to cut the most visible and tangible benefits.

I then extend the analysis to two sets of cases that stand at opposite ends of the postcommunist spectrum in terms of representativeness and the concentration of executive power. The first set, Poland and Hungary, became parliamentary democracies with more inclusive electoral and legislative institutions and less potential for concentration of political power than Russia. The second set, Kazakhstan and Belarus, became electoral-authoritarian or plebiscitary regimes with much more restrictive representative institutions and concentrated executive power than Russia.[4] Although the politics matters literature does not deal explicitly with differences in regime types, its analysis implies that retrenchment and liberalization should be more limited in the democratic states, where representative institutions are stronger and power is less concentrated, and should be more extensive in the authoritarian states. But many scholars argue that representative institutions across the postcommunist space are uniformly weak and unable to constrain change, implying that democratic politics should have little effect on welfare outcomes here.[5] The evidence presented in this book shows that democratic

---

[4]   For regime classification, see Larry Diamond, "Thinking about Hybrid Regimes," *Journal of Democracy* 13, no. 2 (2002): 21–35. Diamond classifies Belarus as competitive authoritarian and Kazakhstan as hegemonic electoral authoritarian.

[5]   See, for example, Marc Morje Howard, *The Weakness of Civil Society in Post-Communist Europe* (Cambridge, UK: Cambridge University Press, 2003); Stephen Crowley and David Ost, eds., *Workers after the Workers' State: Labor and Politics in Postcommunist Eastern Europe,* (Lanham: Rowman and Littlefield, 2001); Paul Kubicek, "Organized Labor in Postcommunist States: Will the Western Sun Set on It, Too?" *Comparative Politics* 32 (October 1999): 83–102; Steven Levitsky and Lucan Way, "Between a Shock and a Hard Place: The Dynamics of Labor-Backed Adjustment in Poland and Argentina," *Comparative Politics* 30, no. 2 (1998), 171–92. For a view that challenges prevailing concepts of a weak labor movement in Poland, see Maryjane Osa, "Contention and Democracy: Labor and Protest in Poland, 1989–1993," *Communist and Post-Communist Studies* 31, no. 1 (1998): 29–42.

representation and bargaining in Poland and Hungary *have* mattered for
maintaining welfare expenditures and moderating liberalization. Societal constraint here is considerably weaker than in European industrial
democracies but still quite significant.

Outcomes for the authoritarian cases prove more complicated.
Kazakhstan fits the theory's expectations for more extensive reform.
Liberalization and retrenchment were more rapid and deeper here than
in the democratic cases or semi-authoritarian Russia. In Kazakhstan, a
strong liberalizing executive excluded societal welfare constituencies
and weakened bureaucratic stakeholders, permitting radical reforms and
partial dismantling of the inherited welfare state. By contrast, Belarus
apparently contradicts the politics matters theory, maintaining an extensive welfare state and comparatively strong welfare effort despite the
weakness of societal influence. How can this difference be explained?

I argue that the influence of bureaucratic-statist welfare interests and
their place in executive coalitions have been the key factors influencing
welfare outcomes in both authoritarian states. In Kazakhstan the executive's power was increasingly based in the private energy economy, whereas
welfare and other state bureaucracies were politically marginalized. In
Belarus, by contrast, economic reform proved abortive and the inherited statist-bureaucratic structures remained strong, forming the base of
presidential power. The pressures to reform welfare provision during the
prolonged recession were blocked, and statist actors maintained nearly
unaltered welfare structures. Although my analysis places statist stakeholders and executive politics at the center of the explanation for welfare
state outcomes, two other explanations must be considered for Belarus.
First, some analysts argue that electoral-authoritarian regimes are subject
to limited electoral pressures for welfare maintenance, that plebiscitary
democracy encourages presidential populism and the continuation of old
social contracts.[6] Second, it might be argued that Belarus's abortive economic reform produced weaker structural pressures for welfare reform
than the more extensive market transformations in the other cases. I
address these challenges to my argument in the book's conclusion.

While I argue that domestic political institutions and coalitions are
central to the explanation of postcommunist welfare state change, state

[6]   Nita Rudra and Stephan Haggard, "Globalization, Democracy, and Effective Welfare
Spending in the Developing World," *Comparative Political Studies* 38, no. 9 (2005): 1015–49;
Andrew March, "From Leninism to Karimovism: Hegemony, Ideology, and Authoritarian
Legitimation," *Post-Soviet Affairs* 19, no. 4 (2003): 307–36.

capacity, a factor that is of marginal concern for industrial democracies, must be integrated into the analysis. During the transition, postcommunist states suffered varying degrees of deterioration in core state capacities to extract revenue and enforce compliance. Governments lost administrative control over parts of their economies and welfare states. Informal sectors grew to between 20 and 40 percent of GDP, and tax evasion became endemic.[7] When they attempted to restructure welfare, transitional states often could not implement the complex institutional changes needed to make new private welfare markets work. State capacity varied considerably across the five cases, acting as an enabling or disabling condition for effective welfare state reform.

DEFINING THE WELFARE STATE, RETRENCHMENT, AND LIBERALIZATION

In conceptualizing and categorizing welfare states, I largely follow Gøsta Esping-Andersen's classic formulation, defining them in terms of how much they spend; what they do; their institutional properties or programmatic content; and how they interact with the market and alternative private arrangements, both formal and informal.[8] Esping-Andersen distinguishes three broad types of welfare states: a universalist or social-democratic model that is broadly inclusive and equality-enhancing, a conservative model that preserves stratification and the traditional family, and a liberal model that contents itself with a residual safety net and deemphasizes public provision. The old communist welfare state combined a dominant universalism (i.e., broad social security coverage and access to basic social services) with stratified provision that better fits the conservative model. The liberal model captures well the direction of welfare state change in the contemporary world toward greater market conformity. Its key principles are the withdrawal of the state toward a residual role of providing for the poor and the replacement of public expenditures by privatized provision and social security markets. Its major features include:

- Means-tested poverty benefits as the major form of state social assistance.

[7] Janos Kornai, Stephan Haggard, and Robert R. Kaufman, eds., *Reforming the State: Fiscal and Welfare Reform in Post-Socialist Countries* (Cambridge, UK: Cambridge University Press, 2001), 276.
[8] Gøsta Esping-Andersen, *The Three Worlds of Welfare Capitalism.* (Princeton: Princeton University Press, 1990), chap. 1.

- Individual, contractual, and actuarially sound social insurance (i.e., medical, disability) provided in the market.
- A mandatory private, invested component in pension provision.
- Privatization and competition, user fees, and vouchers in health, education, and housing.
- Deregulated, flexible labor markets.
- Decentralization of social-sector financing and administration.[9]

Retrenchment is defined here as cutbacks in expenditure—cuts in benefits and entitlements that reduce payments or restrict eligibility but leave in place the basic principles of public financing and state responsibility. *Liberalization* means deep changes in the structures of the welfare state, the dismantling of public programs and administration and their replacement by social insurance markets and privatized social services. In their well-known book, *Development and Crisis of the Welfare State*, Evelyne Huber and John D. Stephens characterize the liberal model as "residual, partial, needs-based, [and] service-poor."[10] In the postcommunist context, liberalization entails sweeping institutional reconstruction and privatization of the welfare state, a shift of provision and responsibility from the public sector to individuals and markets. During the 1990s the liberal paradigm largely defined the terms of the debate over social policy in postcommunist states. Its proponents set the reform agenda.

I also pay attention to an important dimension of postcommunist developments that is not included in the standard welfare state models— the informalization and corruption of social sectors. As the transition progressed, shadow processes of distribution developed in social sectors. Control over social security funds was parcelized among state elites. Access to the extensive inherited networks of social facilities was, to varying degrees, "spontaneously privatized" by poorly paid service providers and elite professionals.[11] In the weaker states, particularly Russia and Kazakhstan, these practices became institutionalized, producing what I call informalized welfare states that were to a significant extent governed neither by state authorities nor by market principles.

---

[9]   Decentralization was not included in Esping-Andersen's model, but it has become part of liberal orthodoxy for the reform of centralized communist and import-substitution industrialization (ISI) welfare states.

[10]   Huber and Stephens, *Development*, 87.

[11]   For a discussion of broader processes of corruption in the Russian economy see Joel Hellman, Geraint Jones, and Daniel Kaufmann, "Seize the State, Seize the Day: State Capture, Corruptions, and Influence in Transition," (Washington, D.C.: World Bank Policy Research Working Paper No. 2444, Sept. 2000).

In sum, my book contributes to the comparative study of welfare states by extending the politics matters framework to the postcommunist context. This context is distinctive in three main aspects. First, democracy in the region is weaker than in the advanced industrial states for which the framework was developed, and the cases include semi- and nondemocratic regimes. Second, the postcommunist economic crises of the 1990s were deeper than any experienced in postwar Western Europe. Third, the statist welfare inheritance is considerably stronger here than elsewhere. The study of welfare reform under postcommunist conditions also adds to the standard liberal model a focus on informalization and corruption as key dimensions of contemporary welfare state change. I propose the category informalized welfare state to capture the mix of weak state and market regulation and informal mechanisms that emerged in the control and distribution of welfare resources.

INTERESTS, REPRESENTATION, AND THE WELFARE STATE

According to Esping-Andersen, "One of the most powerful conclusions in comparative research [on welfare states] is that political and institutional mechanisms of interest representation and political consensus-building matter tremendously in terms of managing welfare."[12] I begin with the major claims of this research as it relates to retrenchment and liberalization in the industrial democracies and to the much more limited treatment of Latin America. Power concentration or dispersion through institutional and constitutional structures also matters. Here I focus especially on the capacities of liberalizing executives to unify their governments around coherent reform strategies, as well as on the roles of veto actors that can block welfare state change.

There is a general consensus among political scientists that democratic welfare states built in strong political defenses. Welfare programs and entitlements create constituencies of beneficiaries, service providers, and administrators, who have vested interests in sustaining them. By the 1980s, almost half of the electorate in many industrial democracies received transfer or work income from the welfare state, producing dense interest group networks and strong popular attachments.[13] Welfare state

[12]   Esping-Andersen, *Welfare States in Transition,* 6.
[13]   They included the recipients of pensions, unemployment, and other benefits, as well as those employed in education, health, and social services; see Paul Pierson, "Coping with Permanent Austerity: Welfare State Restructuring in Affluent Democracies," in Pierson, *New Politics,* 412.

constituents built political alliances and used electoral rights to block
spending cuts and programmatic changes. Retrenchment proved especially difficult where it imposed tangible costs on large, concentrated
groups of voters. Overall, in democratic conditions social security systems were backed by powerful interest aggregations.[14] These interests
generally succeeded in defending entitlements even against strong
executives who were ideologically committed to welfare retrenchment
and privatization. Welfare states, in other words, were subject to democratic constraint; given broad coverage of core welfare programs, resistance to most entitlement cuts was widespread and for a time fairly
successful.

As evidence of welfare retrenchment in the industrial democracies
mounted from the 1980s, however, scholars recognized a crisis of the
welfare state and the weakening of democratic constraint. Economic
factors such as increasing global integration, trade expansion, and
especially capital mobility were producing downward economic pressures on governments to reduce expenditures and to liberalize social
provision. A theory of diminished democracy pointed to the
weakening ability of democratic institutions to sustain public policies
that departed from market-conforming principles.[15] But economic
determinist arguments proved inadequate; efforts to demonstrate the
independent effects of factors such as trade or capital mobility on welfare retrenchment produced inconsistent results.[16] Instead, a combination of economic pressures and domestic factors, especially high
unemployment and growing social expenses for aging populations,
seemed to be narrowing the field of political choice and forcing
reductions in entitlements.[17] At the same time, governments also increased social spending selectively to compensate politically influential groups for lost benefits or new risks brought by globalization

[14] Although trade unions and left parties have been seen as central to the creation
and expansion of Western welfare states, Pierson argues that union and left party strength
was no longer key to sustaining them. Rather, maturing social programs created their own
constituencies or bases of support.

[15] See Swank, *Global Capital.*

[16] See, for example, Geoffrey Garrett, *Partisan Politics in the Global Economy* (New York:
Cambridge University Press, 1998).

[17] Huber and Stephens argue, for example, that a combination of high unemployment, growing dependency ratios, capital mobility, and "conjunctural factors" such as the
economic disruptions brought on by the Soviet collapse and German unification contributed to a loss in policy-making discretion in the major European welfare states in the 1990s;
Huber and Stephens, *Development.*

(the compensation hypothesis), and the overall effects on welfare provision were ambiguous, differing across cases.[18]

One of the most promising approaches focused on political-institutional factors to help explain differing patterns of welfare state change. The institutionalist literature stressed that states responded differently to the pressures of globalization, that welfare state change followed distinct national trajectories. Some states retrenched more than others under similar economic constraints. More significantly, the deeper structural changes associated with globalization—privatization, radical social security cuts, and abandonment of programs—remained exceptional in established democracies. The different political and constitutional structures of states helped to explain the outcomes. According to Duane Swank, for example, "fundamentally, *political institutions determine the forms and quality of representation of domestic interests.* . . . [I]nstitutions provide (or restrict) opportunities for those that are adversely affected . . . to seek compensatory policies and for those ideologically opposed to—or materially harmed by—the common neo-liberal responses to globalization to resist unwanted policy change."[19] Democratic constraint, in sum, varied across polities.

According to the institutionalist analysis, two factors are central in explaining the different responses to pressures on welfare states in the industrial democracies: representation of interests and structures for labor bargaining. Where representative institutions are more inclusive, where electoral and political systems provide broad opportunities for the representation of societal interests, welfare states have been more strongly defended. Where representation is more restricted, for example by the single-member district (SMD) electoral system and majoritarian politics, defenses have been weaker. Social-corporatist structures for labor bargaining strengthen the representation of pro-welfare state interests, and the political alliance prospects available to labor are key to its influence. The organization of the preexisting welfare state also matters—universal and conservative systems that provide broader coverage are better defended than liberal systems. Universalism, a feature of communist welfare systems, in particular produces broad political coalitions and strong popular support for the maintenance of the welfare state. Liberal welfare states, by contrast, fragment interests and produce much weaker defenses.

[18] For a review of these arguments, see Miguel Glatzer and Dietrich Rueschemeyer, "An Introduction to the Problem," in Glatzer and Rueschemeyer, *Globalization and Future of Welfare States*, 1–22.

[19] Swank, *Global Capital*, 6, 35 (emphasis in original).

Political institutions and constellations of power also matter for welfare outcomes in Latin America. This region can provide particular insight into the postcommunist cases because its 1980s debt and economic crises more closely parallel the transitional recessions than do the relatively modest economic downturns in the industrial democracies. Latin American welfare systems also produced statist-bureaucratic welfare stakeholders more similar to those in the communist states.

The Latin American welfare states that developed during the period of import-substitution industrialization (ISI) were, overall, much less socially inclusive, more fragmented, and more inegalitarian than either their Western or Eastern European counterparts. They typically provided for the urban middle classes and for unionized and public-sector workers in the formal economy, excluding large portions of the poorer, rural, and informal-sector workers from benefits and social services. Welfare state and political institutions in the region did vary, however, and these differences strongly influenced the states' responses to the debt and economic crises. In polities with more inclusive and stronger representative institutions (i.e., Costa Rica and Uruguay) politically powerful defenders of the welfare state were able to maintain higher levels of public provision and universalism, despite pressures for retrenchment and restructuring that led to deep cuts elsewhere in the region. Here, too, politics functioned as a counterweight to globalizing pressures.[20]

Political institutions also shaped welfare outcomes during the later period of economic recovery and democratization in the 1990s. In Brazil, for example, weak representative institutions privileged elite and particularistic interests over the broader societal interests that are represented in developed democracies. Popular pressures for greater distributive equality during periods of economic growth were stymied, not mainly by economic constraints but by the lack of encompassing interest associations and the failure of political parties to represent popular aspirations. According to Kurt Weyland, "Weak party organization hindered the articulation of redistributive proposals in the electoral arena; narrow interest associations . . . [gave] better-off sectors direct access to the state to defend their privileges."[21] Although significant social reforms were implemented later under Fernando Cardoso, in

---

[20] Evelyn Huber, "Globalization and Social Policy Developments in Latin America," in Glatzer and Rueschemeyer, *Globalization and Future of Welfare States*, 75–105.

[21] Kurt Weyland, "Obstacles to Social Reform in Brazil's New Democracy," *Comparative Politics* 29, no. 1 (Oct. 1996): 1; see also Kurt Weyland, *Democracy without Equity: Failures of Reform in Brazil* (Pittsburgh: University of Pittsburgh Press, 1996).

the early democratic period the limits of representation preserved fragmentary welfare state benefits for elite constituencies against claims for greater universalism.

Interest Representation in the Postcommunist States:
Societal Welfare Constituencies and Statist Stakeholders

The transitional postcommunist countries combined welfare states that were structurally closer to the European mix of universalism and conservatism—although at a much lower real level of provision—with political institutions more like the Latin American, ranging from weak democracy to authoritarianism. Postcommunist states had mature social security systems, with virtually universal coverage of their labor forces by retirement pensions. More than 15 percent of employees worked in the social sectors, mainly in health and education.[22] Employment protections for both men and women were extensive. But unlike in Europe, and to at least some extent in Latin America, popular demand making had played almost no role in the construction of communist welfare states. Labor and political repression had prevented the formation of autonomous supporting interest groups in society.

Postcommunist political economies were characterized by strong popular attachments to the welfare state without dense societal interest-group networks that could defend it.[23] Societal welfare constituencies were relatively weak in these states. However, to the extent that they gained effective democratic rights and representation in the postcommunist period, some beneficiaries in the general population, public-sector unions, and professional associations found possibilities to defend their interests and bargain politically over welfare reform, to gain compensation, or to veto changes in welfare states.

More organized elite welfare stakeholders, including trade union leadership, social-sector administrators, welfare ministries, and other bureaucracies, had never been accountable to their rank and file or societies during the communist period. They held privileged positions in the welfare state. When the communist systems collapsed, these social-sector elites split into a reformist group of liberalizing technocrats who allied with executives and statist groups that defended the old system

[22]   See, for example, *Trud i Zaniatost' v Rossii: ofitsial'noe izdanie* (Moscow: Goskomstat Rossii, 2003), 187.

[23]   A wealth of survey and public opinion data attests to these attachments. See the discussion below in Chapter 1.

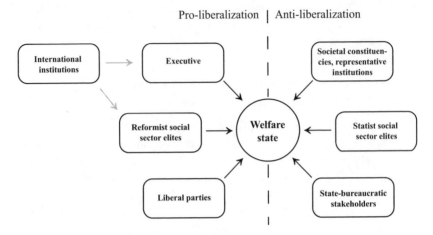

Figure I.1 Main actors in postcommunist welfare state reform

(figure I.1). Where statist stakeholders remained strong, they focused on preserving resources and prerogatives or on bargaining to have losses compensated through both formal and informal strategies.

Opportunities for influence by societal welfare constituencies and statist stakeholders varied across the postcommunist cases. Poland and Hungary featured relatively accountable labor organizations and political parties; statist elites were weakened by rapid economic and political reforms in these cases. Representative institutions were strongest in Poland, which had produced an independent labor movement and other autonomous organizations before the transition. In Russia during the mid-1990s, democratization also created possibilities for political parties and unions to defend claims on the welfare state and produced a polarizing deadlock over welfare policy. I compare the influence of political parties and unions in Russia and the two East Central European cases (Poland and Hungary) focusing on the political alliance prospects of labor and other organizations that defended the welfare state, the legislative roles of parties that favored welfare state maintenance, and the effects on welfare policy.

In the less democratic cases, the statist stakeholders tended to dominate defense of the welfare inheritance. In the semi-authoritarian conditions that developed in post-1999 Russia (as in the Brazilian polity characterized by Weyland) the weakness of representative institutions allowed narrow elite associations direct access to the state to defend their interests while broader societal constituencies were for the most part marginalized. In the electoral-authoritarian states Kazakhstan and Belarus, trade unions and political parties were subject to repression. The defense of the welfare state fell mainly to bureaucratic stakeholders and depended on their place in state structures and executives' coalitions.

LIBERALIZING EXECUTIVES AND THEIR ALLIES

The unity and concentration of executive power are key factors in success of liberal welfare state restructuring.[24] In the quintessential case of radical neo-liberal welfare state transformation, that of Chile under Augusto Pinochet, the extreme power concentration in the executive is understood to account for the rapidity and depth of reforms. Here the president, confronting an economic crisis, was able to push through change with little effective legislative or stakeholder resistance. Such effective liberalizing executives must be able to formulate policy and unify their governments around a reform project. According to Rossana Castiglioni's analysis of Chile, for example, "The extreme concentration of power in the figure of General Pinochet and the minister of finances, together with the presence of a highly cohesive monetarist technocratic team, explains the dramatic departure from the traditional system of social protection."[25]

In the postcommunist states, initiatives for welfare state restructuring came first and foremost from the executives. Committed to programs of macroeconomic stabilization and faced with sharp economic contractions and fiscal crises, executives sought to reduce state obligations and expenditures for welfare and to make spending more effective. Presidents, finance and economic development ministries, and technocratic reform teams advocated the liberalization and privatization of inherited welfare states. They were supported by reformist social policy elites, who had formulated programs of welfare state rationalization and modernization and who were appointed to head social-sector ministries and reform-oriented centers and think tanks. Pro-liberalization political parties in postcommunist legislatures, especially pro-presidential parties of power, also weighed in the pro-reform political balance.

[24] See, for example, Stephan Haggard and Robert Kaufman, *The Political Economy of Democratic Transitions* (Princeton: Princeton University Press, 1995).

[25] Rossana Castiglioni, "Welfare State Reform in Chile and Uruguay: Cross-Class Coalitions, Elite Ideology, and Veto Players" (paper prepared for delivery at the 2000 Meeting of the Latin American Studies Association, Miami, March 16–18, 2000), 27.

TABLE I.2
Main actors in domestic political-power balances for welfare state reform

Pro-reform (liberalizers)	Anti-reform (welfare state stakeholders, veto actors)
Executive Presidents, prime ministers Finance, economics ministers Reformist social-sector ministers Economic and social-sector reform teams Pro-executive political parties	*Societal constituencies, representative institutions:* Pro-welfare political parties Trade unions Public-sector employees (health, education, etc.) Public-sector professional associations Benefit recipients
Reformist social-sector elites, societal constituencies Liberal social-policy specialists, experts, governmental advisors Activist reformers within professions Liberal trade union elites Liberal political parties	*Statist social-sector elites* Elite professional associations
International institutions (contingent influence): Global social policy networks International financial institutions	*State-bureaucratic stakeholders:* Social-sector ministries State social-fund managers Social-sector administrators at central, regional, and local levels

The effectiveness of these pro-restructuring interests varied across the cases. Where executives had nearly unconstrained power, as in Russia during the early 1990s and Kazakhstan through most of the period, they could push through rapid, non-negotiated liberalization. Where power was disorganized and coordinating mechanisms were weak, even in formally strong presidencies, reform efforts accomplished little. Where power was dispersed under more democratic conditions, reforms had to be negotiated with the representatives of societal constituencies (table I.2). As in the more developed welfare states studied by Huber and Stephens, "Dispersion of political power enables potential losers to mobilize opposition and effectively resist cuts, whereas concentration of political power enables governments to implement cutbacks despite widespread political opposition."[26]

Veto Actors and Compensation Strategies

The presence or absence of veto actors in political systems also has strong effects on welfare state change. I consider as veto actors governmental,

---

[26]   Huber and Stephens, *Development*, 23.

state, and other collectives whose cooperation is necessary to legislate or implement welfare reforms.[27] The presence of multiple veto actors may enable the defenders of the welfare state to slow, blunt, or block reforms. Their absence, by contrast, facilitates retrenchment and rapid welfare state change. Where veto actors are present, their effects are influenced by the policy distance between major political actors such as the executive and legislature. Where the policy distance is modest, it may be negotiable, resulting in compromise or compensation. Where the policy distance is great, it can produce polarization or policy deadlock.

One group of organized stakeholders, social-sector ministries and state social fund managers (table I.2), played especially important veto roles within postcommunist states, blocking implementation of reforms after they had been legislated or decreed. Welfare ministries had vested interests in protecting their roles, resources, and clienteles against pressures to retrench, decentralize, and privatize. Threatened with displacement or reduced resources in a restructured system, they often defended the status quo. The permanent staffs of social ministries, in particular, could form effective veto groups with strong status-quo preferences, driven by the logics of bureaucratic self-preservation and supported by lower-level administrative bodies that were articulated through regional and local levels in postcommunist states.[28]

Powerful executives might place reformist leaderships at the tops of ministries, but those at lower levels tended to retain old orientations, modes of operation, and connections with elites in the sectors they oversaw. Ministries could try to reverse reforms, to dilute their effects, or to demand compensation. As Janos Kornai, Stephan Haggard, and Robert R. Kaufman argue in their study of postcommunist fiscal and welfare reforms, "The most important question is the extent to which reforms imply losses for groups with significant political power and the capacity to block their passage."[29] In dealing with these groups, compensation strategies must become an integral part of the overall welfare reform strategies. The efforts of bureaucratic stakeholders to veto reforms or gain compensation are a major part of the story of postcommunist welfare states.

---

[27] George Tsebelis, "Decision Making in Political Systems: Veto Players in Presidentialism, Parliamentarism, Multicameralism and Multipartyism," *British Journal of Political Science* 25 (1995): 289–325. I depart from Tsebelis in including actors that may veto implementation, not only those necessary to pass decisions, because implementation is critical in disorganized political systems with weak rule of law.

[28] Kaufman and Nelson, *Crucial Needs, Weak Incentives.*

[29] Kornai et al., *Reforming the State,* 13.

The Contingent Role of International Institutions

International financial institutions (IFIs) and global social policy net-works also sought influence over welfare state restructuring in postcom-munist states, providing both pressures and resources for liberalizing elites. The World Bank in particular promoted the dismantling of inher-ited welfare systems and the construction in their place of safety nets tar-geting the poor and unemployed. The Bank provided governments with extensive policy-planning assistance, sponsored projects in every sector of the welfare state, and provided hundreds of millions of dollars in policy-based loans that linked disbursement to reforms. The IFIs included wel-fare reform in fiscal stabilization packages that could lead to inflows of international credit and investment, which were the central concerns of finance and economic ministries. Reformist social policy elites estab-lished ties to global policy networks that advocated rationalization and decentralization in health, education, and other areas in order to deal with the rigidities and inefficiencies of inherited welfare states.[30]

The influence of international institutions on postcommunist welfare reform has been a subject of dispute among scholars. Bob Deacon, for example, argues that IFIs played a dominant role, that for these states during transition "the locus of key [social] policy decisions lies far from national governments and inside global banking organizations."[31] Other scholars also attribute a major influence to international organizations in explaining postcommunist social policy change.[32] On the other hand, many analysts contend that such international pressures are usu-ally thwarted by domestic actors, that ministries and politicians protect resource flows to themselves and their constituencies against external pressures for re-allocation.[33]

[30]   For the role of international influences in Latin American social policy reforms, which has been studied extensively, see, Kaufman and Nelson, *Crucial Needs, Weak Incentives*; Kurt Weyland, ed., *Learning from Foreign Models in Latin American Policy Reforms* (Baltimore: Johns Hopkins University Press, 2004).

[31]   Bob Deacon with Michelle Hulse and Paul Stubbs, *Global Social Policy: International Organizations and the Future of Welfare* (London: Sage, 1997), ix.

[32]   See, for example, Mitchell A. Orenstein and Martine R. Haas, "Globalization and the Future of Welfare States in Post-Communist East-Central European Countries," in Glatzer and Rueschemeyer, *Globalization and Future of Welfare States*, 130–52; Katharina Muller, *The Political Economy of Pension Reform in Central-Eastern Europe* (Cheltenham: Edward Elgar, 1999).

[33]   For representatives of this argument, see Wendy Hunter and David Brown, "World Bank Directives, Domestic Interests, and the Politics of Human Capital Investment in Latin America," *Comparative Political Studies* 33, no. 1 (2000): 113–43; Paul Mosley, Jane Harrigan and John Toye, *Aid and Power: The World Bank and Policy-Based Lending, vol. 1, Analysis and Policy Proposals* (New York: Routledge, 1991).

In this study, I pay attention to the influence of international institutions (including the World Bank's telling self-assessments of its successes and failures in postcommunist social-sector reform), but their influence is treated as contingent on the power of reformers in domestic politics. IFIs and other global actors relied on the cooperation of governments and the availability of like-minded governmental counterparts for access to domestic polities.[34] International institutions played an important role in defining the reform agenda, especially on means testing, pension privatization, and medical insurance. But their efforts were sometimes influential and sometimes thwarted, depending on the outcomes of domestic political struggles between advocates and opponents of reform. The evidence shows that in Russia and Eastern Europe IFIs had variable success, that in Kazakhstan they shaped much of the reform program, and that in Belarus they were largely excluded.

STATE CAPACITIES AND SOCIAL-LIBERAL VERSUS INFORMALIZED WELFARE STATES

As previously noted, state capacities declined during the postcommunist transition. Three aspects were especially important for welfare: the weakened powers of revenue extraction and distribution, the loss of administrative control over parts of the social sector, and the limited ability of postcommunist institutional systems to implement and regulate new market-based welfare models.

The state's ability to deliver programs of social welfare depends first on its capacity to penetrate its territory and implement decisions, particularly to extract revenues (tax) and redistribute them.[35] When a state's performance in taxing and delivering welfare to its population is dramatically lower than its own legislation and policies require, its capacities are weak. Postcommunist governments suffered from both tax evasion and weak control over the use of revenues that were collected. With the breakdown and diversification of state-administered economies starting in the late 1980s, the communist-era monitoring and control mechanisms were undermined. Tax administrations were left with limited

---

[34] Deacon et al., *Global Social Policy.*

[35] Michael Mann, *The Sources of Social Power,* vol. 11, *The Rise of Classes and Nation-States* (New York: Cambridge University Press, 1993); Joel S. Migdal, *Strong Societies and Weak States: State-Society Relations and State Capabilities in the Third World* (Princeton: Princeton University Press, 1998).

abilities to track transactions and financial flows in the new privatizing economies, even as high wage taxes were put in place to fund inherited social insurance programs. From the outset, evasion and strategies of minimal compliance were widespread, and varying proportions of post-communist economies moved into the informal sector. In the weaker states, Kazakhstan as well as Russia during the Yeltsin period, politically powerful economic actors or oligarchs penetrated the state, negotiating tax exemptions, privileges, and offsets. I examine taxing and fiscal capacities in the five cases during recession and economic recovery.

During the 1990s, most postcommunist states also lost administrative control over parts of their social sectors, producing varied levels of informality and corruption. Governments cut social-sector salaries while leaving most personnel in place, even expanding staffs. In response to low salaries, social-service providers crafted strategies of survival, establishing de facto private control over access to some health and education services and requiring shadow payments that closed out poorer strata. At the same time, the restructuring of social sectors involved institutionally complex changes that required new administrative and regulatory capacities. This was especially true for the postcommunist states, which sought to introduce social markets even as they established for the first time the financial and insurance markets in which social markets must be embedded.

Taxing capabilities, levels of informality and corruption in economies and social sectors, and regulatory capacities varied across the cases. As a consequence, all postcommunist welfare states mixed elements of state, market, and informal provision. But differences in state capacity in the end produced distinctive sets of welfare state outcomes: states with stronger capacities, Poland and Hungary, moved toward a more market-conforming social-liberal model; states with weaker taxing and regulatory capacities, Russia and Kazakhstan, moved toward an informalized welfare model featuring weak coverage, poorly regulated social security markets, and prevalent informal controls over access to welfare services. (The main features of communist, liberal, and informalized welfare states are shown in table 1.4.)

CASE SELECTION, METHODS, AND EVIDENCE

This study relies on structured within-case and across-case comparisons. I begin with the within-case comparison of three distinct periods in Russia's postcommunist political development to determine whether differences in representativeness and power concentration, key explanatory factors in the politics matters literature, can account for different welfare state outcomes. I then focus on four other cases, two democratic and two authoritarian, in order to maximize variation on the same political factors. Other factors that could explain divergent welfare outcomes, including prior welfare state structures and expenditures, levels of economic development, and differing intensities of transitional recessions, were controlled for as well as possible. At the end of the communist period all five cases had similar welfare state structures, featuring centrally administered, budget-financed, comprehensive though poor-quality, social provision. Welfare effort varied within a limited range; the best available pre-reform estimates are presented in Tables 1.1 and 5.3. In the late Soviet period all five fell within lower- or upper-middle income categories.[36] All followed postcommunist trajectories of transitional recession and then resumed growth and recovery (see figure 1.1). Recessions were comparatively mild in Poland and Hungary but much deeper in the three post-Soviet states.[37] At the same time, Kazakhstan and Belarus had the strongest recoveries among the postcommunist states with authoritarian outcomes, making them the most comparable economically.[38]

Case studies were designed to see whether the political strength of antirestructuring interests could restrain retrenchment and liberalization. The multiple pressures against maintaining inherited welfare states, including their comprehensiveness, the collapse of their structural underpinnings, and the intensity of downward economic pressures, make these "least likely" cases for the "politics matters" argument.[39]

The case studies rely on causal process-tracing, with the theoretical framework serving as an analytical guide.[40] I look at how the supporters and opponents of retrenchment and restructuring were situated within

[36]   In the late Soviet period, the World Bank ranked Hungary as consistently upper middle and Poland variously as upper or lower middle. In 1993, the first time that post-Soviet states were included, Russia and Belarus were ranked as upper middle and Kazakhstan as lower middle.

[37]   World Bank, *Transition: The First Ten Years: Analysis and Lessons for Eastern Europe and the Former Soviet Union* (Washington, DC: World Bank, 2002).

[38]   With the exception of Uzbekistan, which falls below the middle-income category; World Bank, *Transition: The First Ten Years*. 5.

[39]   For a discussion of the methods used, see Henry E. Brady and David Collier, eds., *Rethinking Social Inquiry: Diverse Tools, Shared Standards* (New York: Rowman and Littlefield, 2004).

[40]   See Alexander L. George and Andrew Bennett, *Case Studies and Theory Development in the Social Sciences* (Cambridge, Mass.: MIT Press, 2004) 205–33.

political institutions; who initiated efforts to cut, reform, or preserve the existing programs and entitlements across major areas of the welfare state; which actors and interests prevailed in political and bureaucratic struggles to legislate and implement reforms; and what the outcomes were for welfare state structures, expenditures, and provision.

The Russian case is based on a systematic study of governmental and legislative records, party programs, and other primary materials. It draws on more than one hundred interviews with social policy experts, legislators, and officials from social-sector and economic ministries and the World Bank's Moscow office, conducted during eight research trips to Moscow between 1993 and 2005. Interviews were open-ended, focusing on questions about the design and implementation of reforms and the sources of support or resistance. I was able to re-interview social policy experts, including some who were directly involved in the government's policy planning, at several points over the course of the transition.[41] The four additional country cases are based on documentary and secondary sources.

The five cases allow for an empirically rich account, especially the in-depth study of the Russian case, but the number of cases is too small for testing the causal weight of explanatory factors or making generalizable claims. My purposes, rather, are to present original research on little-studied welfare states, to integrate these cases into the broader theoretical discussion on politics and welfare, and to explore an innovative application of the politics matters theory.

THE ARGUMENT

In this section, I briefly lay out the book's argument, first for the three periods in Russia and then for the other four cases. In each I look at the strength of pro- and antireform interests in power constellations and explain how variations in these constellations as well as in state capacities broadly account for patterns of welfare state change and outcomes.

Three Stages of Welfare State Restructuring in Russia

In the first postcommunist stage (table I.3), 1991–1993, concentrated executive power facilitated very rapid welfare state change. Russia went through

[41] The study also makes limited use of twenty-six interviews with women Duma deputies, which were conducted for the author by the Levada Center, Moscow, in 2004, and several interviews with health-sector specialists, conducted independently by Judyth Twigg in 1997.

TABLE I.3
Three stages of welfare state restructuring in the Russian Federation

Stage	Executive	Representation of welfare stakeholders	Policy process	Outcome
1. 1991–1993	Strong liberalizing executive	No effective representation of statist or societal welfare interests	Non-negotiated liberalization	Unconstrained policy change
2. 1994–1999	Moderate liberalizing executive	Representation of statist and societal welfare interests; ministries and legislature play veto role	Contested liberalization	Policy deadlock
3. 2000–2004	Strong liberalizing executive	Representation of statist elite and bureaucratic interests; bargain for institutional Interests	Liberalization negotiated within elite	Policy change with elite compensation

a period of virtually uncontested or non-negotiated welfare state liberalization that has no counterpart in democratic systems. Policy power in the social sphere was assigned to insulated technocrats, who were placed in key ministerial positions in a unified radical-liberal government. Welfare state interests, including elite and statist stakeholders, were disorganized by the massive institutional breakdown of state structures and had minimal representation or influence. President Boris Yeltsin largely ignored the protests of the legislature against his reforms and, in the end, forcibly dissolved it.

During this period, liberal reformers and technocratic elites were responding to the deep economic shock of transition and a severe fiscal crisis. They eliminated massive subsidy programs and fundamentally reorganized the welfare state, decentralizing health and education, introducing privatization and insurance mechanisms, and off-loading social security obligations from the federal budget. Many of these unilateral policy decisions were poorly implemented or failed, partly because of weak state capacities, but they did withdraw the federal government from large areas of social provision and initiate the liberalization of the Russian welfare state.[42] In chapter 2, I show that they contributed to

---

[42]   The Russian polity in this period may be classified as a delegative democracy, a system characterized by low-quality policy; see Guillermo O'Donnell, "Delegative Democracy," *Journal of Democracy* 5, no. 1 (1994): 55–69.

increases in poverty and inequality and to growing regional and income disparities in access to health and educational services. These radical reforms of the early 1990s illustrate the potential for rapid welfare state liberalization by a strong executive facing neither effective democratic constraints nor bureaucratic veto actors, a pattern that is repeated in Kazakhstan throughout the postcommunist period.

In the second stage (table I.3), 1994–1999, the Russian polity underwent a process of incipient democratization that allowed some representation of pro-welfare interests. Presidentialism and electoralism remained central and most formal democratic institutions remained shallow, but, as Michael McFaul characterizes the changes, "the core of a multiparty system emerged within the Russian parliament."[43] Political parties and the lower house of the legislature (the Duma) took on a limited representative function and transformed the politics of welfare. Societal welfare state constituencies supported legislative parties such as Women of Russia and Yabloko, which pursued a moderate reformist policy, seeking to preserve social protections and public-sector spending. Health and especially education workers engaged in activism on a significant scale, becoming the most strike-prone sector of Russia's labor force. Chapter three focuses on the political alliances built by trade unions, the representation of women's interests in the Duma, and social-sector strikes. I show that the passivity of these groups in the face of retrenchment and liberalization has often been exaggerated. Significant numbers did mobilize through new political institutions, but they remained too weak and politically fragmented to play a major role.

The major legislative opposition to restructuring emerged instead from the hard left. Communist successor parties that were supported electorally by diffuse groups of older, poorer, and more state-dependent Russians, especially pensioners, formed a dominant legislative coalition in the mid-1990s. Their agenda was to restore the communist-era welfare state rather than to negotiate reform. The legislature became a key veto actor, refusing to approve changes in the core legislative base of the old welfare state. The executive and legislature polarized over welfare reform, producing policy deadlock. Executive power was also weakened during this period. Although his constitutional mandate remained strong, Yeltsin failed to unify his cabinet around welfare restructuring, ministerial leadership was highly unstable, and technocratic liberalizers lost power to statist

---

[43]   Michael McFaul, "Explaining Party Formation and Non-Formation in Russia: Actors, Institutions, and Choice," *Comparative Political Studies* 34, no. 10 (2001): 1171.

elites. The social-sector ministries also emerged as veto actors, waging a rear-guard campaign against destatization and privatization, dividing the government. Growing federalization fragmented the state. Multiple veto actors—the legislature, state welfare administrators, and regional authorities—slowed, blocked, or blunted restructuring efforts.

In sum, the balance of political and bureaucratic power shifted against liberalization, locking much of the old welfare state in place despite a severe economic decline that lasted until 1999. Politics blocked the adjustment of welfare state structures to new economic constraints, producing an incoherent policy of retrenchment without restructuring that led to the decay and corruption of Russia's welfare state. Like the broader economy, the welfare state underwent a process of informalization, spontaneous privatization, and parcelization of control over social security funds and social assets.

At the end of the 1990s, another major shift in domestic political constellations and strengthening of state capacities created enabling conditions for welfare state liberalization in Russia. A shift toward a pro-executive legislative coalition in the December 1999 Duma elections ended the left's dominance and the legislature's veto role. A deeper change in the political system, to managed democracy and presidential dominance, brought a decay in the representative function of political parties.[44] Established parties, both reformist and hard left, were replaced with new parties that had shallow roots in the electorate and very weak programmatic commitments. Their control of the legislature greatly lessened political and societal constraints on welfare state change. At the same time, Vladimir Putin unified the government, building consensus around a liberalized welfare state reform model. In sum, limits in representative institutions combined with the consolidation of executive power to enable liberalization.

In the third stage (table I.3), between 2000 and 2004, the Duma approved changes in the legislative base across most areas of the welfare state, shifting direction from a decayed statist model toward a more market-conforming one. It reformed the pension system, passed major legislation on housing privatization and deregulation of labor markets, and initiated further marketizing changes in the health and education sectors. Only the broadest and most visible benefit cuts were resisted by the legislature for fear of popular response.[45] Liberalizing policies

[44]   Timothy J. Colton and Michael McFaul, *Popular Choice and Managed Democracy: The Russian Elections of 1999 and 2000* (Washington, D.C.: Brookings, 2003).

[45]   This is in line with Pierson's thesis that broadly visible and tangible benefit cuts prove the most difficult; see Pierson, *Dismantling the Welfare State* (1994).

were legislated during a period of strong and sustained economic recovery. But this was not a return to the non-negotiated liberalization of the initial transition period, shaped by a nearly unconstrained executive and insulated technocrats. Although democratic decay restricted the representation of broader societal interests, social-sector elites and state-based bureaucratic stakeholders retained influence over welfare politics. Managed democracy produced its own distinctive mediation process of liberalization negotiated within the elite, a process that accommodated and compensated social-sector elite and bureaucratic interests.

As I show in chapter 4, trade union leaders and university rectors' associations negotiated to protect their privileged positions, social-sector ministries were appeased by compensation strategies, and the Pension Fund's war with the Economic Development Ministry produced compromise over pension privatization. Societal interests did continue to impose some constraint on those reforms with the broadest and most tangible effects, cuts in social subsidies and benefits, requiring the government to adopt a strategy of chipping away. In most areas of the social sector, however, politics became less about the welfare function of the state and more about the competing interests of elite and state-based actors in controlling pools of social security funds, access to social institutions, and other social-sector resources.

Comparative Cases, Democratic and Authoritarian

Welfare state liberalization also proceeded in Poland and Hungary during the 1990s. Welfare constituencies were weaker than in the European industrial democracies, but retrenchment and restructuring efforts were subject to democratic bargaining. As a result, even in the depths of transitional recessions some societal constituencies gained compensation for welfare losses, and the process of liberalization was gradual and negotiated, involving much more societal representation, contestation, and compromise than in Russia. Moreover, state capacities weakened considerably less than in Russia. As I discuss in chapter 5, stronger, more democratic trade unions; more stable, moderate, and socially oriented political parties; and stronger governmental accountability gave societal constituencies greater possibilities for representation. And once their economies recovered, the east-central European states stabilized at higher levels of welfare state effort and lower levels of corruption and informality than Russia.

Political fragmentation and polarization were also much more limited in Poland and Hungary. For most of the period, power was coordinated through parliamentary mechanisms and legislatures were dominated by right and left centrist political coalitions that compromised on welfare state change. Bureaucratic welfare stakeholders did resist reforms, but the dispersion of power away from the state in the democratic transitions had greatly lessened their influence. Welfare constituencies were weaker and less organized in Hungary than in Poland, and liberalization and retrenchment went further, but the similarities between the cases outweigh the differences.

In the authoritarian states of Belarus and Kazakhstan, apparently similar authoritarian political institutions produced different welfare outcomes, mainly because of the differing power of bureaucratic welfare stakeholders within those institutions. As I discuss in chapter 5, in Belarus executive power relied on inherited state and collectivist economic-administrative structures and state capacities remained comparatively strong. The executive, postcommunist parties in the legislature, and state-based welfare bureaucrats combined to preserve old structures despite deep economic recession and some social discontent.

In Kazakhstan, by contrast, executive power relied on economic-oligarchic elites that favored liberalization. There was extreme polarization between the liberalizing executive and the communist-dominated legislature, but the legislature proved virtually powerless and statist elites nearly so. State capacities suffered severe declines. In Kazakhstan, liberalizing elites succeeded much more quickly and deeply than in Russia. In both states, extended periods of economic growth coincided with continued low welfare effort and high levels of privatization, informalization, and corruption.

CONCLUSION

There is considerable evidence that politics did matter as postcommunist governments sought to resolve the conflicts between old welfare commitments and the demands of market transformation. Economic pressures were strongly mediated by domestic factors, especially states' levels of democratization and the balance between supporters and opponents of welfare liberalization. Although all retrenched and most liberalized, their trajectories varied, with political institutions and coalitions prominent among the reasons. Domestic and international promoters of liberalization proved most effective where representative institutions were weak and executive power was strong. On the other hand, even relatively weak democratic institutions provided the means for societal constituencies to gain compensation for welfare losses and moderate or block liberalizing changes.

At the same time, my research suggests both a limitation and a modification of the politics matters approach. First, the theory's focus on formal political institutions and actors misses processes of corruption and informalization that have been important in the postcommunist context. Especially where states are weak and recessions prolonged, actual developments in social sectors may become disconnected from both politics and markets and may be determined partly by spontaneous and localized processes. My research also suggests a need for more focus on statist-bureaucratic interests when there is an inheritance of large, centralized welfare systems. For the semi-authoritarian cases, bureaucratic stakeholders mattered more than societal constituencies in defending welfare claims and shaping policy during transitions. The case studies provide evidence for both of these points, and I return to a discussion of them in the conclusion.

1

Old Welfare State Structures and Reform Strategies

Communist-era welfare states were part of a distinctive developmental model that gave them unique features. Communist state bureaucracies controlled and planned their economies, allocating most material and human resources. The model entailed much more comprehensive and intrusive employment and income policies than are found in Western Europe, Latin America, and other regions. It maintained full employment and kept wages low and income differentials narrow. Planning authorities set prices according to state priorities rather than costs, privileging heavy industry and defense while subsidizing and cross-subsidizing both production and consumption. Legal private markets and private productive assets were largely prohibited, and the system was protected from international markets as well as competitive pressures.[1] Economic growth was based on an extensive strategy that mobilized increasing supplies of labor, energy, and materials at comparatively low levels of efficiency and productivity. Developed in the Soviet Union during the 1930s and extended to Eastern Europe in the aftermath of World War II, this model, despite its overcentralization and inefficiencies, produced steady and at times impressive increases in GDP until the mid-1970s.

---

[1] The major exceptions to communist-era prohibitions on private markets and productive assets were the maintenance of large-scale private agricultural holdings in Poland throughout the communist period and the legalization of limited markets by the New Economic Mechanism in Hungary from 1968.

A comprehensive, state-controlled, and budget-financed system of welfare provision was embedded in the communist development model. Soviet planners first constructed this system in the 1930s to meet the industrializing state's needs for human capital and political control. Communist governments later expanded it to Eastern Europe, where pre-existing private providers and social insurance schemes were forced out or absorbed into the state system. During the 1960s and 1970s, communist welfare states reached the peak of their development, extending over rural populations and steadily increasing expenditures and entitlements. States provided basic health care and education, pensions and other types of social insurance, housing, family benefits, and social goods at artificially low prices. Communist welfare states expanded as part of a social contract that was intended to help secure the acquiescence of societies to authoritarian political controls and in response to pressures from state social bureaucracies for increased allocations in growing communist economies.[2]

Levels and quality of welfare provision were quite low by Western standards, and the bureaucratic planning process built in rigidities and inefficiencies. Social service facilities were overstaffed and underequipped, and housing and subsidized goods were in chronic shortage. At the same time, communist welfare states were considerably more comprehensive and egalitarian than those in other non-Western systems. According to Haggard and Kaufman's recent study, at full development East European welfare states were "generous by comparison with other regions and exhibit[ed] strong similarities *within* the region . . . set . . . apart from both the stratified welfare systems in Latin America and the very small public welfare systems established in East Asia."[3] Their strength was in breadth of coverage and the satisfaction of basic needs.

By the end of the 1980s, communist economies had exhausted their potential for innovation and growth and were collapsing. New leaderships turned to programs of marketizing reform that had two key objectives. The first was to facilitate economic transformation by privatizing production and liberalizing prices and trade, measures that would bring an end to full employment and most subsidies. The second objective was to stabilize

---

[2]   Linda J. Cook, *The Soviet Social Contract and Why It Failed: Welfare Policy and Workers' Politics from Brezhnev to Yeltsin* (Cambridge, Mass.: Harvard University Press, 1993); for Eastern Europe, see Stephan Haggard and Robert Kaufman, "Revising Social Contracts: The Political Economy of Welfare Reform in Latin America, East Asia and Central Europe" (draft manuscript, October 2006), chap. 5, 17–20.

[3]   Haggard and Kaufman, "Revising Social Contracts," chap. 5, 40, 51. The quotation refers specifically to East Central Europe but may be applied in a more limited way to communist welfare states generally.

economies that had fallen into deep recession and confronted fiscal crises. Stabilization demanded reductions in fiscal burdens that would weaken the financial base for welfare provision. Transitional economies, in sum, could neither afford inherited welfare states nor sustain them structurally.

This chapter looks at the structure and financing of communist-era welfare states, the pressures on welfare provision caused by transitional recessions and market transformations, and the welfare reform strategies that postcommunist governments adopted. It sets the stage for the political contestation and negotiation over welfare state change that is the book's main subject.

STRUCTURE AND FINANCING OF THE INHERITED WELFARE STATE

Although communist-era welfare states differed in some significant respects, there was broad uniformity across the region. The following discussion applies to all five cases included in this book, with the most important variations among them covered in the concluding section.

Social Services and Subsidies

Communist states financed comprehensive systems of preschool, primary, and secondary education that were run by central ministries. The early decades of welfare state development brought dramatic improvements in educational attainment, including both rural-urban and gender equality, throughout the region. In the Russian Republic, for example, literacy rates increased from 61 percent overall in 1926 to 90 percent in 1939 and 99 percent in 1959.[4] In Eastern Europe as well, school attendance and literacy became virtually universal over the communist decades. By the late communist period, education was guaranteed and in most states ten years was compulsory, close to industrial nation norms. Enrollment rates were high from kindergarten, and extensive systems of subsidized preschool child care were in place, in part to facilitate women's participation in the labor force.[5]

---

[4] For women, the 1926 figure was 46 percent; for the rural population 55 percent, and for rural women 39 percent; *Narodnoe Khoziaistvo RSFSR za 60 let: Statisticheskii Ezhegodnik* (Moscow: Statistika, 1977), 18–19.

[5] Mark Bray and Nina Borevskaya, "Financing Education in Transitional Societies: Lessons from Russia and China," *Comparative Education* 37, no. 3 (2001): 345–65.

Although a basic education was broadly accessible, the educational system was stratified from the primary level, with differentiation between rural and urban areas and among economic branches, and specialized elite schools in large cities, research, and defense industry centers. The state also subsidized a comparatively limited system of higher specialized and university education that was disproportionately accessible to privileged strata. The educational system was narrowly vocationalized to serve manpower planning needs, tracking a majority of young adolescents into technical training with little choice and limited opportunities for general education. It was characterized by rigid, uniform curricula and pervasive political interference.

Systems of national health care were also in place, planned and managed by health ministries and financed from state and enterprise budgets. Access to basic care was nearly universal. Medical services were at the same time explicitly stratified. In the Soviet Union, for example, the health-care system was legally divided into six distinct subsystems—departmental, elite, capital city, industrial, provincial city, and rural. Each subsystem served different population groups at differing levels of financing and standards of care, with less than 0.5 percent of the population having access to the elite system and about half of the population served at the lowest quality, rural district level.[6] The system was very effective in administering broad public health measures to control infectious diseases, screen for illness, and vaccinate. It had markedly positive effects on health outcomes in both the Soviet Union and Eastern Europe, helping to bring adult and infant mortality close to industrial nation norms temporarily in the 1970s. In Poland and Hungary, for example, infant mortality declined by more than 50 percent between 1965 and 1985 as the public health system expanded.[7] But it could not modernize to provide the more sophisticated treatments required for complex health problems such as cancer and heart disease.[8] Health indicators worsened in the 1980s, leading to judgments that the system had become outdated

---

[6]   Christopher M. Davis, "The Organization and Performance of the Contemporary Soviet Health System," in *State and Welfare, USA/USSR: Contemporary Policy and Practice,* edited by Gail W. Lapidus and Guy E. Swanson (Berkeley: University of California Press, 1988), 114–30.

[7]   Haggard and Kaufman, "Revising Social Contracts," chap. 4, 38.

[8]   See Ellie Tragakes and Suszy Lessof, *Health Care Systems in Transition: Russian Federation,* edited by Ellie Tragakes (Copenhagen: European Observatory on Health Systems and Policies, 2003), 22–25; Alexander S. Preker and Richard G. A. Feachem, "Health and Health Care," in *Labor Markets and Social Policy in Central and Eastern Europe: The Transition and Beyond,* edited by Nicholas Barr (New York: Oxford University Press, 1994), 288–300.

and ineffective. It was also deficient in comparative international terms, relying on high rates of hospitalization and high provider-patient ratios, while utilizing low levels of medical technology and generally poor health facilities.

Communist welfare states provided broad consumer subsidies and social privileges. Subsidies for food and housing constituted the largest category of social spending. Demand for subsidized goods was very high and shortages were endemic, but subsidies helped make access to basic food and shelter nearly universal. Housing at nominal cost and strong tenancy rights had come to be considered an entitlement, especially in the urban parts of the Soviet Union. States also provided myriad particularistic social privileges, both monetary and in-kind—special supplements, bonuses, exemptions from payment for housing, utilities, and transport, among others—granted to civil servants, veterans, teachers serving in rural areas, those working in harsh climates, and other categories. Social privileges were used by the state to reward loyalty, especially for the wartime generation. In the 1950s and 1960s, privileges became an instrument for differentiating remuneration under the constraint of suppressed wage differentiation.[9] Over the decades, they grew by accretion into a massive and convoluted set of entitlements that would become the bane of rationalizing reformers.

Social Security and Social Assistance

At the beginning of transition, communist states had in place fully articulated, mature systems of social security that carried extensive financial obligations to their populations. These included pensions and sickness, disability, and survivor benefits covering most workers and their families and financed from state budgets partly through taxes on enterprises, usually with no direct worker contributions.[10] Given the very high labor force participation rates for both men and women, social insurance and pension coverage were nearly universal for those retiring at the end of

---

[9]   L. N. Ovcharova, ed., *Dokhody i Sotsial'nye Uslugi: neravenstvo, uiazvimost' i bednost'*: *Kollektivnaia monographiia* (Moscow: GU-VShE, 2005), chap. 4, available at http://www. socpol.ru/publications/.

[10]   The best source on the Soviet social security system remains Alastair McAuley, *Economic Welfare in the Soviet Union: Poverty, Living Standards, and Inequality* (Madison: University of Wisconsin Press, 1979); for Eastern Europe, see Nicholas Barr, ed., *Labor Markets and Social Policy in Central and Eastern Europe: The Transition and Beyond* (New York: Oxford University Press, 1994), 192–200.

the communist period. In the early 1990s, for example, almost 25 percent of Russia's population received pension payments, considerably higher than the 15–19 percent in developed Organisation for Economic Cooperation and Development (OECD) welfare states.[11] At the same time, payment levels were relatively low, leaving little scope for reductions without serious damage to welfare.

An important subset of protections was directed at women. Whereas most social security systems were originally structured for families with male breadwinners, the communist states had early dual-breadwinner systems that built in accommodations for families.[12] Protective policies socialized part of the cost of familyhood with extended maternity leaves, subsidized child care, and so forth. Especially in Eastern Europe, family benefits provided a nearly universal and substantial supplement to wages.[13] Women depended on these protections for access to employment and earnings. These policies had a clear pro-natalist intent, being most protective of pregnant women and those with very young children. They were also double-edged, making woman less desirable as employees and contributing to vertical segregation of labor forces and gender-based wage inequality.[14] Communist welfare states have been ranked fairly highly in meeting women's needs, although they did channel women into the poorly paid public sector for employment. In addition, the underdevelopment of the service sector made women's dual role as workers and homemakers a heavy double burden, and the absence of an income guarantee (discussed later) left a significant number of single-earner and other female-headed households in poverty.[15]

Communist welfare states were least developed in the area of social assistance or safety nets. Although they provided assistance for designated

[11]   Organisation for Economic Cooperation and Development, *Social Crisis in the Russian Federation* (Paris: OECD, 2001), 118. The main factor distinguishing communist states was the low retirement age, typically fifty-five for women and sixty for men.

[12]   On the male breadwinner model and women's employment entitlements, see Diane Sainsbury, *Gender, Equality, and Welfare States* (New York: Cambridge University Press, 1996).

[13]   Branco Milanovic, *Income, Inequality, and Poverty during the Transition from Planned to Market Economy* (Washington, D.C.: World Bank, 1988), 21. In 1988, the family allowance for two children equaled 17 percent of average earnings in Poland and almost 25 percent in Hungary.

[14]   Alastair McAuley, *Women's Work and Wages in the Soviet Union* (London: Allen and Unwin, 1981).

[15]   For an attempt to rank the communist welfare systems comparatively in meeting women's needs, see Bob Deacon with Michelle Hulse and Paul Stubbs, *Global Social Policy: International Organizations and the Future of Welfare* (London: Sage, 1997), 42.

groups of the unemployable needy (i.e., orphans and invalids) and family benefits served as a hedge against child poverty, especially in Eastern Europe, there was no civil or human right to subsistence. Need or income poverty per se did not entitle one to assistance, and social transfers for the poor remained residual, fragmentary, and discretionary. Various estimates set the pretransition poverty rate at between 2 and 11 percent in Russia, between 5 and 15 percent in Kazakhstan, 6 percent in Poland, and 1 percent in Hungary during the 1980s.[16] Except in Hungary, unemployment compensation was also absent or poorly developed at the start of transition. In general, access to income and transfer benefits was tied to employment, reflecting the bureaucratic compulsion to work.

Although it is not a standard part of welfare state categorizations, the regional dimension of welfare distribution plays a prominent role in the discussion here, especially for the Russian Federation, and should be considered. The major available study, by Donna Bahry, covers the Soviet Union as a whole and finds modest levels of inequality in republic and local social expenditures in the post-Stalin period. According to Bahry, in education and health-care financing, "decisions have explicitly been tied since the Stalin years to a standard of equal per capita spending. Differences in per capita outlays [across republics and regions] have been extremely modest since Khrushchev proposed to base republic budgets on the size of their populations."[17] Bahry finds slightly higher expenditures for both sectors in more developed regions and concludes that Soviet-era fiscal policies were driven mainly by social and economic, as opposed to political, factors.[18]

Institutional and Programmatic Features

Communist welfare states do not fit any of the available Western models or typologies and are probably best categorized as statist- or

---

[16] See Jeanine D. Braithwaite, "The Old and New Poor in Russia," in *Poverty in Russia: Public Policy and Private Responses,* edited by Jeni Klugman (Washington, D.C.: World Bank, 1997), 29; World Bank, *Kazakhstan: Living Standards during the Transition* (Washington, D.C.: World Bank, Human Development Sector Unit, 1998), 1; Barr, *Labor Markets,* 233; Milanovic, *Income,* 68–69.

[17] Donna Bahry, *Outside Moscow: Power, Politics, and Budgetary Policy in the Soviet Republics* (New York: Columbia University Press, 1987), 121–23.

[18] Bahry finds that appropriations were rather evenly distributed irrespective of such political factors as whether republics had representation in the Politburo, titular nationals as top leaders, etc.

authoritarian-paternalist. At the same time, these typologies can be useful for elucidating comparative tendencies toward social stratification or equalization produced by communist-era welfare distribution. As explained in the introduction, Esping-Andersen's classic typology of European welfare regimes distinguishes three variants.[19] In the conservative-corporatist variant, social rights attach to and preserve class stratification and status differentials, loyalty and service to the state are rewarded through privileged benefits for civil servants, and the welfare state plays a protective but virtually no redistributive role. The universalist variant, by contrast, promotes equality, dilutes differentials, and guarantees a broad range of social rights. The communist welfare system mixed elements of these two models, although the state rather than the market created the underlying status groups and monopolized distribution. It had strong conservative features. Most social goods and services were distributed through restricted-access networks that were vertically subdivided (i.e., closed stores and tiers of privilege). There was a great deal of administrative discretion in the awarding of benefits. Production managers, for example, systematically manipulated access to divide and stratify workers. The system privileged political, state, security, and military elites as well as some categories of industrial workers.

At the same time, the communist welfare system had strong universalist features. Stratification was superimposed on a system of narrow, state-dictated income differentials and broad subsidies. Access to at least basic health and educational services was widespread. A comparatively very high percentage of the working-age population was eligible for social insurance, a key marker of universalism.[20] According to Branco Milanovic's analysis, nomenklatura (i.e., party and administrative elite) privilege pulled up income inequality while subsidies, generally favoring the poorer, pulled it down, producing an "overall income distribution [that] was more egalitarian than in most market economies."[21] By the 1970s, the welfare state had extended over all strata of society, including,

---

[19]   Gøsta Esping-Andersen, *The Three Worlds of Welfare Capitalism* (Princeton: Princeton University Press, 1990).

[20]   Ibid., 73.

[21]   Milanovic, *Income,* 15. Milanovic's conclusion here is echoed by Janos Kornai in his major study, *The Socialist System: The Political Economy of Communism* (Princeton: Princeton University Press, 1992), 332. Kornai, although very critical of the low living standards and repressed potential for economic growth under communism, concludes, "if one considers all dimensions of material welfare ... , inequality is less than it is under the present capitalist system" (332).

TABLE 1.1
Social expenditures in the Soviet period (collective consumption as % of GDP, 1976)

	Education	Health	Welfare	Total
Socialist countries				
Bulgaria	3.9	3.1	10.3	17.3
Czechoslovakia	3.9	3.8	16.3	24.0
East Germany	4.9	5.1	11.7	21.7
Hungary	*3.4*	*5.3*	*11.6*	*20.3*
Poland	*3.2*	*3.3*	*7.1*	*13.6*
Soviet Union	*3.7*	*2.6*	*9.3*	*15.6*
Capitalist countries				
Austria	4.6	4.6	21.1	30.3
Italy	5.0	6.1	14.8	25.9
United States	5.0	2.9	11.3	19.2
West Germany	3.8	5.1	20.6	29.5

Source: Janos Kornai, *The Socialist System: The Political Economy of Communism* (Princeton: Princeton University Press, 1992), 314.

last and at the meanest level of provision, the collective farmers, leaving no significant informal sector or excluded strata.

Expenditure and Financing

Social expenditure data from the middle of the Soviet period compiled by Janos Kornai show spending for health, education, and welfare by communist states at 14–20 percent of GDP, considerably below Western levels but relatively high compared with states at similar levels of economic development (see table 1.1). Total social spending at the beginning of transition is estimated at 15–25 percent of GDP.[22]

Two factors complicate comparison, particularly with the nonsocialist systems. The first is that historically communist state enterprises financed some expenditures that would be in the public sector in a market economy, mainly for health and education. Estimates show that toward the end of the Soviet period Russian enterprises spent 3–5 percent of GDP on social provision and that East European firms spent about half this amount, and it remains unclear how much of this spending is included in budget social expenditures. Large Russian enterprises provided up to

[22] See Dina Ringold, "Social Policy in Postcommunist Europe: Legacies and Transition," in *Left Parties and Social Policy in Postcommunist Europe*, edited by Linda J. Cook, Mitchell A. Orenstein, and Marilyn Rueschemeyer (Boulder: Westview Press, 1999), 15; Milanovic, *Income*, 195–219.

40 percent of social expenditures, including public housing infrastructure, in some regions.[23] The communist systems also provided consumer subsidies (for food, housing, etc.) that are not included in comparative welfare data, costing almost 11 percent of Soviet GDP in 1989 and 14 percent of Russian GDP before the 1992 price liberalization.[24] Food subsidies were a major burden on states' budgets, and attempts to cut these subsidies were a source of otherwise rare labor unrest in Poland and Russia well before the transition. Janos Kornai famously characterizes communist welfare states as "premature," that is to say, too extensive for their economies' resources.[25]

Kornai's judgment holds in that welfare was chronically underfinanced in terms of the communist states' own commitments. Given free access or nominal cost for social goods and services, demand was high and shortages and rationing were endemic throughout the social sector. Health and education were undercapitalized, social infrastructure was poorly maintained and equipped, and the communist states fell far behind the developed world in health care and other technologies. International comparisons show that resources were systematically misallocated and inefficiently used. In health care, for example, there was a "massive but lopsided buildup in acute-care hospitals and excessive specialization," queues, and waiting lists despite high doctor-patient ratios.[26] Public-sector salaries fell near the bottom of national salary scales. Pensions and other social payments were not indexed to wages or hidden inflation and tended to decline in real terms over time.[27]

The sharp economic slowdown of the 1980s exacerbated these problems, making it increasingly difficult for communist states to deliver

[23]   For estimates, see Christine I. Wallich, ed., *Russia and the Challenge of Fiscal Federalism* (Washington, D.C.: World Bank, 1994), 126; Simon Commander, Qimiao Fan, and Mark E. Schaffer, eds., *Enterprise Restructuring and Economic Policy in Russia* (Washington, D.C.: World Bank, 1996), 53. According to Wallich, in some single-company Russian towns enterprises provided all the social infrastructure, with no social expenditures in public budgets.

[24]   For the 1990 figure, see Anders Aslund, "Gorbachev, Perestroika, and Economic Crisis," *Problems of Communism* 40, no. 1–2 (1991): 25; for 1992, see *OECD Economic Survey: The Russian Federation 1995* (Paris: OECD, 1995), 126.

[25]   Kornai, *Socialist System*, quoted in Ringold, "Social Policy in Postcommunist Europe," 15.

[26]   Preker and Feachem, "Health and Health Care," 296.

[27]   Walter D. Connor, "Social Policy under Communism," in *Sustaining the Transition: The Social Safety Net in Postcommunist Europe*, edited by Ethan Kapstein and Michael Mandelbaum (New York: Council on Foreign Relations, 1997), 10–46.

on their welfare commitments. Basic health and welfare indicators deteriorated throughout the region. Family benefits fell as a proportion of family incomes, and the real value of pensions declined by as much as one-third over the decade. According to Haggard and Kaufman, "beneficiaries experienced declining real transfers, [and] features of the shortage economy became increasingly manifest in the delivery of social services."[28]

Corruption and Informality before Transition

Because corruption and informalization play a major part in my analysis of welfare state change during the transition, it is important to consider the extent of these phenomena during the communist period. Informal payments, including the well-known gratuities commonly given to health-care personnel, were certainly present in communist-era welfare states. As in any economy characterized by scarcity, bribery and connections played a role in access to social goods. Although accurate information about their extent remains unavailable, most assessments conclude that informal allocational mechanisms did not compromise either the near-universality of access to basic services and social insurance or the state-imposed system of stratification. In his study of the structure and stratification in the Soviet health care system, for example, Chris Davis concluded that while the second economy had some effect, it was "more influential in distributing scarce resources within a subsystem. . . . It is unlikely that even a substantial side payment would enable a member of the public to obtain medical care in a closed subsystem (elite, departmental, industrial) in the absence of official entitlement to access . . . . [T]he second economy probably has only a small influence on distribution."[29] The communist state, in other words, financed and authoritatively allocated most welfare.

COMMITMENT, ATTACHMENT, DEPENDENCE, AND DISAFFECTION

There is considerable evidence that communist states' thick commitment to social provision was complemented by a strong popular

---

[28] Haggard and Kaufman, "Revising Social Contracts," chap. 5, 48.
[29] Davis, "Organization," 130; on patients' payments to health-care personnel, see Mark G. Field, "Postcommunist Medicine: Morbidity, Mortality, and the Deteriorating Health Situation," *The Social Legacy of Communism*, edited by James R. Millar and Sharon L. Wolchik, 187–89 (Cambridge, UK: Cambridge University Press, 1994).

attachment to the welfare state. A mass of attitudinal data shows that communist-era populations believed the state should be responsible for social security and services and that these beliefs persisted through the 1990s. Data from the Soviet period are scarce and unrepresentative, but surveys of Soviet World War II refugees in the early 1950s and of Jewish émigrés in the 1980s showed that high percentages valued full employment and free health and educational services, indeed that these were counted among the few positive features of the Soviet system.[30] Surveys for Russia, Poland, and Hungary at various points from the early 1990s through 2000 show that large majorities of respondents—in many cases more than 80 percent and sometimes more than 90 percent—favored state guarantees for jobs, health care, education, pensions, and social benefits (see table 1.2).[31] (The one exception here is spending on unemployment, a new program instituted or expanded during the transition, which has much lower levels of support.) A separate survey during this period found that 81 percent of respondents in Belarus agreed that "government should spend more on education, health, and pensions."[32] Support for state expenditures is somewhat lower than for state responsibility, although still strong, with majorities favoring increased spending for most policies.

It should be noted that some surveys in postcommunist societies have found contradictory results, that is, evidence of stronger individualist and weaker collectivist attitudes. More significantly, the surveys cited above found weaker support for the state's welfare role among those

[30]   On the post–World War II surveys, see Alex Inkles and Raymond A. Bauer, *The Soviet Citizen: Daily Life in a Totalitarian Society* (Cambridge, Mass.: Harvard University Press, 1961), 233–54; on the 1980s émigré interviews, see Brian Silver, "Political Beliefs of the Soviet Citizen: Sources of Support for Regime Norms," in *Politics, Work, and Daily Life: A Survey of Former Soviet Citizens,* edited by James Millar, (New York: Cambridge University Press, 1987), 103–5. Respondents at the same time complained of deficiencies in the actual provision of social welfare.

[31]   See Amy Corning, *Public Opinion and the Russian Parliamentary Election* (Rfe/Rl Research Report 2, no. 48, Dec. 3, 1993); James L. Gibson, "The Russian Dance with Democracy," *Post-Soviet Affairs* 17, no. 2 (2001): 113–15; Christine S. Lipsmeyer, "Welfare and the Discriminating Public: Evaluating Entitlement Attitudes in Post-Communist Europe," *Policy Studies Journal* 31, no. 4 (2003): 545–64; Hubert Tworzecki, "Welfare-State Attitudes and Electoral Outcomes in Poland and Hungary," *Problems of Post-Communism* 47, no. 6 (2000): 17–28.

[32]   The remainder of the questions read, "even if it means people like myself paying more taxes." Richard Rose and Toni Makkai, "Consensus or Dissensus about Welfare in Post-Communist Societies?" *European Journal of Political Research* 28 (1995): 203–24, quotation on p. 208; it should be noted, however, that Rose and Makkai do not interpret these answers as indicating support for collectivist welfare provision.

TABLE 1.2
Attitudes toward government's welfare role in Hungary, Poland, and Russia, 1996[a]

It should be government's responsibility to:	Hungary	Poland	Russia
Employment/unemployment			
Provide a job for everyone	85.4	86.4	91.6
Provide a decent standard of living for unemployed	60.4	71.6	75.9
Spend more on unemployment benefits	33.1	41.0	59.5
Health care & education			
Provide health care for the sick	97.7	95.2	97.3
Spend more on health care	91.6	90.6	94.2
Spend more on education	79.9	79.0	87.5
Retirement			
Provide decent standard of living for old	97.1	96.1	98.0
Spend more on retirement	82.9	79.0	90.0
Housing			
Provide decent housing	73.2	83.1	89.0

Source: Adapted from Christine S. Lipsmeyer, "Welfare and the Discriminating Public: Evaluating Entitlement Attitudes in Post-Communist Europe," *Policy Studies Journal* 31, no. 4 (2003): 551–553 based on the International Social Survey Program (ISSP, Role of Government III), 1996.

[a] Percentage agreeing that government "definitely should" or "probably should" take responsibility for policy area or should spend "more" or "much more" in policy area.

better-positioned in socioeconomic terms (i.e., education, incomes, age, or occupation) in the transitional economies. There is also evidence of considerable dissatisfaction with the services and benefits actually provided. Both the attitudes of the better-off strata and broad dissatisfaction with delivery open opportunities for social support of reform policies.

Communist-era welfare states also created dependence. In addition to providing benefits for broad populations, welfare states employed substantial parts of national labor forces as social service providers and supported large bureaucratic apparatuses to plan and administer the social sectors. The near absence of private alternatives or personal wealth as well as low incomes enforced the populations' dependence, especially in the post-Soviet states where the system had been longest and most deeply entrenched. The ongoing expansion of welfare obligations was built into the system, with the numbers eligible for benefits (especially pensions) growing rapidly as populations aged.[33] As for social service providers, health and education workers, dependent on the state for jobs, income, and professional status, made up more than 15 percent of the Russian labor force in 1990, at the beginning of transition.[34] A massive system of central social ministries and related bureaucratic structures, articulated through the regions and municipalities of communist states, also had vested interests in public spending and centralized administration. As postcommunist governments promoted programs of welfare state restructuring and retrenchment, these societal constituencies and state-based stakeholders adopted strategies of political defense, bureaucratic bargaining, and self-preservation that shaped welfare policy and provision.

At the same time, disaffection with welfare states had developed among academic social scientists and policy specialists in the late communist period. By the start of *perestroika* in the mid-1980s, many had come to view the old welfare system as both intrinsically deficient and inimical to continued social and economic development. Prominent social scientists pointed to its overcentralization and inefficiencies, and they argued that it promoted a disabling, morally debilitating dependence of society on the state. In their view, egalitarianism produced disincentives to work and talent, stifling initiative and ambition, while excessive paternalism frustrated society's aspirations for participation and accountability.[35] As communist states opened up to international influences, elite social scientists became acutely aware of the backwardness and deficiencies of their welfare system in comparative international terms, and greater internal openness exposed its declining performance domestically. By the late 1980s these reformist social-sector elites were in communication with global social policy networks and had begun articulating programs for dismantling and restructuring old welfare states that would help define the agendas of reformist leaderships.

Comparisons among Cases

By the beginning of transition, all five postcommunist cases had mature welfare states, broadly similar in structure and financed almost entirely

[33]   The number eligible for pensions in the Soviet Union had grown by 143 percent between 1960 and 1981; see Connor, "Social Policy under Communism," 33.

[34]   *Trud i Zaniatost' v Rossi: ofitsial'noe izdanie* (Moscow: Goskomstat Rossii, 2003), 187; defined as those working in "health care, sport, and social protection" and "education, culture, and art."

[35]   In the Soviet Union, the well-known sociologists Abel Agenbegian and Tatiana Zaslavskaia, prominent in the Novosibirsk School, were especially important; see, for example, Tatiana Zaslavskaia, "Chelovecheskii factor razvitiia ekonomiki i sotsial'naia spravedlivost'," *Kommunist* 13 (1996): 61–73; Cook, *Soviet Social Contract*, 82–93.

from state budgets. Welfare expenditures and standards were somewhat higher in east-central Europe, especially in Hungary, than in the post-Soviet states (see table 1.1).[36] The two least-known cases, Belarus and Kazakhstan, had fully developed welfare states. Belarus showed among the highest indicators of social well-being in the Soviet Union, with 5–6 percent of GDP going to education and key indicators such as infant and maternal mortality rates "compar[ing] very favorably on a European-wide level."[37] Kazakhstan, the least developed of the five cases, was the least poor of the central Asian republics, with the full range of social security and social assistance programs and universal state-run education and health care. According to a 1998 World Bank study, "This system of social provision underlies the strong achievements in the field of human development that [are] characteristic of the FSU (Former Soviet Union) countries. At independence, most human development indicators were higher in Kazakhstan than in countries with comparable levels of income."[38]

THE STRATEGY OF ECONOMIC REFORM: PRIVATIZATION, LIBERALIZATION, STABILIZATION

The shift toward market economies at the end of the 1980s had deep implications for the welfare state. The transitional governments moved to privatize productive and other property and to cut production subsidies, putting enterprises on a profitability basis. By 1997, for all the cases except Belarus, the private sector constituted more than 55 percent of GDP and the majority of output and employment were generated there.[39] Economic reform strategies also called for price liberalization, which eliminated most consumer subsidies and allowed prices to rise to market

[36] Janos Kornai, "Paying the Bill for Goulash Communism: Hungarian Development and Macro Stabilization in a Political-Economic Perspective," in *Struggle and Hope: Essays on Stabilization and Reform in a Post-Socialist Economy* edited by Janos Kornai (Northampton, Mass.: Edward Elgar, 1997), 121–79.

[37] Kathleen J. Mihalisko, "Belarus: Retreat to Authoritarianism," in *Democratic changes and authoritarian reactions in Russia, Ukraine, Belarus, and Moldova* edited by Karen Dawisha and Bruce Parrott (Cambridge, UK: Cambridge University Press, 1997), 235, citing a 1993 World Bank study.

[38] World Bank, *Kazakhstan*, 1.

[39] Ringold, "Social Policy in Postcommunist Europe," 29, citing the European Bank for Reconstruction and Development (EBRD); Anders Aslund, *Building Capitalism: The Transformation of the Former Soviet Bloc* (New York: Cambridge University Press, 2002), 279.

levels (although the remaining subsidies would become a major source of political contention). The five states implemented these reforms at different rates, with Russia and Poland initially relying on very rapid or "shock therapy" reform and the others beginning more slowly, and they pursued reforms unevenly and incompletely, but all set out in marketizing directions. These changes meant the collapse of the developmental model that underpinned the old welfare states.

Irrespective of their reform strategies, all five states experienced major declines in GDP during the regionwide recession of the 1990s (see figure 1.1). The failure or contraction of many enterprises and the rapid decline of trade among communist states led to a collapse in output, especially in industrial sectors. Fiscal crises developed, caused to a significant extent by this collapse. Budget deficits reached about 7 percent of GDP in Poland and Hungary, and approached 20 percent of Soviet GDP before the demise of the Soviet Union at the end of 1991 (see table 1.3). Price liberalization contributed to high levels of inflation in all cases and to episodes of hyperinflation in the three post-Soviet states. Programs of fiscal stabilization called for cuts in government expenditures in order to contain deficits and reduce inflation.

The effects of transition on welfare were dramatic. The restructuring of privatized enterprises toward more efficient labor utilization and the fall in production produced dismissals and mass layoffs. Unemployment emerged everywhere, reaching double digits in Poland, Russia, and Kazakhstan. Declining wages contributed to the growth of poverty. The fall in the size of the labor force and wage bill weakened the tax base and worsened the ratios of active workers to pensioners and other benefit recipients. In the largely unregulated new market sectors, competitive pressures, corruption, and informality led to significant and sometimes dramatic growth in inequality. Price liberalization produced an explosion in the costs of basic needs and social inputs. Governments faced new pressures to address unemployment and poverty and to pay the real costs of their inherited welfare commitments. Transitional states could no longer assume the entire financial burden for welfare. (Statistics on the growth of unemployment, poverty, and inequality can be found in tables 2.2 and 5.1.)

Many studies of welfare reform, including those discussed in the introduction, focus on global integration as the major source of pressure on welfare states. It is important to note that, for the transitional postcommunist states, the biggest factors were the exhaustion of the communist development model and the adoption by the governments of transformation strat-

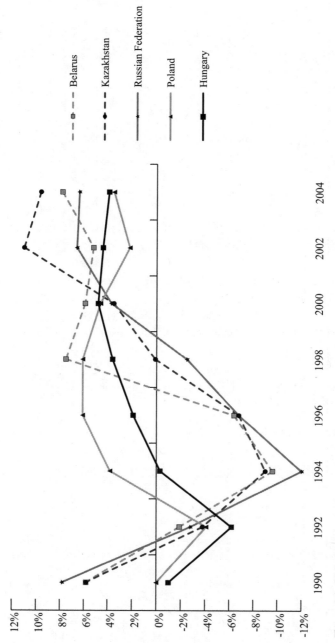

Figure 1.1 GDP annual percentage change (three-year moving average based on calculations using values of GDP based on the purchasing-power parity valuation of each country)

Source: International Monetary Fund, World Economic Outlook Database: September 2004 and April 2006, available at www.imf.org.

TABLE 1.3
Annual inflation and general government balances, 1989–2002[a]

	1989	1990	1991	1992	1993	1994	1995	1996	1997	1998	1999	2000	2001	2002[b]
Hungary														
Inflation	17	29	35	23	23	19	28	24	18	14	10	10	9	5
Fiscal balance	—	0	-2.1	-5.4	-6.6	-7.5	-3.1	0.8	-1.8	-4.0	-3.8	-3.4	-4.7	-9.9
Poland														
Inflation	244	586	70	43	35	32	28	20	15	12	7	10	5	2
Fiscal balance	—	3.7	-6.7	-4.9	-3.4	-3.2	-3.3	-3.6	-3.3	-3.0	-2.5	-3.2	-5.4	-5.7
Russian Federation														
Inflation	—	6	93	1,354	895	305	189	47	15	28	100	21	21	16
Fiscal balance	—	—	—	-21.8	-8.7	-11.3	-5.8	-8.7	-7.6	-7.8	-7.6	3.0	2.9	1.4
Belarus														
Inflation	—	5	94	970	1,188	2,221	709	53	64	73	150	168	61	43
Fiscal balance	—	—	—	-2.0	-5.6	-3.6	-2.8	-2.0	-2.3	-1.1	-1.8	-0.6	-1.4	-0.4
Kazakhstan														
Inflation	—	19	87	1,623	1,256	1,158	35	39	17	7	6	13	8	6
Fiscal balance	—	—	-9.0	-6.9	-0.7	-6.5	-3.2	-3.2	-3.7	-3.7	-4.8	-1.0	-0.9	0.0

Sources: Johannes F. Linn, "Ten Years of Transition in Central Europe and the Former Soviet Union: The Good News and the Not-So-Good News," in *Transition: The First Decade*, edited by Mario I. Blejer and Marko Skreb, 16–19 (Cambridge, MA: MIT Press, 2001); IMF 2006 International Financial Statistics Online, available at www.imf.org; European Bank for Reconstruction and Development, *EBRD Transition Report Update 2003*, 19–20, available at www.ebrd.com/pubs, *Republic of Belarus: Statistical Appendix* (IMF country Report 05/218, June, 2005)

[a] Annual inflation as percentage change in consumer product index (CPI); fiscal balance as percentage GDP.
[b] Balances for 2002 are estimates.

egies, leading to the collapses of domestic production and intercommunist trade. For the most part, these processes preceded global integration. The later opening of capital and trade regimes created pressures on welfare (discussed later), but internal sources were by far the greatest cause of structural and financial pressures on communist welfare states.

WELFARE REFORM STRATEGIES

The governments' actual strategies of postcommunist welfare state change depended on the outcomes of political struggles between reformers and defenders of inherited structures. Reformist governments and their domestic and international supporters pursued an overall direction of change toward retrenchment and liberalization. Their goal was to make postcommunist welfare more market-conforming, that is, privatized, competitive, efficiency-oriented, and means-tested. Here I set out the key dimensions and available measures of liberal restructuring and retrenchment that are used in the study and discuss some limits of the data.

The major goal of liberalization was to reduce the welfare responsibilities of the state and pressure on the budget, to "contain the explosion of social sector budgets" by re-organizing both delivery and financing of welfare.[40] Reforms were designed to shift the provision of social services toward the private sector, to diversify providers and sources of financing, and to rationalize and improve cost-effectiveness. They were also supposed to make the relationship between individuals' contributions and receipt of benefits closer and more transparent, to put social insurance on a self-financing and actuarially sound basis, and to free shrinking state resources for use as poverty-targeted assistance. There were four main mechanisms for restructuring.

The first mechanism was to decentralize social services, assets, and responsibilities from the central state to regional and municipal governments. Decentralization was widely promoted for the administration and financing of education and social assistance, as well as for health-sector management. It took a different form in the divestiture of social assets such as housing, utility networks, and schools from the central states and large-scale enterprises to municipalities. Decentralization was supposed to replace rigid central controls, to mobilize local tax resources and involve communities, and to improve the efficiency and responsiveness of social sectors.

---

[40]   Barr, *Labor Markets*, 23

The second mechanism was to shift responsibilities for financing health, pensions, unemployment, and other types of social insurance from state budgets, first, to independent social funds financed by employer-employee wage taxes and then to private insurance markets. Health insurance, run by private companies and based on competitive contracting, would replace the single-payer system for the employed population, promoting consumer choice and providing incentives for efficiency. Pension systems would be developed into multi-tiered configurations, including individual private investment accounts as major components. States would organize and regulate social insurance markets but, except for the poor or a subsistence guarantee, would not for the most part directly fund benefits.

The third mechanism was to legalize private providers and services in health and education, mobilize private resources, and move toward public-private mixes in provision. The measures here included the introduction of user fees, co-payments, vouchers, capitation formulas, and other mechanisms designed to promote competition, choice, and efficiency. The opening of social service markets formed part of the general deregulation and flexibilization of labor markets in the transition.

The last major mechanism was the replacement of subsidies, broad entitlements, and price controls by means-tested or poverty-targeted benefits that re-allocated state spending toward the poor. In the liberal paradigm, the state's major responsibility, the main appropriate use of its limited resources, is to provide for those whose incomes fall below an established minimum. Effective targeting was supposed to both help the socially vulnerable and contain costs while nongovernmental organizations (NGOs), charities, and self-help groups supplemented state aid.

The strategy of welfare state liberalization just presented is stylized and more integrated and coherent than any implemented in practice.[41] Actually, postcommunist governments often pursued reforms piecemeal, focusing on one or two policy areas or benefit programs. During the early transition years, they did so in a chaotic policy environment, sometimes expanding in an ad hoc fashion the very programs they were committed to cutting. Liberalizing measures were often poorly designed and implemented, contributing to policy failures and corruption in social sectors. Table 1.4 sets out the main features of communist and

---

[41] For other summaries of postcommunist welfare reform strategies see ibid., especially chap. 6; Haggard and Kaufman, "Revising Social Contracts," chap. 6, 13–14.

TABLE 1.4
Main features of communist, liberal, and informalized welfare states

	Communist (Statist)	Liberal (Market)	Informalized (Liberalization + weak state capacities)
Financing	Public, state budget	Predominance of private over public	Mixed public, private, and informal
Administration	Centralized state monopoly	Mixed state administration and market regulation	Weak state and market regulation, informal private controls on access
Coverage	Universal, state-stratified	Partial: state coverage of eligible poor; social security markets predominant	Fragmentary: weak state coverage of eligible poor; corruption in social security markets
Welfare Policy Areas			
Pensions, Social Insurance	Single-pillar Collective tax base Risk-pooling	Multi-pillar, wage-tax based PAYG and personal capitalized pension accounts Individualization of risk	Multi-pillar PAYG and/or capitalized accounts Low wage tax collections Low contribution rates to capitalized accounts
Health and Education	Centralized, Budget-financed	Decentralized Private practices, schools Health insurance Competitive criteria Co-pays, fees, vouchers, tuition, student loans	Informal control over access to subsidized services Poorly regulated private services Prevalence of shadow payments
Social Subsidies, Social Assistance, Poverty Relief	Universal social subsidies Little poverty-targeted assistance	Means-tested, poverty-targeted assistance predominant	Residual subsidies Poorly-targeted poverty relief
Labor Market, Labor Code	Full employment Centralized wage regulation Rigid labor market rules and protections	Unemployment with insurance benefits Competitive wage bargaining Flexible labor markets, codes	Large informal sector with unregulated wages Few formal legal protections De facto flexible labor markets

liberal welfare state types, as well as the informalized type that resulted from liberalization under conditions of weak state taxing and regulatory capacities.

Most significantly, liberalization was contested. Central ministries resisted decentralization, and resource-poor municipalities sometimes refused or failed to take on social services and divested assets. Employers, and workers whose wages were declining, evaded the new social security taxes. Health-care and pension-fund administrators opposed insurance schemes that would take away their control over finances; and doctors, teachers, and university rectors resisted reforms in their sectors. People of many social strata whose incomes were falling opposed cuts in entitlements and sub-sidies, and pressed for benefit increases to compensate for their losses. Political parties, trade unions, and social-sector bureaucracies defended these claims with varying degrees of effectiveness, variously failing, mod-erating changes, or producing policy deadlock. I trace these processes of political bargaining over welfare reform and show how they contributed to divergent trajectories and outcomes across the five cases.

MEASURES OF LIBERALIZATION, RETRENCHMENT, AND OUTCOMES

The chapters that follow track liberal restructuring efforts across the major areas of the welfare state, showing where and when decentralization, insur-ance markets, privatization and competition in social sectors, and means testing have been proposed, legislated, and implemented in the five post-communist states and with what effects. The discussion focuses on differ-ent patterns of expenditure and structural change over time and across the cases. Most comparisons are based on descriptive data, with compara-tive quantitative measures presented when available. Data limitations pose many problems for measurement and comparison, particularly for com-parison between the East Central European and the post-Soviet cases. Four cumulative measures of comparative liberalization are presented, based on Esping-Andersen's key indicators of welfare state liberalization: [42]

1. the extent of pension-system privatization
2. public versus private health-care expenditure

[42]   Esping-Andersen's main indicators are the relative weight of means-tested benefits as a percentage of the total social assistance, the private-sector share of total pension ex-penditure, and the private-sector share of total health expenditure; *Three Worlds of Welfare Capitalism*, 73.

3. the effectiveness of social transfers for poverty relief (as a proxy for the proportion of means-tested benefits in social assistance), and
4. structural changes toward efficiency in health sectors

Whereas liberalization entails changes in the fundamental organization and modes of financing the welfare state, retrenchment means cuts in expenditure that need not involve structural change. Retrenchment may be accomplished by restricting eligibility for existing programs; cutting funds; or reducing, delaying, or failing to pay mandated benefits and public-sector salaries. All five postcommunist welfare states retrenched in that they cut real spending across some areas of welfare provision during their recessionary crises. However, accurate measures of real comparative spending are complicated by a number of factors. The uncertainty of Soviet-era data at the starting point, much re-organization of social-sector financing between central and local governments, and frequent gaps in cross-country data all present problems.[43] While real expenditure data are provided for Russia, for the comparisons I have relied mainly on measures of welfare effort (spending as a percentage of GDP), which are available for most cases throughout the period under study. This measure has limitations, but shifts in welfare effort over time constitute the best indicator of changes in the states' overall commitment to welfare and their priorities, central concerns of this book.

Finally, I look at the comparative outcomes of the different trajectories for welfare provision in contemporary postcommunist states, including levels of poverty and inequality, access to health and education services, coverage of major social security programs, and levels of corruption and informalization. The transition has produced three types of welfare outcomes: the statist model that persists in Belarus, a mixed state and market model in Poland and Hungary, and a more liberalized model in Russia and Kazakhstan in which informal mechanisms play a major role.

Chapters 2–4 trace the political struggles over welfare in the newly independent Russian state, beginning with the administration of Russia's

---

[43] For a related discussion of data problems and limits, see Ringold, "Social Policy in Postcommunist Europe," 12–13; according to Ringold, for the transition states, "Accurate and comparable data on social sector spending are not widely available, as accounting systems differ and data are often fragmented across government ministries" (12). See also Barr, *Labor Markets*, 82.

first popularly elected president, Boris Yeltsin, and continuing through the Putin administration. Chapter 5 looks at welfare politics and outcomes in Poland, Hungary, Kazakhstan, and Belarus. The conclusion draws the comparisons and explores their implications for the comparative study of welfare states.

2

Non-negotiated Liberalization

Decentralizing Russia's Welfare State and Moving It Off-Budget

As the Soviet Union collapsed in the last half of 1991, a radically reformist leadership established itself at the head of the new Russia state. In the aftermath of his strong victory in the June 1991 Russian presidential election, Boris Yeltsin was granted extensive decree powers by the holdover legislature, the Supreme Soviet. He appointed a reform team headed by Deputy Prime Minister Egor Gaidar, an economist who committed the government to policies of liberalization, privatization, and fiscal stabilization that were designed to deal with the economic crisis and transform the old command system into a market economy. As part of its stabilization project, the government set out to cut federal budget expenditures and scale back the welfare state. The Finance Ministry played a key role in these reforms, and a central part of its strategy was to shift responsibility for most social expenditures away from the federal budget.

POWER CONCENTRATION AND THE REFORMIST COALITION

The welfare state that Russia inherited was a top-down creation, established under conditions of society's political exclusion. Except at the margins in the later Soviet period, the society had never mobilized to make claims or shape provision.[1] Trade unions served mainly as administrators rather

---

[1] There were instances of societal influence on educational policy in the Khrushchev period and on child care policies in the Brezhnev period.

than demanders of welfare. The professional groups that provided social services—doctors, educators, and so forth—belonged to mandatory associations but had no experience with organizational autonomy and little with interest articulation. State administrators had controlled the professions. Within the state, social-sector ministries and other institutions had been disorganized by the collapse of the Soviet Union and the transition to a separate Russian Federation government. In sum, during the initial stage of transition, both societal constituencies and statist stakeholders were in weak positions to defend their interests in the inherited welfare system.

Russian social-sector elites themselves were divided over the future of the welfare state. As noted in chapter 1, since the start of Mikhail Gorbachev's *perestroika* in the mid-1980s academic social scientists and activist professionals had been developing critiques of the old system, focusing on its overcentralization, rigidities, inefficiencies, and excessive paternalism.[2] This reform movement now spread within the professions, where ad hoc groups developed agendas for modernizing and democratizing the social sector. As the Soviet political system opened up, some of these professionals became politically active, winning election to the new legislature, the Supreme Soviet, and taking leadership positions on social policy committees. They also connected with global social policy networks that promoted reform models through publications, conferences, and other mechanisms. The approach of the global networks was broadly liberalizing.[3] They became important sources of programmatic innovation and direction for Russian social reformers.

In the early 1990s, a synergy of these three influences—economic liberalizers in the executive, reformist domestic social-sector elites, and global social policy networks—began restructuring of the Russian welfare state. Executive liberalizers were primarily interested in reducing budgetary expenditures and the welfare role of the state to achieve fiscal stabilization and market transformation. Social-sector reformers wanted to decommunize and democratize the welfare state, to make it more effective and responsive. They were influenced by models of welfare reform then being promoted by global networks and were

---

[2]   For earlier critiques of the Russian welfare state, see, for example, T. Serebrennikova, "Ekonomicheskie i Sotsialnye Funktsii Raspredeleniia," *Ekonomicheskaia Gazeta* 41 (1996): 8; on the educational reform movement in the 1980s, see Stephen L. Webber, *School, Reform, and Society in the New Russia* (New York: Palgrave, 2000).

[3]   Robert R. Kaufman and Joan M. Nelson, eds., *Crucial Needs, Weak Incentives: Social Sector Reform, Democratization, and Globalization in Latin America* (Baltimore: Johns Hopkins University Press, 2004).

TABLE 2.1
Politics of non-negotiated liberalization in Russia, 1991–1993

Pro-reform; liberalizers	Anti-reform; welfare state stakeholders
Executive	*Societal constituencies, representative institutions*
Strong	**Weak**
Unified liberalizing government	No coherent parties
Reformist social sector ministers	Weak legislative-society links
Gaidar reform team	Ineffective Supreme Soviet
Reformist social-sector elites	*Statist social-sector elites*
Strong	**Weak**
Access to policy power through social ministries	Transition disorganizes
Domination of legislative committees (health, housing)	Organizations disbanded
Articulated reform programs	
Global policy networks, IFIs[a]	*State-bureaucratic stakeholders*
Strong	**Weak**
Models of decentralization and privatization shape reform	Transition disorganizes
	Decentralization undermines power and leverage

Outcome
Non-negotiated liberalization

[a] IFIs, international financial institutions.

empowered because their ideas fit the agendas of powerful actors in the economic and finance ministries who drove the broader transition process. (The main actors in Russian welfare politics, and the pro- and antireform political balance during this period, are shown in table 2.1.)

Constitutionally, the executive and legislature held dual power in Russia during this period, but the president effectively dominated the polity through his stronger claim to electoral legitimacy, unilateral control of ministerial appointments, and decree powers. Yeltsin and his aides "focused primarily on strengthening executive authority so that they could insulate economic policymaking and enhance economic policy implementation. . . . [They] believed that economic policymakers had to be protected from populist politics."[4] In fall 1991, Yeltsin appointed

[4] Michael McFaul, *Russia's Unfinished Revolution: Political Change from Gorbachev to Putin* (Ithaca: Cornell University Press, 2001), 147.

himself prime minister and put Gaidar and a team of young economists in charge of economic reform. Prominent reformers, including
Aleksandr Shokhin and Ella Pamfilova, were placed at the heads of social
ministries, unifying the government around a reform agenda.[5] Until
the end of 1992 (when Gaidar was removed and Victor Chernomyrdin
appointed prime minister), economic, fiscal, and welfare policies
were largely driven by Gaidar, Privatization Committee Chair Anatoly
Chubais, and Finance Minister Boris Federov. There was a broad per-
ception within the government that Yeltsin had a popular mandate to
carry out radical change

Supreme Soviet deputies, who had been elected before the transition to an independent Russian state, had weaker claims to democratic
legitimacy. With the exception of the Communist Party members, they
also had few clear partisan affiliations. The broad movement-parties
that had mobilized against communism collapsed during this period,
and new ones did not emerge. The legislature provided some voice for
industrial and agrarian lobbies, but was otherwise weakly linked to societal interests. According to Vladimir Mau, who served as an advisor to
the Russian government during this period, "Russian parliamentary lobbying had a number of specific features distinguishing it from its foreign counterparts. Russian lobbying was almost exclusively limited to the
material production sphere. Russian deputies did not experience organized pressure from public, women's and veterans' organizations, con-
sumers' groups, etc. Russian lobbyists actually spoke on behalf of large
monopolist formations."[6]

The legislature did mount growing opposition to the economic reform
program, pressing for increased expenditures and continued subsidies
but with few effects on welfare, except to slow industrial restructuring and
prop up employment. Yeltsin relied heavily on decrees to implement his
policies, vetoed spending increases, and ignored many decisions of the
legislature, which he dismissed as a Red-Brown (i.e., Communist-Fascist)
coalition of extremists. The legislature's passage of a high-deficit budget
in 1993 was a precipitant of its forcible dissolution by the president.

Welfare reform legislation remained "under the radar" during these
larger struggles. Social policy was not a major cleavage issue in the

---

[5] Shokhin became Deputy Prime Minister for Social Affairs and retained the Labor
Ministry; Pamfilova was appointed Minister for Social Affairs.

[6] Vladimir Mau, *The Political History of Economic Reform in Russia, 1985–1994* (London:
Centre for Research into Communist Economies, 1996), 80.

increasingly polarized legislature.[7] Small, organized groups of reformist deputies dominated the social committees and shepherded through framework restructuring legislation on health, education, pensions, and housing in 1991 and 1992, with little debate or apparent comprehension on the part of most legislators. During this early period there was, in the words of a deputy department chair from the Ministry of Economic Development and Trade, "a unique situation—all laws were written from scratch. A law could be prepared in a week. Since then, if we look at the laws the Duma is accepting, there are very rarely new laws."[8]

In sum, political and institutional balances favored welfare state liberalization during this period. Power was concentrated in the executive, and economic and social reformers dominated the government. Welfare interests were weak in political and state structures. The legislature did not serve as a veto actor on programmatic change and, in any case, had little influence. Reformers faced very few constituency pressures. As in some Latin American cases, under such political conditions the economic crisis "opened a window of opportunity for [a] technocratic group of policy-makers to seize power . . . and redefine the role of the state, the market, and state-society relations."[9] Over the years 1991–1993, they initiated major re-organizations of the welfare state, including the decentralization of social services, competitive contracting for health care, privatization of housing, and the transfer from state budgetary financing of most social security programs. Some of these social-sector reforms did confront resistance in the implementation stage, but most opposition came later. This early period in the transition permitted nearly uncontested welfare state change, a non-negotiated liberalization that has no parallel in more established, non-authoritarian polities.

THE ECONOMIC CRISIS AND THE REFORM STRATEGY

The Russian economy entered the new decade in crisis. Productivity was declining, inflation stood at close to 100 percent in 1991, and shortages of consumer goods were acute. The budget deficit inherited from

[7] See Thomas Remington, *The Russian Parliament: Institutional Evolution in a Transitional Regime, 1989–1999* (New Haven: Yale University Press, 2001), esp. chaps. 4–5.
[8] Deputy department chair, Ministry of Economic Development and Trade, interview with author, Moscow, May 6, 2001.
[9] Alejandra Gonzalez Rossetti, "Change Teams and Vested Interests: Social Security Health Reform in Mexico," in *Crucial Needs, Weak Incentives*, edited by Kaufman and Nelson, 68.

the collapsed Soviet state was estimated at 20 percent of GDP. The crisis derived in part from the accumulating structural deficiencies in the Soviet economy and the breakdown of Russia's intercommunist trade. It was exacerbated by the partial, failed economic reform efforts of the Gorbachev period (1985–1991), which had eliminated many administrative controls without creating markets in their place, thereby worsening price and other distortions.[10] The new Yeltsin administration saw rapid and comprehensive economic transformation, or "shock therapy," as the necessary road to economic recovery.

It is important to recall that globalization was not the main cause of Russia's economic contraction and the resulting pressures on the welfare state. The collapse was precipitated by failed Gorbachev-era reforms that destabilized the Soviet economy and led to the breakup of the trade block the Soviets dominated. The Soviet economy was not deeply integrated into global markets, although energy exports were significant.[11] It had very little foreign investment. It was a protected system that had exhausted its potential for growth. In an economic sense, the causes of the collapse were largely endogenous. Social spending generally fell in line with GDP, with the decline most precipitous in 1992–1994.

In late 1991, Gaidar's reform team set three main strategic goals that were designed to end the crisis: price liberalization, fiscal stabilization, and privatization of productive and other assets. In early 1992, the government freed 90 percent of consumer and 80 percent of producer prices, effectively ending most state price subsidies and allowing the market to set prices according to supply and demand. The budget deficit was to be eliminated within the year, mainly by cutting subsidies to enterprises and placing them on a profitability basis.[12] Anatoly Chubias's State Privatization Committee set out to achieve the rapid transfer of Russia's huge industrial sector to private ownership. The reformers' intent was to establish a market economy with low inflation and stable economic growth, creating conditions for Russia's integration into the global economy. They viewed themselves as a

[10] On the reform programs, see Anders Aslund, *How Russia Became a Market Economy* (Washington, D.C.: Brookings Institution, 1995).

[11] High oil revenues in the 1970s had been used to fund consumer imports and subsidies. The fall of oil prices in the 1980s contributed to the decline of welfare in the late Soviet period. See Petr Aven, "Problems in Foreign Trade Regulation in the Russian Economic Reform, in *Economic Transformation in Russia*, edited by Anders Aslund (New York: St. Martin's Press, 1994), 80–93.

[12] E. Gaidar and G. Matiukhin, "Memorandum ob Ekonomicheskoi Politike Rossiiskoi Federatsii," *Ekonomiki i Zhizn* 10 (1992): 4–5.

"kamikaze" government whose task it was to carry out an irreversible transformation of the state-run system in the shortest possible time.

The reforms did not halt the economic decline. Russia's GDP continued to fall until the end of the decade, declining almost 20 percent in
1992 and more than 10 percent in 1993 and again in 1994—an estimated
40 percent overall by 1999, a decline comparable to the Great Depres-
sion. During this period, the government continued policies of economic liberalization, opening Russia's trade and capital regimes. Exports
were heavily dominated by energy and other raw materials because most
Russian finished goods proved to be too poor in quality to compete in
international markets. Foreign direct investment remained very low, estimated at $1–3 billion annually, much lower per capita than in the East
Central European transition economies and highly concentrated in a
few regions and sectors.[13] Most inflows of capital came in the form of
short-term portfolio investment, mainly in government securities. The
opening of capital markets, at the same time, facilitated large-scale capital
flight, and Russia remained a net exporter of capital throughout the
decade. Integration into the international economy during the 1990s
had negative effects on welfare overall, and the benefits that did materialize accrued mostly to a small number of regions with natural resources
or the few competitive industries and to urban centers that developed
financial services.

The Reform Strategy and the Welfare State

The economic reform strategy had major implications for the welfare
state. Real prices replaced administrative allocations in the new economy,
making the costs of welfare transparent. The reform eliminated old protections, reduced resources, and created new needs. The Gaidar team did
not pay much explicit attention to welfare reform or map out a comprehensive strategy, but indications of its approach can be found in various
sources. In his policy statements, Gaidar stressed the need to "divest the
state of functions (that are) inappropriate under market conditions."[14]
Privatization would be extended to the social sphere. Pensions and
other benefits would be financed by wage taxes paid into social funds.
In a major exposition on the economic reform program, Gaidar made it

[13]   Organisation for Economic Cooperation and Development [hereafter OECD],
Economic Surveys: Russian Federation, 2000 (Paris: OECD, 2000).
[14]   Egor T. Gaidar, "The Most Correct Policy Is a Responsible Policy, Not Populism,"
Problems of Economic Transition 37, no. 4 (1994): 10.

clear that the budget would no longer bear responsibility for social security, that "the payment of pensions and social insurance grants must be limited to the Pension Fund's and Social Insurance Fund's own available resources at a given time. The government will not subsidize these funds in 1992. . . . The government is planning to take steps to stimulate the development of private pension funds and to privatize the state pension system."[15] Housing would be privatized and the costs of maintenance and utilities would be transferred to residents. Gaidar called for an acceleration of laws on medical insurance to help finance health care, although at the same time he favored maintaining the public health system. Social Affairs Minister Pamfilova, Gaidar, Yeltsin, and others also stressed their commitment to creating a new system of social protection that would replace inherited subsidies with targeted assistance for the most vulnerable groups, especially families with children.[16] The overall logic of social-sector reform was both to reduce budget financing and to make the state's role in welfare more limited and poverty-targeted.

FISCAL POLICY, WELFARE EFFORT, AND EXPENDITURE

Russia's economic reformers moved quickly to cut budget expenditures and scale down the size and scope of the public sector. Consolidated budget spending declined from about two-thirds of GDP before the transition to 32 percent in 1996. Federal expenditures fell from 27 percent of GDP in 1992–1993 to about 18 percent in 1995, while regional expenditures increased slightly.[17] Consumer subsidies were reduced from 14 to 7 percent of GDP after the 1992 price liberalization. Enterprises shed welfare functions, and their social expenditures declined by about half, or 2 percent of GDP.[18] The costs of food and other necessities increased by multiples, contributing to hyperinflation and a spiking of the poverty level. Communist-era restrictions on worker dismissals were eased to

[15] Gaidar and Matiukhin, "Memorandum ob Ekonomicheskoi Politike Rossiiskoi Federatsii," 5.

[16] Tatyana Khudyakova, "The Budget Can't Sustain Social Programs," *Izvestiia* (Sept. 23, 1992): 2, trans. in *Current Digest of the Post-Soviet Press* 44, no. 38 (1992): 30–31.

[17] Augusto Lopez-Claros and Sergei V. Alexashenko, *Fiscal Policy Issues during the Transition in Russia*, (Washington, D.C.: IMF, 1998), 23.

[18] On subsidies, see OECD, *Economic Surveys: Russian Federation, 1995* (Paris: OECD, 1995), 126. On the estimated decline in enterprise social expenditures, see Elena Vinogradova, "Analiticheskaia Zapiska: Rossiiskie Predpriiatiie: Zaniatost, Zarabotnaia Plata, Sotsial'naia Podderzhka Rabotnikov" (Xerox, 1996).

permit labor force cuts and enterprise closings. Both open and hidden unemployment emerged and continued to grow through the decade.[19] Because some industrial subsidies were retained until the mid-1990s, the collapse of the industrial economy and rise in unemployment proved more gradual in Russia than in some other transition economies, but the effects on social provision were dramatic. The core of the old welfare system—collective social provision and guaranteed employment in enterprises shielded by the state from competitive pressures—was collapsing.

The changes in major social indicators—poverty, unemployment, and inequality—are shown in table 2.2. Official statistics placed one-quarter to one-third of the population below the poverty level throughout the 1990s, and alternative estimates by the World Bank indicate considerably higher levels. Officially, unemployment rose from about 5 percent in 1992 to more than 13 percent in 1998; other estimates, including various types of hidden unemployment, pushed the percentage several points higher. The World Bank placed total unemployment at close to 15 percent in 1997.[20] (It should be noted that the growth of informal economic activity called both sets of figures into question, with some analysts arguing that even the official figures might be inflated and that the real levels of poverty and unemployment in the mid-1990s were indeterminate.)

Inequality grew at an extremely rapid pace, far exceeding the growth in East Central European transition economies, moving Russia from a European pattern of income distribution to a pattern more closely approximating the less egalitarian Latin American states. Poverty was concentrated especially among families with children, households with unemployed members, and elderly women living alone on minimum pensions. The overall effects are summarized in the United Nations Development Programme (UNDP) Human Development Index (HDI), which combines measures of life expectancy, real per capita income, and access to schooling. As table 2.2 shows, in 1992 Russia had a ranking of 0.848, placing it at the lower end of the "high human development" cluster. With the rapid decrease in HDI of just over 100 points, to 0.747

---

[19] Hidden unemployment encompassed sending workers on involuntary leaves, reducing workers to part-time or irregular work, or maintaining them on employee rolls with no or irregular pay.

[20] World Bank, "Report and Recommendation of the President of the International Bank for Reconstruction and Development to the Executive Directors on a Proposed Social Adjustment Protection Loan in the Amount of US$800 million to the Russian Federation," Wahsington, D.C., June 5, 1997, 4.

TABLE 2.2
Selected social indicators for the Russian Federation, 1991–2002[a]

	1991	1992	1993	1994	1995	1996	1997	1998	1999	2000	2001	2002
Poverty (% pop)												
Goskomstat	11.7	33.5	31.5	22.4	24.7	22.1	20.7	23.3	28.4	29	27.5	24.6
World Bank[b]	—	26.8	36.9	37.6	41.1	43.2	24.1	31.4	41.5	35.9	26.2	19.6
Unemployment (%)	—	5.2	5.9	8.1	9.5	9.7	11.8	13.3	13.0	10.5	9.1	8.0
Inequality (Gini coefficient, Goskomstat)	0.26	0.29	0.39	0.40	0.38	0.38	0.38	0.40	0.40	0.40	0.40	0.40
HDI	—	0.848	0.833	—	0.790	0.780	0.747	0.771	—	0.781	0.779	0.795

Sources: Sotsial'noe polozhenie i uroven' zhizni naseleniia Rossii: statisticheskii sbornik 1997 (Moscow: Goskomstat Rossii, 1997), 107; 2003, 137, 146; 2005, 150, 162; *Trud i Zaniatost' v Rossii: ofitsial'noe izdanie* (Moscow: Goskomstat Rossii, 2003), 109; *Rossisskii Statisticheskii Ezhegodnik: Ofitsial'noe Izdanie 1999* (Moscow: Goskomstat Rossii, 1999) 109, 163. World Bank data from Lawrence Thompson, *Russia: Bank Assistance for Social Protection* (Washington, D.C.: World Bank, 2002), 27, for 1992–1996, based on RLMS; World Bank, *Russian Federation: Reducing Poverty through Growth and Social Policy Reform* (Report no. 28923-RU) (Washington, D.C.: World Bank, 2005), 14, for 1997–2002; UNDP, *Human Development Report 1997: Russian Federation* (Human Rights Publishers, New York 1997), 11; UNDP, *Human Development Report 2000: Russian Federation* (Moscow: UNDP, 2001), 36; WHO/Europe, European HFA Database, June 2006.

[a] HDI, Human Development Index; HFA Database, Health for All Database; RLMS, Russian Longitudinal Monitoring Service; UNDP, United Nations Development Programme; WHO, World Health Organization.

[b] The higher poverty figures from the World Bank are based on the RMLS for 1992–1996 and a recommended World Bank methodology that differs from Goskomstat's for 1996–2003.

in 1997, Russia fell out of the "high human development" group of countries, mainly because of declines in GDP and life expectancy.

Estimates of the Russian government's welfare effort and expenditure
in the early 1990s are complicated by the transition from Soviet to Russian states in 1991, the economic crisis, and the lack of official data. The
best available estimates, by Mikhail Dmitriev and Branco Milanovic, are
presented in tables 2.3 and 2.4. Table 2.3 shows that welfare effort (social
expenditure as percentage of GDP) remained fairly stable across major
expenditure categories and even increased slightly for some categories
in 1993 and 1994. Liberal analysts (such as Anders Aslund and Dmitriev,
himself) argue that the welfare state was relatively well protected during
the transition.[21]

Even sustained welfare effort, however, meant a dramatic decline in
real expenditures. Table 2.4 shows that estimated real spending fell by
more than 40 percent in education and 30 percent in health from 1990
to 1995. Family allowances collapsed, unemployment benefits remained
marginal, and estimated pension spending fell to less than half of its
pretransition level at the height of the payment arrears crisis in 1995.
Although expenditure declines varied somewhat across policy areas,
they broadly followed the decline in GDP. There appears to be a significant degree of path dependence in the early retrenchment process, with
welfare effort following established patterns, expenditure decline driven
mainly by economic factors, and relatively little adjustment to new transitional needs.

Political decisions to restructure the welfare state had deep effects
on the distribution of these diminished expenditures and on the
reform's social costs. The liberalizing structural changes did diversify
the financing of the welfare state, but they also weakened redistributive
and administrative capacities. Russia's insulated, executive-dominated
policy process facilitated rapid liberalization but often produced poor-
quality policies. Some reforms followed imported models that did not
fit the Russian context. In the end, reformers re-organized the welfare
state in ways that worsened disparities in access to services and benefits across regions, disorganized coordinating mechanisms, and left
the federal government with little ability to address rising poverty and
unemployment.

[21]   See Aslund, *How Russia Became a Market Economy*, 283–89; Mikhail Dmitriev, *Biudzhet-naia Politika v Sovremennoi Rossii* (Moscow: Carnegie Center, 1997).

TABLE 2.3
Social expenditures in the Russian Federation, budget and off-budget funds, 1992–1995 (% of GDP)

Type of public expenditure	1992	1993	1994	1995
Expenditures of the budget system as a whole				
Consolidated budget	45.8	42.7	45.2	38.9
Federal budget (excluding transfers to territorial budgets)	27.1	17.5	18.5	16.9
Territorial budgets (regional and local)	12.2	16.2	17.5	14.5
Off-budget funds	6.5	9.0	9.2	7.5
Health				
Consolidated budget	2.45	3.58	4.09	3.41
Federal budget	0.27	0.34	0.37	0.21
Territorial budgets	2.18	2.82	2.76	2.33
Education				
Consolidated budget	3.58	4.03	4.36	3.40
Federal budget	1.21	0.76	0.87	0.52
Territorial budgets	2.37	3.27	3.49	2.88
Social policy				
Consolidated budget	0.63	0.85	1.20	1.25
Consumer subsidies[a]				
Housing-communal economy	—	—	4.60	3.66
Social transport	—	—	0.56	0.75
Off-budget social funds				
Pension fund	4.83	6.06	5.92	5.33
Employment and unemployment fund	0.66	0.22	0.38	0.33

Source: Mikhail Dmitriev, *Biudzhetnaia politika v sovremennoi Rossii* (Moscow: Carnegie Center, 1997), 22, 47–48. Table constructed by Elena Vinogradova.

[a] Territorial budgets are the only source of housing and transport subsidies.

RESTRUCTURING SOCIAL SERVICES: DECENTRALIZATION AND THE BEGINNINGS OF PRIVATIZATION

The first major structural change was decentralization, the delegation to subnational governments of greater responsibility for the administration and delivery of welfare services. In the early 1990s, "the center's basic strategy [was] to push the deficit downward by shifting unfunded spending responsibilities down to the oblasts [regions] . . . to force oblast governments to discontinue some public sector expenditures."[22] Between

[22]   Christine I. Wallich, "Russia's Dilemma," in *Russia and the Challenge of Fiscal Federalism,* edited by Christine I. Wallich (Washington, D.C.: World Bank, 1994), 6; Jorge Martinez-Vazquez, "Expenditures and Expenditure Assignments," in *Russia and the Challenge of Fiscal Federalism,* edited by Christine Wallich (Washington, D.C.: World Bank, 1994), 105.

TABLE 2.4
Real Russian government social expenditures 1990–1995[a]

Category of expenditure	1990	1991	1992	1993	1994	1995
Pensions	36.3	29.1	18.7	25.5	21.5	17.1
Family allowances	10.8	5.0	1.3	2.5	2.4	0.2
Unemployment benefits	—	0.1	0.2	0.3	0.5	0.7
Education	19.6	21.5	16.8	17.1	16.0	11.3
Health	12.9	14.5	11.6	13.4	11.5	8.1
Estimate of enterprise-financed benefits	—	29.0	11.6	—	—	—
Total transfers[b]	79.6	101.2	65.4	67.7	61.4	41.0

Source: Branko Milanovic, *Income, Inequality, and Poverty during the Transition from Planned to Market Economy* (Washington, D.C.: World Bank, 1998), 199.

[a] 1987 rubles, in billions of rubles per year, deflated by the cost of living index.

[b] Includes small residual categories: child allowances, sick leave, scholarships, etc.

1991 and 1993, increased responsibility for financing education, social protection, and remaining consumer subsidies was transferred to the regional and local levels, generally without corresponding increases in tax or expenditure assignments or fiscal transfers. The main goal of the executive and the Finance Ministry was to reduce the deficit and decrease the size of the state sector in the medium term, as part of its larger structural adjustment program. Subnational governments initially favored decentralization and autonomy, assuming that they would get increased tax assignments or control over other resources that carried revenue-raising potential.[23]

The social-sector elites who championed decentralization had somewhat different motivations and priorities than their executive allies. Their key concern was to make Russia's social services more modern and responsive, to overcome the backwardness and authoritarianism of Soviet legacies. They were, in Kurt Weyland's terms, "specialists [who] have a direct interest in promoting innovative solutions to policy problems because such initiatives enrich their professional experience and bolster their career prospects."[24] They were receptive to foreign models that came from more successful socioeconomic systems, models

[23] Martinez-Vazquez, "Expenditures and Expenditure Assignments," 97.

[24] Kurt Weyland, "Learning from Foreign Models in Latin American Policy Reform: An Introduction," in *Learning from Foreign Models in Latin American Policy Reform,* edited by Kurt Weyland (Washington, D.C.: Johns Hopkins University Press, 2004), 15.

that carried prestige and promised to resolve long-standing problems. From their positions in the social ministries and Supreme Soviet social policy committees, largely unencumbered by organized societal or professional resistance, they incorporated these models into framework laws that passed through the legislature. The further elaboration and implementation of social legislation was accomplished mainly by presidential decrees.

The models of decentralization that were promoted by global networks and IFIs fit multiple political and economic agendas of the reformist state and professional elites. According to its proponents, decentralization would provide greater efficiency in the face of declining resources, thereby easing the effects of budget cuts. It would give subnational governments incentives to collect and use revenues effectively. Local decision makers were closer to local preferences and conditions, making them more responsive and accountable than their predecessors at the center had been. Decentralization of education and health administration was supposed to allow for greater participation, strengthen democratic institutions, give service providers more autonomy, and empower local communities. It also justified the devolution of power and responsibilities to regional elites. As Wendy Hunter states the case in her study of educational decentralization in Latin America, "Disparate forces could see decentralization as consistent with their own positions and unite under the same banner."[25]

According to the comparative literature, both social-sector bureaucracies and public-sector unions generally resist such restructuring measures. Administrators and service providers have a strong stake in the status quo. According to Joan Nelson, "Throughout the world, doctors and other health service providers predictably oppose aspects of reform that seem to them to threaten their income, status, independence, and established work routine. . . . They bitterly contest reforms that shift some control . . . to provincial or municipal governments."[26] Health and education workers' unions typically oppose decentralization because it breaks up centralized wage bargaining, and they resist privatization and efficiency measures that threaten jobs and security. The capacity of unions to block reform or to negotiate compensation such as salary increases, however, varies with

[25] Wendy Hunter, "The Diffusion of Decentralizing Reforms in Latin America: The Case of Education" (draft paper, 2006), 12; cited with the author's permission.

[26] Joan M. Nelson, "The Politics of Health Sector Reform: Cross-National Comparisons," in Kaufman and Nelson, *Crucial Needs, Weak Incentives*, 33–34.

their strength and potential to find political allies.[27] In the early 1990s, Russian public-sector unions, which in any case had never engaged in meaningful wage bargaining, had neither political-party allies nor influence in government ministries. Social-sector bureaucracies and elite professional organizations were disorganized and, in some cases, had been literally disbanded.

The decentralization of education and health care were promoted by global policy networks and IFIs throughout Latin America and Eastern Europe in the late 1980s and early 1990s to address problems of overcentralization and inefficiency in post-ISI and postcommunist states. Some of the claimed benefits are supported by experiences in developed democracies, although other studies conclude that, even here, decentralization typically has the negative effect of fragmenting welfare states.[28] But there was less evidence of its effectiveness in the transitional context. In democratizing Latin American states, for example, "Many international and domestic economists expected decentralization [of education] to encourage more efficient and effective delivery of social services . . . although by the early 1990s this view was contested by at least some policy specialists."[29] Though decentralization brought benefits in some cases, results were uneven and often disappointing.

Transplanted to the political and fiscal conditions of the new Russian Federation, decentralization largely failed to bring anticipated benefits. It was carried out very rapidly and simultaneously across several sectors, often overwhelming local fiscal and administrative capacities. No precise estimates of the additional fiscal burden on the subnational governments were made. The regional and local governmental share of education spending increased significantly from 1992 to 1996 (figure 2.1), and local responsibility for social protection expenditure increased by a factor of five (figure 2.2).

[27]   Maria Victoria Murillo, "Recovering Political Dynamics: Teachers' Unions and the Decentralization of Education in Argentina and Mexico," *Journal of Interamerican Studies and World Affairs* 41, no. 1 (1999): 31–57.

[28]   See, respectively, Robert Putnam, *Making Democracy Work: Civic Traditions in Modern Italy* (Princeton: Princton University Press, 1993); Duane Swank, *Global Capital, Political Institutions, and Political Change in Developed Welfare States* (New York: Cambridge University Press, 2002).

[29]   Robert R. Kaufman and Joan M. Nelson, "The Politics of Education Sector Reform: Cross-National Comparisons," in *Crucial Needs, Weak Incentives,* edited by Kaufman and Nelson, 270.

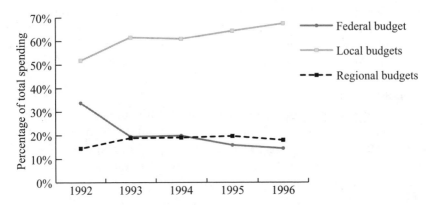

Figure 2.1 Education, distribution of expenditures between government levels, 1992–1996
Source: Jorge Martinez-Vazquez and Jameson Boex, *Russia's Transition to a New Federalism*
(Washington, D.C.: World Bank, 2001), 15.

The subnational governments initially expected compensating tax
assignments, but shifts in the rules for revenue-sharing and declining
tax bases left most in deficit.[30] Again, as Wallich puts it, "most additional (social) expenditures will be borne subnationally, most additional
revenue (from trade and energy taxes) will likely accrue to the *federal*
government . . . [or] will flow only to the three or four resource-producing
oblasts [regions]."[31] Transfers from the center did play a modest equalizing role, but the bulk of transfers were caught up in the opaque and
politicized bargaining that characterized Russia's fiscal federalism. Regions
responded by withholding taxes and accumulating social-sector wage
and benefit arrears. Significantly, expenditure responsibilities were transferred downward just as market transition and global integration had
begun to increase differentials in the economic bases of Russia's regions.
Overall, decentralization contributed to growing regional disparities in
social expenditures and service provision throughout the transition.

Reforming Education, Reducing Guarantees

The initiative for restructuring Russia's educational system came from a
team of reformist professional educators within the Ministry of Education

[30]   Martinez-Vazquez, "Expenditures and Expenditure Assignments," 97.
[31]   Christine I. Wallich, "Intergovernmental Finances: Stabilization, Privatization,
and Growth," in *Russia and the Challenge of Fiscal Federalism,* edited by Christine Wallich
(Washington, D.C.: World Bank, 1994), 77(emphasis in original).

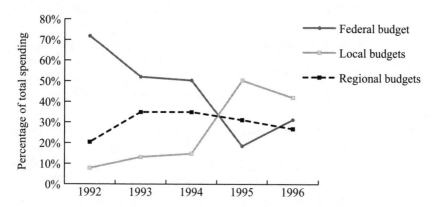

Figure 2.2 Social protection, distribution of expenditures between government levels, 1992–1996
Source: Jorge Martinez-Vazquez and Jameson Boex, *Russia's Transition to a New Federalism* (Washington, D.C.: World Bank, 2001), 15.

led by Edward Dneprov. Dneprov's group had emerged in the late 1980s as critics of what they viewed as bureaucratic tyranny and the dictatorial regime of uniformity in the Soviet educational system. They advocated the end of the state monopoly over education (destatization or *razgosudarstvlenie*), depoliticization, and humanization of the schools. Their Pedagogy of Cooperation harked back to the experiments of the Soviet 1920s, stressing personal autonomy, diversity, initiative and creativity for teachers and students. Dneprov saw the way to these goals through decentralization, the dismantling of authoritarian controls, and the development of educational markets.[32] He was closely tied to global policy networks, cultivating international financial and technical assistance to such a degree that he was perceived by many as having exclusively Western contacts. Under his stewardship of the Education Ministry, several large bilateral and multilateral aid efforts were launched in 1991–1992 and "Anglo-American 'conservative' solutions (such as privatization and the use of vouchers) [were] chosen over more continental solutions that stressed labor market planning and state direction."[33] Dneprov later justified his commitment to radical decentralization, privatization,

[32]   See Ben Eklof and Edward Dneprov, eds., *Democracy in the Russian School: The Reform Movement in Education since 1984* (Boulder: Westview, 1993); Edward Dneprov, *Chetvertnaia Shkol'naia Reforma v Rossii* (Moscow: Interfax, 1994).
[33]   Mark Johnson, "Western Models and Russian Realities in Postcommunist Education," *Tertium Comparationis: Journal für Internationale Bildungsforschung* 2, no. 2 (1995): 120, 122.

and vouchers in part by reference to World Bank and other external influences.[34]

The reform movement gained some adherents among educators and support from the pedagogical press in the late 1980s.[35] According to Stephen Webber, who has done the most in-depth study of the reform, "the educational community, politicians, the mass media, and the public at large seem to have been convinced . . . that the problems of the schools were extensive, and fundamental reform was required."[36] But the agenda of Dneprov's group did not succeed in mobilizing broader support. It failed to win a majority at the 1988 All-Union Teachers' Congress, and the alternative pro-reform Creative Teachers' Union quickly collapsed.[37] Dneprov was appointed Minister of Education in July 1990 and confronted major resistance from the conservative educational bureaucracy, including the Academy of Pedagogical Sciences and the official educators' union. Those barriers fell with the collapse of the Soviet Union in the last months of 1991. According to a participant in the reform movement,

> After the failure of the coup, [the last-gasp attempt of the old guard to preserve the Soviet Union] the ministry enjoyed an interval of roughly four months in which it had unprecedented freedom to pursue its agenda: the State Committee on Education was abolished in November, the Academy of Pedagogical Sciences finally disbanded in December, and the belief spread that now, finally, real change could begin. In May 1992, the minister won approval for his long-advocated Statute on Non-Government Educational Institutions—essentially a charter for private schools. But since the end of 1991 optimism has rapidly eroded. The collapse of the economy has exacerbated already severe shortages in the schools.[38]

Dneprov adopted a Gaidar-style "kamikaze" approach, determined to make the transformation of the educational system irreversible in order to prevent the re-assertion of communist controls.[39] He presided over the dismantling of the centralized educational system until he was

---

[34]   Edward Dneprov, *Shkol'naia reforma mezhdu vchera' i zaftra* (Moscow: Russian Academy of Education, 1996); Johnson, "Western Models," 128.

[35]   The main source here is *Uchitel'skaia Gazeta* (Teachers' Newspaper).

[36]   Webber, *School*, 14.

[37]   Johnson, "Western Models," 121.

[38]   Eklof and Dneprov, *Democracy in the Russian School*, 18.

[39]   Janet Vaillant, commenting on a talk given by the author, May 11, 2004, at the Davis Center for Russian and Eurasian Studies, Harvard University, stressed the significance of preventing a return of communist control as a motive for reformers' rapid institutional change of the system.

forced out of the government at the end of 1992, along with other radical reformers, and subsequently dismissed from his position as Yeltsin's education advisor at the end of 1993.

During 1991–1992, the Education Ministry engaged in a chaotic rush to decentralize financial, administrative, and curricular responsibilities for most education to the regional and municipal levels. The July 1992 Law on Education formalized this devolution, retaining only higher education at the federal level.[40] It ended the state monopoly, legalizing the establishment of private schools by individuals and by religious and public organizations, and promising state funds (vouchers) to those that passed accreditation. It provided greater freedom for public schools to change curricula and to engage in instructional and pedagogical innovation.

The Law on Education also reduced the guarantee for the provision of free, compulsory public education from eleven to nine years (from ages 17 to 15), breaking the Soviet commitment to universal secondary education. Overall, it was a profound revision of the existing system, made with very little preparation. The reform was shaped by a confluence of the Education Ministry's reformist politics and the economic imperatives of the Finance Ministry, which pressed Dneprov to move forward with cost-cutting measures. It passed through the Supreme Soviet quickly, with minor opposition. Reformers operated in something of a vacuum, with carte blanche to change the existing system.

Sources agree that the reforms, although they provided for more innovation in and diversification of schools, were detrimental to access, equity, and overall quality in the Russian educational system. These declines had multiple causes, including expenditure cuts and the growth of poverty among children and families, but the educational reforms had some distinct distributive effects. The withdrawal of the federal guarantee of education through grade 11 had an immediate impact on access, permitting public schools to adopt selective admissions policies and to reject students. For a time, many children, especially adolescent boys, were denied access to schools. This led to a substantial *otsev* (dropping out) from the system, mostly at grade 10, although some children were rejected even at the primary level.[41] The rates of exclusion and drop-out

---

[40] "Zakon Rossiiskoi Federatsii ob Obrazovanii," *Uchitel'skaia Gazeta*, no. 28, 4 Aug. 1992, 10–15.

[41] Webber, *School*, 183–84. Educational reformers were critical of the quality of the last two grades, believing that these had been added with inadequate planning. Webber reports that 1.7 million age-eligible children were not in school in 1992–1994; the exclusion of weaker students, particularly adolescent boys, was popular with many teachers.

rose further in the mid-1990s. The Law also blurred the public-private boundary in the upper grades, opening the way for public schools to charge fees for educational services that were no longer mandated.

The Russian state's abandonment of the guarantee to a full secondary education did not stand (for the politics of its reversal, see chapter 3.) But attendance rates did not return to their prereform levels. Elementary school enrollments fell slightly. Enrollment levels fell significantly at the upper secondary level. The percentage of 15- to 18-year-olds in school declined from 79 to 69, and in vocational-technical schools from 54 to 42, with high drop-out and low graduation rates becoming common.[42] At the same time, enrollments in academic secondary and post–secondary schools increased slightly. Enterprises also withdrew financing from their kindergartens, with one-third of all kindergartens in Russia closing between 1992 and 1994.[43] In sum, the reform affected disproportionately preschool children and poorer, less academically capable adolescents in vocational-technical programs, excluding substantial numbers of both from the educational system. Significant numbers of mid- and late adolescents, out of school and unable to enter the shrinking labor force, began to appear on the streets of Russian cities and towns.

The declining state commitment to education also had effects in more remote and indigenous regions. According to an advisor to the Russian parliament interviewed by the author in 1999, in indigenous regions during the Soviet period, "there was some state involvement to bring people into education and industry. . . . now they are on their own. . . . In the past all children went to school. Now even in cities some children are not in school at all. . . . [I]n Siberia the situation is worse. There are no possibilities for school in remote regions, no transportation, or it is too expensive."[44]

The fiscal and administrative dimensions of decentralization affected regional equity. Per capita spending on education became more dependent on regional income, and expenditure differences across regions rose.[45] The majority of teachers' salaries and other education costs were

[42]   Sue E. Berryman, *Hidden Challenges to the Education System in Transition Economies* (Washington, D.C.: World Bank, 2000), 110–17.

[43]   Jorge Martinez-Vazquez and Jameson Boex, *Russia's Transition to a New Federalism* (Washington, D.C.: World Bank, 2001), 16.

[44]   Advisor, Fund for the Development of the Russian Parliament, interview with author, Moscow, February 1, 1999.

[45]   Mary Canning, Peter Moock, and Timothy Heleniak, *Reforming Education in the Regions of Russia* (Washington, D.C.: World Bank, 1999); the coefficient of variation of the share spent on education increased from 0.17 in 1994 to 0.22 in 1996 (36).

transferred to local allocations. By 1995, educational financing across the Russian Federation was very diverse, with the systems adequately funded in some regions and almost collapsing in others. The biggest spenders tended to be the oil and gas regions in the far north and Siberia.[46] Reform also had major impacts on the administration of education. The 1992 legislation envisioned the establishment of regional centers of educational development to build local administrative capacity for the reform's implementation, but only a few of these appeared and capacities remained highly uneven. Internationally funded or partnered projects that were mounted to help with this and other aspects of reform tended to produce isolated experiments with innovation.

Politically, decentralization weakened the Ministry of Education within the government and left it with little leverage to influence developments in the regions. The Finance Ministry took control of the education budget and refused to provide transparent information about financing to Education Ministry officials. Major initiatives in education policy were taken without consulting or even informing the Education Ministry. The Finance Ministry pressed for further decentralization, including the transfer of some higher educational institutions to local budgets, measures that were strongly opposed by both education officials and the rectors of the higher schools.[47] The Education Ministry was marginalized, experiencing a steady erosion of its political, administrative, and budgetary resources.

The fundamental claims for decentralization were that it would produce greater efficiency in the face of declining resources and empower local actors. External assessments by the World Bank and Organisation for Economic Cooperation and Development (OECD) found no efficiency gains from the reforms. According to a 1996 World Bank report, the educational decentralization in Russia "suffer[s] from a lack of clearly defined responsibilities between governing agencies . . . an incomplete legal framework and lack of transparency in the allocation and use of public funding."[48] As to the effects for local actors, available evidence

[46] Webber, *School,* 68–71; E. Zhirkov, "Den'gi, Den'gi. Nichego Krome Deneg," *Uchitel'skaia Gazeta,* no. 25, 6 June 1995, 17.

[47] Andrei Baiduzhy, "The Collapse of the Schools—That Is What Adopting the Decisions That Are Ripening in the Bureaucracy Could Bring," *Nezavisimaia Gazeta,* 14 Dec. 1993, 6, trans. in *Current Digest of the Post-Soviet Press* 45, no. 50 (1993): 17–18; OECD, *Reviews of National Policy for Education; Russian Federation* (Paris: OECD, 1998), 35–55.

[48] World Bank, *Russia: Education Innovation Project, PID* (Report no. PIC2127) (Washington, D.C.: World Bank, Sept. 20, 1996), available at www.worldbank.org; OECD, *Reviews of National Policy for Education,* 55–87.

shows that some teachers did value the new curricular and other freedoms. However, the majority believed that they had little influence over the course of the reforms and felt little or no sense of ownership. Survey evidence indicates that most saw the reforms as controlled mainly by bureaucratic actors, the Ministry of Education and especially regional education authorities.[49]

The reform would later provoke political opposition from regional and central education authorities, teachers' and rectors' unions, and political parties. The Dumas of the mid-1990s rolled back some provisions. It resulted in very limited privatization or other formal structural change. Many changes to education came as informal adaptations to budget cuts and wage declines and arrears.

Restructuring Health Care

Russian health care also underwent radical restructuring during the early 1990s. As with education, the health-care system was "carried along in the tidal wave of decentralisation," but other major changes were also initiated.[50] A central goal of reform was to replace the existing system of single-payer public-budget financing with mandatory health insurance that would be financed from payroll taxes and other sources. New legislation also legalized private insurers and health-care providers. The initiative for restructuring again came from two sources: the executive, especially the Finance Ministry; and reformers within the medical profession, mainly a group of doctors and academics acting through the Supreme Soviet's Committee for Health Protection. These reformers were initially supported by the health workers' trade union, whose members hoped that the reform would bring increases in health-care spending and salaries.[51]

In fall 1990, Dr. Viacheslav Kalinin, a reformer committed to the introduction of an insurance medicine model, was appointed to head the Ministry of Health. Reformers also dominated among the ninety-seven doctors who served as legislative deputies, and the critical reform legislation was shepherded through the Supreme Soviet by the Health

---

[49]   Webber, *School*, 118. Webber's survey is based on a limited sample of 132 teachers but is informed by his excellent study of the overall reform process.

[50]   OECD, *The Social Crisis in the Russian Federation* (Paris: OECD, 2001), 102.

[51]   A. Askalonov served as the chair of the Committee on Health Protection. Michael Ryan, "Russia Report: Doctors and Health Service Reform," *British Medical Journal* 304 (Jan. 11, 1992): 101–3.

Committee with opposition only from Russia's holdover trade union federation. The infant insurance industry, a new private interest that had a stake in the expansion of social security markets, also made its appearance. According to one of the architects of the reform, "There were only about 12 people at the time who really understood the implications [of the health insurance law,] so it was easy to get it through the legislature. . . . at the time, an insurance industry was being created in other sectors (not health), but people in the industry began to see that they could make money in health insurance. So, their lobbyists began to push it in the legislature."[52] Within a year, Kalinin had been replaced by a minister who lacked enthusiasm for insurance medicine, and the Health Ministry spent the remainder of the decade trying to gut the reform. But, as with education, the changes of the early 1990s proved highly consequential, amounting to a radical departure from traditional lines of responsibility for financing and delivery, an "overnight massive de-statization of medical care . . . extending 'shock therapy' into the health care system."[53]

Restructuring legislation re-organized the financing of medical care and created two new sets of institutions: Compulsory Medical Insurance Funds and Health Insurance Organizations.[54] The Funds would collect and manage payroll-based employer contributions for the employed and contributions from municipal budgets for nonworkers, with most of the monies being raised and spent at the regional level. The Funds would contract with insurers, who would in turn purchase medical services from providers. This competitive contracting model was supposed to introduce competition and choice into the health-care system, to improve quality and efficiency. Separating purchasers from providers was supposed to facilitate the elimination of excess hospital and other capacity, one of the major problems of the inherited system. The legislation also legalized supplementary, voluntary private medical insurance and private medical practices, which would provide choice. The reform was supposed to keep in place guaranteed access to free and comprehensive health services. Insurance would be universal, compulsory, and publicly financed for those outside the labor force; mandatory out-of-pocket payments were

[52] Senior Russian health economist, interview with Judyth Twigg, Moscow, May 21, 1997 (transcript provided to the author).

[53] Judyth Twigg, "Balancing State and Market: Russia's Adoption of Obligatory Medical Insurance," *Europe-Asia Studies* 50, no. 4 (1998): 586.

[54] "Zakon o Meditsinskom Strakhovanii Grazhdan," *Meditsinskaia Gazeta*, no. 8, 29 June 29 1991, 8–9.

rejected. A decentralized, competitive, public-private mix replaced centralized state control, planning, and finance.[55]

The health-care reform represents one of the clearest cases of Russian reformers abandoning a more moderate, domestically generated policy built on indigenous institutions in order to adopt a radically new foreign model that could not be fit to Russian conditions. A health-care reform experiment, the New Economic Mechanism, had been developed in Russia in 1989–1991. Based on existing polyclinics as fundholders and capitated payments, it showed initial promise but collapsed under the financial strain of the early reform years. At the same time, in the early 1990s a great deal of attention in global social policy networks was focused on health-care reforms, capped by the World Bank's *World Development Report 1993: Investing in Health*, which promoted competition, choice, and other elements of the liberal model.[56]

Russian reformers drew on these internationally generated ideas as well as on European health-care systems, particularly those of the Netherlands and Germany, which were diffusing throughout Eastern Europe in this period.[57] Their belief in the market, model shopping, and freedom to shape policy change are well captured by an expert who was involved in designing the reforms:

> Back then (in 1991) we, the architects of the health insurance legislation, were "naïve and silly." We didn't really understand the difference between mandatory and voluntary health insurance; we didn't understand risk assessment and the ability of insurance companies to choose whom they would cover; we didn't think about . . . the need for a socially responsible body to regulate the system. . . . [W]e thought we could rely on the market; we thought market forces would do it all. Also, we had traveled to the Netherlands, and thought those ideas could work in Russia.[58]

Health-care restructuring confronted major limitations of institutional capacity in Russia. A 2001 OECD report stated the problems

[55]   Technical Assistance to the CIS [hereafter TACIS], *Public-Private Mix in the Health Care and Health Insurance System: Current Situation, Problems, Perspectives* (anthology of reports prepared by experts in TACIS Project no. EDRUS 9605) (TACIS, Moscow, 1999).

[56]   World Bank, *World Development Report 1993: Investing in Health* (Oxford: Oxford University Press, 1993).

[57]   According to Judyth Twigg (personal communication, March 16, 2003) ideas were taken from Germany and the Netherlands or from a hybrid of German and U.S. models. There was no attempt to copy wholesale. Russian reformers were looking for ideas.

[58]   Senior Russian health economist, interview with Judyth Twigg, Moscow, May 21, 1997 (transcript provided to the author).

succinctly: "This 'competitive contracting' model should in theory promote efficiency; but it is too complex, and requires numerous institutions that are not well-developed in Russia, such as health care insurers
and many independent providers in each health care market."[59] In practice, most Russian municipalities held a monopoly on health facilities
in their area, and competing private providers emerged in significant
numbers only in major urban areas. Insurance companies appeared but
remained concentrated in a few major cities, with no competitive market
developing in a majority of regions.

The implementation of restructuring legislation remained very uneven. About one-third of health-care expenditures shifted to contract
relations while most spending continued to follow previous patterns.[60]
The proportion of spending on in-patient hospital care did not decline
significantly nor did other measures of efficiency improve. Although the
reform did introduce some mechanisms for competition and quality
control, in the short term especially it disorganized the health-care sector rather than making it more efficient, leaving multiple institutions—
funds, insurance companies, private providers—unevenly distributed
and poorly regulated.[61]

Decentralization also weakened central coordinating mechanisms, fragmenting the health-care system and disrupting public health sub-systems.
The Health Ministry now controlled limited funding, leaving federal authorities with few levers to influence developments in the regions. During
the first half of the 1990s, child vaccination rates fell temporarily; mortality
from infectious and parasitic diseases nearly doubled; and tuberculosis
rates grew sharply, placing Russia among the top ten countries for prev-
alence worldwide.[62] The overall health and demographic crisis in Russia
has many causes; among them, decentralization contributed to weakening
public health measures that had been one strength of the old system.

As with education, decentralization also exacerbated fiscal and administrative inequalities across regions. The ability of regional health

[59]   OECD, *Social Crisis*, 13.

[60]   Twigg, "Balancing State and Market"; Edward J. Burger, Mark G. Field, and Judyth
Twigg, "From Assurance to Insurance in Russian Health Care: The Problematic Transition," *American Journal of Public Health* 88, no. 5 (1998): 755–58.

[61]   Ksenia Yudaeva and Maria Gorban, "Health and Health Care," *Russian Economic
Trends* 8, no. 2 (1999): 32.

[62]   Ellie Tragakes and Suszy Lessof, *Health Care Systems in Transition: Russian Federation*,
edited by Ellie Tragakes (Copenhagen: European Observatory on Health Systems and Policies, 2003), 13–14. Fear of contracting AIDS from used needles was a factor in the fall in
vaccination rates.

departments to fulfill their roles varied, and in many cases it was inadequate to the tasks that had been carried out by the center. Health-care planning gave way to crisis management in poorer regions, which struggled to maintain basic services while monitoring and regulation were crowded out. In regions that did have resources, expenditure decisions were often ad hoc. There was a growing divide among regions in financing and access to health-care facilities. A later World Bank study estimated variations in per capita public expenditures for health care at seven- to eightfold across Russia's eighty-nine regions, with large rural-urban differences and exclusion from access.[63] According to the OECD, although the severe reduction in overall public financing remained the system's deepest problem, the repudiation of a strong federal role worsened and deepened the catastrophe.[64]

The reform did transfer much health-care financing from public budgets, a key goal of central reformers. Combined federal and regional budget financing fell from 100 percent to about 50 percent of the total during the 1990s, with insurance and household payments making up the difference (see table 2.5). The proportion of household payments for both medical services and pharmaceuticals increased significantly. Reforms also succeeded in establishing payroll taxes as a reliable base for health-care financing. Most regions reported 80–95 percent of payroll taxes paid.[65]

But the reform faced powerful opposition from local administrative organs, which could not block legislation but could play a veto role in the implementation stage. Local health administrators stood to lose control over the budgets of health facilities to the Medical Insurance Funds. Cash-strapped local governments often refused to contribute their shares for insurance of the nonworking population or to cooperate with fund administrators. The insurance mechanism was seriously underfinanced from the outset by their withholding of contributions. In 1996, for example, municipalities in half of Russia's regions made few or no insurance payments. The health-care system became caught up in time-consuming and destructive battles, with continual bureaucratic and institutional in-fighting among major players over responsibilities and control of resources.[66] Local and regional governments progressively undermined

[63] World Bank, *Russian Federation Health Reform Implementation Project* (report no. PID7394) (Washington, D.C.: World Bank, Dec. 3, 2001), available at www.worldbank.org.

[64] OECD, *Social Crisis.*

[65] Burger et al., "From Assurance to Insurance."

[66] Judyth Twigg, "Obligatory Medical Insurance in Russia: The Participants' Perspective," *Social Science and Medicine* 49 (1999): 377.

TABLE 2.5
Main sources of health-care financing in the Russian Federation, 1992–1999 (% of total)

Source of finance	1992	1993	1994	1995	1996	1997	1998	1999
Federal budget	11.3	8.9	8.6	6.4	4.9	7.7	4.6	4.9
Regional health budgets[a]	88.7	75.3	64.7	60.6	58.6	53.1	47.1	44.7
Budget contributions or mandatory health insurance for nonworking population	—	0.5	4.5	6.7	6.3	5.1	5.6	5.2
Mandatory health insurance contributions for working population	—	—	15.6	14.7	15.7	14.5	16.0	15.9
Private contributions to voluntary health insurance	0	0.9	1.5	2.0	2.5	2.7	3.0	3.5
Household payments for medical services[b]	—	1.6	2.2	4.7	6.3	7.3	9.1	8.4
Household payments for pharmaceuticals	—	—	7.8	13.2	13.7	15.6	21.1	24.9

Source: Ellie Tragakes and Suszy Lessof, *Health Care Systems in Transition: Russian Federation* (ed. by Eliie Tragakes) (Copenhagen: European Observatory on Health Systems and Polities, 2003), 98.

[a] Including contributions to mandatory health insurance for nonworking population.

[b] Not including under-the-table payments.

the insurance mechanism.[67] By mid-decade, fewer than half of Russia's eighty-nine regions allowed insurance companies to function, and lower-level governments were withdrawing licenses. Eventually most regions suspended the implementation of the reform and moved to prohibit the operation of insurance funds.

Reforming Social Assistance

In early 1992, the federal government also shifted responsibility for most social assistance and subsidy programs to regional and local governments. These included family allowances and child benefits, cash subsidies for vulnerable groups, welfare programs for elderly, support for the homeless, and consumer subsidies.[68] In terms of percentage of expenditures,

[67] TACIS, *Governance of Social Security: Social Insurance, Medical Insurance and Pensions: Final Report* (Cologne: TACIS, June 1, 2000), 63–64.

[68] Wallich, "Russia's Dilemma," 8.

this was by far the most dramatic devolution. Education and, especially, health financing had had a strong regional component even before reform, but social assistance had traditionally come mostly from federal outlays. The federal government's share of financing declined from almost 72 percent in 1992 to 50 percent in 1994 and to a low of 18 percent in 1995, with most of the burden falling on local governments (see figure 2.2).

According to the major Western experts on poverty in Russia, "The Russian system became decentralized by default . . . since the central government had practically no money to allocate for social assistance. . . . this led to a wide dispersion of the coverage and levels of social assistance in the country."[69] This change was not endorsed by the IFIs, which wanted the federal government instead to establish and fund means-tested antipoverty programs. World Bank publications exhorted the Russian government to recentralize the financing of social assistance, which it gradually did after 1995. According to one publication: "If the adequacy of the social safety net becomes an issue of *national* priority in the difficult transition ahead, it should not be a major responsibility of sub-national governments alone. If it is, some will be able to provide, others will not, and regional differences in well-being will be accentuated."[70]

As this quotation suggests, the devolution of social assistance contributed to the regional concentration of poverty and to a distribution pattern in which the poorest groups received disproportionately little from social transfer programs during the 1990s. As table 2.6 shows, the levels of poverty increased very unevenly across the Russian Federation, remaining well below the average in financial centers such as Moscow and in oil-rich regions such as Tiumensk while increasing to half and more of the population in many other regions. According to a study by a group of Western experts on poverty and income distribution in Russia, "strongly regionalized systems such as the . . . Russian display the tendency to exclude from access to social assistance households living in the 'wrong' regions. . . . decentralized financing systems in a country where territorial income differences are large, lead to large horizontal inequities in treatment of people at the same income

[69]   Branko Milanovic, "The Role of Social Assistance in Addressing Poverty," in *Poverty and Social Assistance in Transition Countries,* edited by Jeanine Braithwaite, Christiaan Grootaert, and Branko Milanovic (New York: St. Martin's Press, 1999), 137–38.

[70]   Christine I. Wallich, "Making—or Breaking—Russia," in *Russia and the Challenge of Fiscal Federalism,* edited by Christine I. Wallich (Washington, D.C.: World Bank, 1994), 247.

TABLE 2.6
Poverty levels in selected regions of the Russian Federation, *1994–1998*
(% population below subsistence)

Region	1994	1996	1998
Nothern Raion			
Republic of Karelia	18.9	21.1	23.4
Repubic of Komi	18.4	20.2	20.6
Archangelsk region	20.8	27.7	37.8
Vologodsk region	19.2	21.4	25.2
Murmansk region	19.1	18.7	18.5
Volgo-Viatskii Raion			
Republic of Mari-El	22.1	56.8	61.0
Republic of Mordovia	24.2	45.5	46.9
Chuvash Republic	23.6	27.4	48.0
Kirovsky Oblast	26.3	30.7	41.5
Nizhegorodsky Oblast	18.7	19.2	21.5
Siberian Raions			
Republic of Buriatiia	33.0	49.4	46.4
Altai Republic	15.3	45.7	46.5
Kemorovsk Oblast	14.3	19.7	22.7
Tiumensk Oblast	11.5	15.8	15.3
Republic of Tuva	66.8	74.7	74.9
Central Raion			
City of Moscow	13.7	17.7	17.6
North Caucasus			
Republic of Dagastan	—	64.7	58.1

Source: *Rossiiskii Statisticheskii Ezhegodnik: Statisticheskii Sbornik* (Moscow: Goskomstat Rossii 1999), 163.

level."[71] Regions coped in various ways. Some experimented with means testing, while many fell back on in-kind benefits for groups of the traditionally poor. Few regions developed programs that reached the new poor created by the transitional economy, the unemployed and households with declining wage incomes that fell below the poverty level.[72]

The restructuring of major components of the inherited welfare state—health, education, and social assistance—shows that the first

[71] Milanovic, "Role of Social Assistance, 151–56.

[72] Jeanine Braithwaite, economist, Poverty Reduction and Economic Management, Europe and Central Asia Unit, World Bank, phone interview with author, January 12, 2000. There was a federal unemployment program, but its funding remained very inadequate.

Russian government had an impressive capacity to legislate change. Both the concentration of executive power and the virtual absence of effective veto actors were critical in explaining this capacity. The government re-organized the administration and financing of social services with minimal negotiation or opposition, paying little attention to the stakeholders who elsewhere slowed or blocked similar reforms. Small groups of reformist professionals, strategically located in the government and legislature and supported by the executive, trumped the weakened statist social-sector elites and ministerial bureaucratic stakeholders who had administered the old welfare state. Policy change was rapid but generally low-quality, relying on broad framework legislation that was implemented by presidential and governmental decrees, with little legal or regulatory basis. Often the expected benefits failed to materialize, while unanticipated negative consequences harmed welfare. Moreover, these policies produced latent resistance.

PRIVATIZING HOUSING

Housing privatization was also initiated in the early 1990s. Housing is not generally treated as a category of welfare state expenditures, but the public housing sector is considered part of the welfare state.[73] At the beginning of the transition, the vast majority of Russia's housing was public, state-owned and -allocated, and heavily subsidized. Management and financing were divided about evenly between municipalities and enterprises, with residents paying minimal costs. Housing and utilities (communal services) were closely tied up with issues of energy prices and subsidies. Energy was one of the major costs associated with housing, and energy prices had been kept under state control when most consumer prices were liberalized at the beginning of 1992. The state now wanted to escape this subsidy burden and transfer the costs to residents. Housing was also connected to a range of social privileges (*l'goty*), mainly exemptions from payment for rent, utilities, telephone service, and so forth that were extended to veterans, the elderly, and myriad other categories.

In 1993, the government set out to privatize most of this housing, to shift ownership, costs, and management to residents, and to create a

---

[73]   See, for example, Paul Pierson, *Dismantling the Welfare State: Reagan, Thatcher, and the Politics of Retrenchment* (Cambridge, UK: Cambridge University Press, 1994).

housing market. This was arguably the one piece of welfare reform that could provide broad compensation: the state would distribute property to much of the population at nominal cost. Privatization to residents had gained considerable support for the destatization of council housing, and the broader liberal reform program, in Margaret Thatcher's Britain.[74] In Russia as well, reformers hoped that the state's grant of ownership rights would generate political support for the reform program. In their scenario, the state would distribute property to households. Residents would gain a tangible asset that they could rent, sell, or use as collateral for small business loans and other purposes. A large number of property owners would be created. It is not too much of an exaggeration to suggest that Russian reformers and their international advisors spun a middle class out of the housing reform.

Privatization of housing was integral to the broader marketizing project in Russia. First, the near-absence of a housing market limited mobility, especially labor mobility, which was essential to developing a labor market. Second, as enterprises privatized and lost subsidies in 1992–1993 they were pressed—indeed required by presidential decrees—to divest housing and other social assets in order to focus on core production and business functions. Third, housing subsidies constituted a large budget item, costing more than 3 percent of GDP annually through the mid-1990s.

The privatization program that was devised involved four stages: (1) enterprises would divest their housing to municipalities, which would hold it temporarily and privatize it to residents; (2) residents would organize their buildings into self-financing, self-managing condominiums that would contract for services and utilities; (3) subsidies would be withdrawn and replaced by residents' payments; and (4) means-tested benefits would be made available to eligible households, limiting the state's role in housing to the provision of targeted assistance for the poor. For municipalities, housing was supposed to be a temporary, federally compensated expense, with residents quickly taking over the costs and management of their buildings.[75]

---

[74]   Pierson, ibid., argues that privatization would not be popular in the United States because most public housing was in large multi-unit buildings (rather than individual houses as in Britain) and because tenants in the United States were relatively poor. The Russian circumstances more closely approximate the American ones.

[75]   V. F. Massarygina, "O Nekotorykh Sotsial'nykh Aspektakh Zhilishchno-Kommunal'noi Reformy," in *Rossiiskie Reformy: Sotsialnye Aspekty* (Moscow: Vysshnaia Shkola Ekonomiki, 1998), 345–49; Raymond J. Struyk, ed., *Restructuring Russia's Housing Sector: 1991–1997* (Washington, D.C.: Urban Institute, 1997).

The Russian government, working mainly through its Economics and Construction Ministries, developed the housing reform program in 1992. A comprehensive piece of framework legislation, the Law on Fundamentals of Federal Housing Policy, was passed by the Supreme Soviet in December with little debate or apparent comprehension.[76] According to a senior fellow at the U.S. Urban Institute, who was involved in housing reform, "a small coalition got it through.... the legislature probably didn't understand it [the 1992 law]."[77] According to the legislation, while households could privatize their dwellings for a nominal fee, all except the poor would see their costs rise dramatically, by five times over a five-year period. Municipal governments were given the right to evict residents and move them to dormitory-style housing for nonpayment. This legislation ended, in principle, the established tenancy rights of the Soviet period. Reformers anticipated the rapid development of a housing market, leaving only a residual public sector. Implementing measures were put into place by governmental and presidential decrees in 1993 and 1994.

The World Bank and other international organizations, particularly the U.S.-based Urban Institute, promoted the housing reform with advice, technical assistance, and demonstration projects. The Bank published numerous studies prescribing privatization and laying out the mechanics of the process.[78] It sponsored technical assistance projects for cities that met implementation goals for divestiture, cost recovery, and privatization. These projects were designed to support reforms that privatized ownership, to change the attitude that housing is a public good that should be heavily subsidized by the state. They were intended to have broad demonstration effects.[79] The prescriptions fit the liberal agenda, pushing for full privatization with only a small residual public sector and replacing subsidies with means-tested assistance. They partook of the market fundamentalism that focused on establishing property rights while paying little attention to the broader institutional context needed for functioning markets.

[76] For a discussion of the legislation and its significance, see T. D. Belkina, *Zhilishchnaia Reforma v Rossii: Problemy i Perspectivy* (Moscow: TACIS, 1999).

[77] Senior Fellow, Urban Institute, Washington, D.C., phone interview with author, April 21, 1999.

[78] Among the numerous World Bank reports on housing reform are *Russia: Housing Reform and Privatization, Vol. 1* (Main Report no. 14929) (Washington, D.C.: World Bank, 1995); *Russian Federation Housing Project* (Staff Appraisal Report no. 13022-RU) (Washington, D.C.: World Bank, 1995); *Russian Federation: Enterprise Housing Divestiture Project* (Staff Appraisal Report no. 15112-RU) (Washington, D.C.: World Bank, 1996).

[79] World Bank, *Russian Federation Housing Project.*

In the event, enterprises did divest most of their housing to municipalities. During the first years of the reform, the total housing stock managed by many municipalities increased by 50 percent or more.[80] But only
about half of eligible households privatized, mainly those whose housing
was in desirable urban locations and elderly residents who gained the
right to will housing to nonresident relatives.[81] For the rest, property
rights apparently did not serve as adequate compensation for increased
housing costs and responsibilities, especially in the face of declining
incomes.[82] Gaps in the institutional system added risks to privatization
and limited the potential benefits. The legal, financial, and regulatory
infrastructure that underpins real estate markets was largely absent in
Russia. The banking sector was too chaotic, and interest rates far too
high, to support a program of mortgage lending or borrowing against
property. When housing was exchanged during this period, it was done
through convoluted series of cash and barter transactions brokered by
creative real estate agents. Those who privatized also had to take on new
risks, such as fire and maintenance, and to depend on existing local
monopolies for services.[83] According to an official of the Institute for
the Economy of the Housing-Communal Sector, "People got the right
to privatize, but we didn't develop mechanisms of realizing ownership
rights . . . so they can't feel themselves owners."[84]

The housing divestiture and municipalization process also confronted
serious legal problems because it was implemented mainly through
governmental and executive decrees. It illustrates the low-quality policies
produced by unconstrained executive authority. According to one Russian
expert, "the legal framework of social asset (mainly housing) municipalization was shaped in an erratic way, resulting from numerous partial decisions made by the executive authorities. . . . the statutes aimed exclusively
at relieving enterprises of social functions, paid inadequate attention

[80]   Elena Vinogradova, "Provision of Social Benefits by Russian Enterprises: Managers'
Behavior and Motivations" (paper presented at the Workshop on Labor and Privatization,
Watson Institute, Brown University, Providence, R.I., March 6, 1999).

[81]   Jennifer Daniell, Alexander Puzanov, and Raymond Struyk, "Housing Privatization
in Moscow: Who Privatizes and Why," (Urban Institute Project 6306-03) (Washington,
D.C.: Urban Institute, 1993); some elderly residents later deprivatized.

[82]   Massarygina, "O Nekotorykh Sotsial'nykh Aspektakh Zhilishchno-Kommunal'noi
Reformy."

[83]   Department head, Institute of National Economic Forecasting, Russian Academy
of Sciences, interview with author, Moscow, June 8, 2000; Research associate, International
Activities Center, Urban Institute, interview with author, Washington, D.C., April 13, 1999.

[84]   Official, Institute for the Economy of the Housing-Communal Sector, interview
with author, Moscow, Feb. 2, 1999.

to institutional and financial conditions enabling local governments to carry the burden."[85] The process left much housing in legal limbo, underfinanced, or totally abandoned. The outcome was a partial privatization that greatly increased the amount of housing owned and managed by municipal governments. Rent increases were put into effect for all tenants, cost recovery from residents increased to 50 percent by 1998, and a rental market began to emerge.[86] But about 40 percent of housing remained in the public sector.[87] Most who privatized lived in buildings with fragmented ownership patterns, and few formed condominiums. Housing and communal services became the largest item in municipal budgets, accounting for 30 percent of total outlays on average at mid-decade and for more than 50 percent in some cities, crowding out expenditures for health and education.[88] Housing subsidies remained at 3.5–4.5 of GDP. And as in other areas, the legislature would roll back the reform in the mid-1990s, insisting on the maintenance of housing as a public good that should be heavily subsidized by the state.

DECENTRALIZATION, FISCAL FEDERALISM, GLOBALIZATION, AND WELFARE

Although couched in the language of administrative re-organization, efficiency, and reliability of financing, the decisions to decentralize, privatize, and introduce insurance mechanisms into social provision were profoundly political in their distributive and welfare consequences. Decentralization weakened the federal role in welfare provision just as the economic transition began. It increased disparities in expenditures and access to basic services, and it institutionalized a fiscal system that would tend to sustain these disparities when economic growth resumed.

Cumulatively, expenditure assignments equaling an estimated 6 percent of GDP were transferred down to the subnational level in the early

[85]   V. N. Leskin and A. N. Shvetsov, *New Problems of Russian Cities: Municipalisation of Social Assets: Legal and Financial Solutions* (Moscow, URSS, 1999), 239.

[86]   A. Z. Astopovich, C. A. Afontsev, and A. A. Blokhin, *Obzor Ekonomicheskie Politiki v Rossii za 1997* (Moscow: Biuro Ekonomicheskova Analiza, 1998).

[87]   Institut Ekonomika Goroda, *Problemy Zadolzhennosti Naseleniia po Oplate Zhilia i Kommunalnykh Uslug, Vypusk 2* (Moscow: Fond Institut Ekonomika Goroda, 1998); director, Department of Living Standards, Russian Center for the Study of Public Opinion (VTsIOM), interview with author, Moscow, Feb. 3, 1999.

[88]   Astopovich et al., *Obzor Ekonomicheskie Politiki v Rossii za 1997*. Housing subsidies were increasingly concentrated on utilities, especially energy.

1990s.[89] The gap between the taxable base and the amount of social obligations in many Russian municipalities was huge. Local governments responded by accumulating public-sector wage and benefit arrears, cutting services, and suspending the payment of benefits. The population's access to social services and assistance became heavily dependent on local and regional resources. Many of the poorest people lived in regions with the greatest inadequacy of funds, the weakest administrative capacities, and the least potential to provide assistance. Disparities in regional levels of per capita revenue collections and expenditures grew steadily during the transition.

Fiscal transfers could have mitigated the inequalities. A regional equalization fund (the Fund for Financial Support of Regions), using formula-based funding that reflected need, was established in 1993 and used to distribute some federal monies.[90] But the bulk of fiscal transfers in the 1990s were ad hoc negotiated subventions, subject to political bargaining between regional leaders and the Finance Ministry. Many regions entered into special fiscal regimes with the federal government[91] Federal distributions were driven mainly by political calculations rather than social need. According to the most influential analyses, fiscal transfers were used to respond to separatist pressures, to appease politically dissident regions, and to placate regions with public-sector strikes.[92]

Meanwhile, as the Russian economy was privatized and opened to international markets, regions performed at widely differing levels, reflecting the structures of their economies and resource bases. Those with natural resources, those with competitive metallurgy and chemical industries, and those able to develop service sectors based on international trade and finance prospered. Foreign direct investment and economic growth were concentrated in a small number of regions, with others stagnating or declining. Although federal revenue assignments improved over time, according to a 2001 analysis, "The transfer system, introduced in 1993, has yet to have a major impact on regional equity. The system is mildly equalizing. It is insufficient to offset more powerful trends creating greater concentration

[89]   Christine Wallich, "Russia's Dilemma of Fiscal Federalism," in *Macroeconomic Management and Fiscal Decentralization*, edited by Jayanta Roy (Washington, D.C.: World Bank, 1995), 105.

[90]   Dmitriev, *Biudzhetnaia Politika*, 33.

[91]   Lopez-Claros and Alexashenko, *Fiscal Policy Issues*, 52.

[92]   See Daniel S. Triesman, *After the Deluge: Regional Crises and Political Consolidation in Russia* (Ann Arbor: University of Michigan Press, 1999); Vladimir Gimpelson and Daniel Triesman, "Fiscal Games and Public Employment: A Theory with Evidence from Russia, *World Politics* 54 (2002): 145–83.

of economic well-being in regions benefiting from reforms, integration into world trade, or natural resource endowments."[93]

MOVING SOCIAL SECURITY OFF-BUDGET

Russia's inherited system of social security was also re-organized at the beginning of the transition. Between 1990 and 1993, the Pension and Social Insurance Funds (covering maternity leave, sick pay, etc.) were moved from budget financing to separate off-budget funds.[94] An Employment Fund was also established to provide unemployment compensation and reemployment services.[95] These three, along with the Medical Insurance Fund (previously discussed), were financed by a payroll tax levied almost entirely on employers (table 2.7). Reformers gave several rationales for these changes. First, they were intended to improve financing by creating a dedicated base of revenue inflows, "a stable and predictable source of funds that would not fluctuate with the budget . . [or] compete with other sectors for its budget allocation."[96] Second, financing of social benefits would become more transparent, and the costs would be more visible to beneficiaries. IFIs encouraged the creation of the off-budget funds as a step in the formation of a contribution-based system of social security.[97] Employers would pay into what were essentially trust funds, and the monies would be held and used only to cover designated expenses. Social security payments would be covered by contributions rather then general revenues, and programs would be financially self-sustaining and actuarially sound.[98] The new pension system, no longer reliant on budget financing for most pensions, was essentially a pay-as-you-go (PAYG) system.

The Funds immediately confronted a number of problems. The social security tax, calculated to cover existing benefits, was set at 38 percent of

[93]   Jorge Martinez-Vazquez and Jameson Boex, *Russia's Transition to a New Federalism* (Washington, D.C: World Bank, 2001).

[94]   The transition to a self-financing, extra-budgetary Pension Fund began in 1990, before the Soviet collapse. The reform was accelerated with the beginning of shock therapy. See Andrea Chandler, *Shocking Mother Russia: Democratization, Social Rights, and Pension Reform in Russia, 1990–2001* (Toronto: University of Toronto Press, 2004), chap. 4.

[95]   A modest system of unemployment insurance had been created in the Gorbachev period, funded from general budget revenues.

[96]   OECD, *Social Crisis*, 102; E. Tragakes and S. Lessof, *Health Care Systems in Transition: Russian Federation* (Copenhagen: European Observatory on Health Systems and Policies 2003:5 [3]), 75.

[97]   See Lopez-Claros and Alexashenko, *Fiscal Policy Issues*, 46–47.

[98]   The system would be coordinated and controlled by the federal government but run on insurance principles, with the legislature setting contribution rates.

TABLE 2.7
Social security funds, 1994

Fund	Supervision	Coverage	Funding
Pension Fund	Ministry of Social Protection	Retirement, disability, social pensions	29% of payroll tax
Employment Fund	Federal Employment Service	Unemployment benefits, retraining, job placement	2% of payroll tax
Social Insurance Fund	Ministry of Social Protection	Maternity benefits, sick pay, sanatorium treatment	5.4% of payroll tax
Medical Insurance Fund	Ministry of Health	Health-care benefits (doctors, hospitalization, some drugs)	3.6% of payroll tax

Source: OECD Economic Surveys: The Russian Federation, 1995 (Paris: OECD: 1995), 127, citing the Ministry of Social Protection.

the total wage, a very high rate by international standards. Social security wage taxes are generally divided between employers and employees; all but 1 percent of the Russian tax was imposed on employers, making it the highest payroll tax paid directly by employers among transition and OECD states.[99] The World Bank views any payroll tax over 25 percent as unacceptably high and likely to generate evasion.[100] In the transitional Russian context, a tax of almost 40 percent contributed to large-scale evasion, avoidance, and minimal compliance. Each of the Funds collected taxes separately. The smaller Medical and Employment Funds proved relatively successful, arguably providing a more reliable revenue base than budget financing would have provided.[101] But, overall, arrears grew rapidly (see table 2.8), especially to the Pension Fund, which accounted for the bulk of the tax (29 percent). The Funds made pay-outs in rapidly inflating rubles during their initial years of operation, allowing them to

[99] International Monetary Fund, *Russia: Policy Development Review* (Washington, D.C.: IMF, June 2003), 17.
[100] World Bank, *Averting the Old Age Crisis: Policies to Protect the Old and Promote Growth* (New York: Oxford University Press, 1994), 263.
[101] Judyth Twigg (personal communication) argues that funding for health care was better than that for education, which remained on the budget; the assessment of employment fund collections is from Elena Vinogradova (personal communication).

TABLE 2.8
Enterprise wage tax arrears to off-budget social funds, 1995–2001

	1995	1996	1997	1998	1999	2000	2001
Amount (billions of rubles)	17.6	97.2	154.3	246.2	297.4	322.1	311.2
Percentage of GDP	0.9	4.2	5.7	9.0	6.3	4.6	3.4

Source: Russian Economic Trends 4, no. 4 (2002): table D37.

run surpluses and to appear financially healthy, but by the mid-1990s inflation was brought under control and the deficits mounted. Moreover, pensioners' real incomes were eroded by inflation, and the president vetoed most legislative initiatives to index payments.

Nor could the design of the Funds have taken account of the impending wage shock. Real wages contracted sharply, by an estimated 40 percent in the early 1990s, undercutting the revenue base for the new Social Security Funds. The tax base continued to erode as production shifted toward informal and unreported activities. At the same time, the economic collapse greatly increased demands on the Funds. Unemployment grew, labor force cuts pushed older workers out of jobs and on to pensions, and the numbers claiming invalid pensions increased significantly.[102] The Employment Fund, at a 2 percent wage tax rate, proved far too small from the outset. Unemployment benefits were paid at a fraction of the subsistence level and, then, only for a small minority of the unemployed. The majority failed to register because of the paltry benefit and high eligibility requirements. The Fund had almost no effect on alleviating poverty among Russia's unemployed.

The problems of the pension system also worsened rapidly. The officially reported ratio between those paying in and recipients reached 1.7 in 1996, an unsustainable ratio. Experts' estimates that took account of tax evasion put the actual ratio at 1.4.[103] In the face of similar pressures, Poland substantially increased spending on pensions and unemployment and Hungary increased expenditures on social assistance to cushion the effects, and both initiated pension reforms. Russia did neither. By mid-decade, pensions were paid at a very low, nearly flat rate, with almost no

[102]   Tatyana Maleva, ed., *Sovremennie Problemy Pensionnoi Sfery: Kommentarii Ekonomistov i Demografov* (Moscow: Carnegie Center for International Peace, 1997), 17; the number of employed declined by more than 5 million between 1991 and 1996, and the number of pensioners grew by more than 3 million.

[103]   See *Rossiiskaia Gazeta,* 23 Aug. 1995.

relation to previous wages or employer contributions, violating the insurance principle the Funds were supposed to embody. Payment arrears undermined confidence in the system and contributed to nonpayment and defection.[104] From 1995, the Pension Fund, especially, confronted a deepening financial crisis driven by revenue shortfalls, a contracting tax base, and weak taxing capacities.

The establishment of the Social Security Funds created new institutions, sets of resources, and interests in Russia's social sector. The Pension Fund became by far the largest pool of money in the social security system, a coveted asset, transferred from the control of the legislature to the government in late 1993. Its internal governance structure provided no representation for contributors. It was effectively shielded from external oversight over money flows and was plagued by problems of weak legal regulation and charges of corruption.[105] Under both Chairman Visilii Barchuk and his successor Mikhail Zurabov, the Pension Fund exemplified the winner-take-all phenomenon in the social sphere: it developed as a semi-independent corporate interest, its management a social-sector version of early winners who had gained nearly unaccountable control over large-scale financial resources in the first stages of reform.[106] Whereas pensioners in Russian society remained weakly organized, the Pension Fund developed a strong interest in the collection and management of contributions and would stand as a major obstacle to both legal regulation and further privatizing reforms of the system.

STATE CAPACITY

The Russian state's capacities were seriously weakened in the transition period (see introduction). The descriptions of several social policy areas presented in this chapter reveal how limitations in taxing, institutional, and administrative capacities damaged or disabled efforts to either finance or reform welfare. First, the state's ability to tax was limited because it could not monitor many transactions in the new privatizing economy or enforce compliance on powerful economic actors. Second, the implementation of

---

[104]   Maleva, *Sovremennie Problemy Pensionnoi Sfery*; Elena Romanova, "Pension Arrears in Russia: The Story behind the Figures," *Russian Economic Trends* 8, no. 4 (1999): 15–23.

[105]   Grigorii Pavlovich Degtiarev, "Pensionnaia Reforma v Rossii: 1991–1999" (paper prepared for the Russian Governance Project, Harvard University, 2001).

[106]   Joel Hellman, "Winners Take All: The Politics of Partial Reform," *World Politics* 50, no. 2 (1998): 203–34.

reform policies was undermined by lack of the institutional infrastructure, regulatory mechanisms, and information flows that would have been necessary to make liberal social policy models, such as medical insurance and housing privatization, work. Third, Russia's system of asymmetrical federalism undercut central administrative capacities, making it impossible for the center to enforce policy or control distribution even in those parts of the welfare state that remained formally centralized.

Taxation and Social Security

The revenue base of the Russian state declined greatly with the fall in GDP during the 1990s, but here I am concerned mainly with the capacity of the state to tax the resources that remained. The problems were both administrative and political. The state needed a new system of revenue extraction that could function effectively in the transition economy. As that economy diversified and privatized through the decade, tax authorities were often unable to penetrate the finances of businesses or to enforce revenue claims. A growing portion of economic activities moved into the informal sector, many relying on barter and other non-monetary exchanges. According to the European Bank for Reconstruction and Development (EBRD), the share of Russia's unofficial economy in GDP grew from 12 percent in 1989 to over 41 percent in 1995, one of the highest among the transition states.[107]

At the same time, the most powerful economic actors, or oligarchs, were able to negotiate tax exemptions, concessions, and other privileges from executive and legislative elites in the Yeltsin era and to accumulate tax debts or arrears, sapping the state's ability to fund the social sector. The largest tax debtors had access to the state through political connections and favoritism, and they could not be held accountable by tax authorities. Among the largest debtors to the Pension Fund, for example, were the natural monopolies Gazprom and United Energy Systems, the oil companies, and the railroads. When it was struggling to pay off arrears in the mid-1990s, the Pension Fund designated thirty companies (out of some 120 with debts of more than R50 billion) to appear before the government's Temporary Extraordinary Commission for Tax and Budget Discipline. The commission threatened a range of sanctions, including threats to sell

---

[107] Janos Kornai, Stephan Haggard, and Robert R. Kaufman, *Reforming the State: Fiscal and Welfare Reform in Post-Socialist Countries* (Cambridge, UK: Cambridge University Press, 2001), 276, citing *EBRD Transition Report, 1997*, 74. In 1995 only Ukraine, Georgia, and Azerbaijan were reported to have higher unofficial shares of GDP.

off parts of the companies, limit their exports, and force them to issue bonds, all to little avail.[108] Essentially, these economic actors had sufficient autonomy vis-à-vis the state to resist efforts at tax collection.

Elite bargaining frustrated the Finance Ministry's efforts to improve collections. According to Gerald Easter, Goskomstat figures for 1996 show that "the amount of revenue lost through tax privileges was close to one-third of the total taxes collected for the consolidated budget, and more than two-thirds of the total taxes collected for the federal budget." Federal tax collections fell sharply, from more than 16 percent of GDP in 1992 to a low of 9.6 percent in 1998, while collections to the consolidated budget underwent a more modest decline.[109]

The impacts of tax evasion and avoidance strategies on the off-budget funds that now financed most social insurance were severe. Employers for about 40 percent of hired workers, especially those in new economic organizations and secondary employment, failed to make contributions into the Social Funds, and other employers accumulated debts.[110] It became routine for employers to rely on strategies of minimal or formal compliance, taking advantage of the state's limited information to understate wages, often paying off the books or in-kind to minimize taxes. Given the resulting low levels of pensions and other social payments, the emergent strata of middle- and upper-income employees were largely indifferent to the social security system and colluded with employers to shelter wages and evade taxes.

Institutional Capacity

The reformers' efforts at liberal restructuring also confronted problems of institutional capacity. In the West, social security markets have been constructed historically with the aid of the state and embedded in stable, functioning financial markets. Russian social reformers were generally hostile to the state, sharing a "pervasive philosophical sense that everything centralized had to be eliminated."[111] In Russia, health insurance reform, implemented in the absence of either insurance companies or

[108]   See *Rossiskie Vesti*, 30 Jan. 1997. The larger story of government officials' struggles with tax debtors is well told in Andrei Shleifer and Daniel Triesman, *Without a Map: Political Tactics and Economic Reform in Russia* (Cambridge, Mass.: MIT Press, 2000), 143–56.

[109]   Gerald Easter, "Building Fiscal Capacity," in *The State after Communism: Governance in the New Russia*, edited by Timothy J. Colton and Stephen Holmes (Lanham, Md.: Rowman and Littlefield, 2006), 26, 36 for quote.

[110]   "Proekt Strategiia Razvitiia Rossiiskoi Federatsii do 2010" [hereafter Proekt Strategiia] (Tsentr Strategicheskikh Razrabotok, 2000), available at www.kommersant.ru/documents/Strat1.htm.

[111]   Judyth Twigg (personal communication, March 16, 2003).

multiple providers in most localities, largely failed to create markets or competition. The housing reform distributed ownership rights but failed to create the financial or regulatory conditions for the buying, selling, or mortgaging of property. Health and education privatization, in the absence of regulatory structures, facilitated corruption and restrictions on access. Reformers, often relying on presidential or governmental decrees and with the urging of IFIs and other international institutions, repeatedly imported models for which Russia lacked the infrastructure and which failed or produced unintended and often perverse consequences.

Administrative Capacity

The third dimension of state capacity has to do with central administrative powers over welfare policy and resource allocation. Weak central power in the Russian Federation was in part a consequence of welfare reform. The decentralization of health, education, and social assistance weakened federal responsibilities and the power of central ministries in those areas. Other parts of the welfare state, including the Social Security Funds, remained formally centralized and federal in nature, but the central government exercised little control over them in Russia's system of asymmetrical federalism. There were serious problems of regional compliance with federal social-sector policies, deriving from the weakness of central control over federal officials in the regions. Interviews by Kathryn Stoner-Weiss with top officials in regional branches of the federal Social Security Funds, for example, reveal that these officials, although formally subordinated to the center, were strongly influenced by regional authorities in the administration of the Funds and regularly refused to transfer money to the center or to follow its policy mandates.[112]

Decentralization was both an outcome of the Russian state's policy and a cause of the further weakening of its capacities. Control over formally centralized Social Security Funds was fragmented or parceled among regional authorities. Most of the money collected by the Funds remained in the regions. Central Funds officials bargained informally with regional political elites over the division of taxes, undermining the uniformity of the social security system.[113] The result was substantial variation in payments across regions and the concentration of arrears in poorer regions and rural areas. The effects were especially damaging

[112]   Katherine Stoner-Weiss, "Resistance to the State on the Periphery," in *The State after Communism: Governance in the New Russia,* edited by Timothy J. Colton and Stephen Holmes (Lanham, Md.: Rowman and Littlefield, 2006), 87–120.
[113]   Romanova, "Pension Arrears in Russia."

in the case of the Employment Fund, which remained very limited in its ability to transfer funds from low- to high-unemployment regions, contributing to the "maldistribution of funds . . . a significant part of the real unemployed receiving no benefits."[114] Nationally, in the regions most negatively impacted by reform, the Russian government created no effective unemployment insurance or active labor market policies during the most difficult transition years, when there was an acute need for national policy and federal backstopping. According to the comparative literature, federalism segments welfare states and militates against their effectiveness. This was particularly true for the Russian Federation's weak state, with its asymmetrical relations between the center and regions. Here the effects of federalism went further, parceling control over the formally centralized social security programs.

CONCLUSION

In the first years of the Russian transition, the balance of influence between pro- and antirestructuring interests leaned heavily toward the former. Russia had an executive with a strong electoral mandate and extensive powers, leading in a time of profound economic crisis, and bound by few mechanisms of accountability to society or other political institutions. Liberalizing professional elites were placed in charge of social ministries and organized in the legislature's social committees, giving them access to policy power. Global social policy networks and IFIs helped to shape the reforms, providing intellectual and programmatic guidance to receptive elites who faced very few organized domestic constituencies.

Among those who benefited from old welfare structures and entitlements, societal constituencies were largely dormant or ineffective in blocking change in Russia's new and unconsolidated democracy. Representative institutions remained weak and largely disconnected from society. The legislature resisted the broader economic reform program, but did not try to block reforms in inherited welfare structures or financing mechanisms. Statist social-sector elites were disorganized, and in some cases their associations had literally disbanded during the transition. Bureaucratic stakeholders, especially those in the central ministries, saw their influence undermined by decentralization. The outcome was rapid, non-negotiated welfare state liberalization. (The major changes introduced across areas of the welfare state are shown in the first column of table 3.5.)

---

[114]   Proekt Strategiia, chap. 4, 76–77.

Liberal reformers used their power to re-organize the welfare state, to decentralize its administration, and diversify its sources of financing. The leadership also promised a new safety net for those who were pushed out of labor markets and into poverty in the transitional economy but, as Gaidar himself admitted, such nets largely failed to materialize.[115] Declines in welfare spending were inevitable during Russia's economic crisis, but most of the evidence suggests that liberal welfare reforms worsened the welfare consequences of expenditure decline. Reforms left the center with limited control over, or responsibility for, how the welfare costs of transition were distributed. Decentralization meant that cuts in expenditures for health, education, and social assistance were distributed very unequally as the economy adjusted and integrated globally. Rapid, nearly simultaneous decentralization across areas of the social sphere loaded administrative and financing responsibilities on to the weakest actors, mainly the municipal governments. Reforms supposed to debureaucratize the system instead led to a proliferation of institutions and generated conflicts over declining resources. The transfer of social insurance programs to wage taxes collected at the regional level weakened the federal government's ability to address unemployment or control pension distribution. Russian reformers faced intense pressures, both from financial decline and from centrifugal forces pulling at the federation. Nevertheless, fewer radical institutional changes and the maintenance of some priority social tasks at the federal center would arguably have eased the social consequences of transition.

The welfare reforms of the early 1990s relied on small groups of elites and executive power, and often produced poor-quality, ineffective policies. There was virtually no participation or consensus-building among affected constituencies in society or within the state. Changes did lead to active and passive resistance, as was evident with the local administrators in health reforms. Resistance grew into political and bureaucratic backlash during the mid-1990s, when elections brought into the legislature left and pro-welfare political parties, and social-sector ministries regrouped under new leadership. The backlash eroded many of the institutional changes that had been made in 1991–1992, although fundamental features of the old system had been eliminated.

---

[115] "The Sixth Congress of Russian Federation's People's Deputies," *Rossiiskaya Gazeta*, 14 Apr. 1992, 3–6, translated in *Current Digest of the Post-Soviet Press* 44, no. 15 (1992): 5. According to Gaidar, speaking in mid-1992, "We consider it necessary to raise the level of targeted social protection . . . to begin thoroughgoing reforms in all systems of social protection and to shift from slapdash emergency measures to reduce the budgetary burden" (5).

3

Contested Liberalization

Russia's Politics of Polarization
and Informalization

In December 1993, Russian citizens elected a new legislature and narrowly approved a new constitution. The 1993 Russian constitution privileged the executive, giving him strong appointment, decree, and veto powers. But the new legislature, especially its lower house, the Duma, did provide some representation for societal interests, and it exercised stronger political constraint on the president than had its predecessor. A broad spectrum of political parties, including moderate-reformist and hard-left, produced programs, ran candidates, and sought electoral support. These first competitive legislative elections produced a backlash against the broader market transition and transformed the politics of welfare. The political constellation that had permitted non-negotiated liberalization in the early 1990s gave way to one in which welfare state change was contested, first (in the 1993 Duma) by a moderate coalition that sought to negotiate change and then (in the 1995 Duma) by a radical coalition that largely obstructed it. During this period, Russia's GDP continued to decline overall, although less sharply than in the early 1990s, falling by about 4 percent in each of 1995 and 1996, growing slightly in 1997, and then declining an additional 5 percent as a result of the 1998 financial crisis. Welfare effort remained fairly stable while real expenditures continued to fall through the decade.

In this chapter, I look at societal and political effects on welfare politics during this period of incipient democratization. I first ask whether the welfare state constituencies that are familiar from the Western literature, particularly trade unions, public-sector workers, and women's organizations, mobilized to defend established benefits and programs and whether Russia's quasi-democratic political process afforded them influence. Did unionists, teachers, and women in Russia organize, find political allies, and affect policy change? I look at linkages between pro-welfare societal constituencies and political parties and map the welfare programs and legislative agendas of parties that played a significant role in the Duma. The evidence shows that public-sector unions, women, and others did organize politically to defend their interests, but in the end their influence was constricted by the weakness and fragmentation of Russia's unions, the instability of political parties, and the nonaccountability of the government. Moderate pro-welfare societal interests played a temporary and diminishing political role in negotiating welfare state change.

Opposition to reform was nevertheless mobilized through Russia's new political institutions. Diffuse groups of older and poorer citizens and nationalist organizations supported hard-left, anti-market communist successor parties that formed a dominant legislative coalition in the mid-1990s. Despite the constitutional limits on its power, the legislature became a key veto actor, blocking the executive's efforts to dismantle statist structures of social provision and to construct new private markets for public goods. Executive and legislature polarized over welfare reform, producing policy deadlock.

Resistance to welfare reform also emerged in the government. Disorganization within the state bureaucracy during the early 1990s had permitted decentralizing changes that greatly weakened the social ministries. But support for these reforms was shallow, largely confined to the Finance and Economics Ministries and the Gaidar government's liberal social ministers, who had been replaced by late 1992. From that point, the social ministries began to resist the loss of authority and resources resulting from the early reforms.[1] Until 1997 President Yeltsin did not make serious efforts to rebuild a social-sector reform team, and the ongoing economic decline limited the possibilities for the government to compensate powerful opponents. State-based

---

[1] On the advantages and disadvantages of reforms carried out with minimal negotiation or consensus building, see "Introduction," in *Reforming the State: Fiscal And Welfare Reform in Post-Socialist Countries,* edited by Janos Kornai, Stephan Haggard, and Robert R. Kaufman (Cambridge, UK: Cambridge University Press, 2001), 1–22.

stakeholders waged a rearguard campaign against the executive's policies of destatization. The governmental elite was deeply divided over welfare reform.

In sum, although the 1993 constitution appeared to privilege executive power, legislative and bureaucratic resistance shifted the balance against welfare state restructuring. The executive continued to pursue a liberalizing agenda in a piecemeal fashion and then more systematically from 1997 when the World Bank intervened to try to revive the restructuring process. I show, however, that the Bank's interventions were largely thwarted by domestic political resistance. Overall, although Yeltsin's government succeeded in cutting social expenditures, it failed to implement its liberalizing agenda in any area of Russia's social sector, and some of the reforms that had been put into place in the early 1990s were rolled back. (The main actors in Russia's welfare politics during this period are shown in table 3.1)

TABLE 3.1
Politics of contested liberalization in Russia, 1994–1999

Pro-reform; liberalizers	Anti-reform; welfare state stakeholders
Executive	*Societal constituencies, representative institutions*
Moderate	**Moderate**
Inconsistent presidential leadership	Fragmentary union-party alliances
Divisions in government ministries	Anti-reform legislative parties
No social-sector reform team	Left-dominated legislature
Weak pro-executive parties	as veto actor
Reformist social-sector elites	*Statist social-sector elites*
Weak	**Moderate**
Limited policy access	Veto actors against new reforms
Weak representation on legislative	Efforts to dilute, reverse
committees	earlier reforms
Failed implementation of	
earlier reforms	
Global policy networks, IFIs[a]	*State-bureaucratic stakeholders*
Weak	**Moderate**
Failure of policy-linked lending	Veto actors against new reforms
Failed interventions to	Efforts to dilute, reverse
reshape policy	earlier reforms
Outcome:	
Contested liberalization	

[a] IFI, international financial institutions.

The outcome was contested liberalization and policy deadlock between the legislature and executive, an incoherent policy of welfare state retrenchment without restructuring. Executive liberalizers were able to cut spending, but lacked the power to eliminate benefit programs, dismantle institutions, or privatize social services. The failure of Russia's political elites to either preserve or restructure the old welfare system had several effects. First, declining expenditures were spread across a stagnant system of entitlements, social-sector institutions, and personnel. Whereas in Poland and Hungary welfare effort was increased in selected areas during economic decline, in Russia public-sector wages, pensions, and other benefits fell and were chronically in arrears. Second, policy deadlock blocked possibilities for the reallocation of spending to the transition's new poor and unemployed. While the East Central European transition states put in place unemployment insurance, poverty-targeted benefits, and other measures to cushion the effects of reform, the Russian welfare state underwent little adjustment. Third, because political conflict blocked the development of legal private markets while public-sector salaries fell below subsistence, health and education workers and social-sector elites turned to informal income-generating strategies. Shadow payments and informal markets corrupted welfare provision and excluded poorer strata while largely unregulated private spending on social services grew. Russia's welfare state became informalized, producing a new type that was to a significant extent governed neither by state authorities nor by market principles.

The conflict over welfare state reform was part of the larger ongoing struggle over the directions of Russia's economic development in the 1990s, a struggle to determine whether the system would continue moving toward the market or retain a large state role in the economy. Anti-reform interests, including communist successor parties, bureaucratic stakeholders, many industrial and agricultural elites (the Red Directors), and statist social-sector elites (i.e., the Red Rectors) pressed for protectionism, the maintenance of subsidies, state-led development, and the regulation of markets, all policies that would help to maintain old welfare state protections. Liberals in the executive and economics ministries sought to dismantle the state-run economy in order to stimulate economic recovery. They saw further cuts in subsidies and public social expenditures as keys to both fiscal stabilization and resumed economic growth. Restructuring the welfare system was a major component of their broader project for systemic transformation, modernization of the state, and integration into global markets.

SOCIETAL WELFARE CONSTITUENCIES: TRADE UNIONS, PUBLIC-SECTOR WORKERS, AND WOMEN

Trade Unions' Dependencies and Strategies

By far the largest societal organization in Russia that might have been expected to defend the welfare state, to oppose liberalizing reforms, or bargain for concessions, was the Federation of Independent Trade Unions of Russia (FNPR). The successor to its Soviet-era counterpart, the FNPR inherited an organizational structure and membership that covered all sectors of the labor force, including industrial, agricultural, and public-sector workers. Most of the unions' members stood to lose in multiple ways from market transition, and the organization itself relied heavily on the control and distribution of threatened social security benefits to attract and hold members.[2] Unions have played a major role in defending Western welfare states, and they have been significant in the transitional welfare politics of East Central European states. In Russia during the 1990s, by contrast, unions did little. Significant pro-welfare labor activism emerged only among public-sector workers.

The comparative weakness of postcommunist, and particularly Russian, labor unions has been explained by various authors as a consequence of the unions' structural position in transitional economies; globalization; and a range of organizational, cultural, and psychological factors.[3] Still, the unions were the dominant civil society organization in postcommunist Russia, claiming 60 million of Russia's 73 million–member labor force in 1992, a number that declined steadily but remained at an estimated 40–45 million in the later 1990s.[4] Unions had

---

[2] See Sue Davis, *Trade Unions in Russia and Ukraine, 1985–1995* (New York: Palgrave, 2001).

[3] For an explanation focusing on structural economic change and globalization, see Paul Kubicek, *Organized Labor in Postcommunist States: From Solidarity to Infirmity* (Pittsburgh: University of Pittsburgh Press, 2004). For a study that focuses on the communist cultural and ideological inheritance, see David Ost, "The Weakness of Symbolic Strength: Labor and Union Identity in Poland, 1989–2000," in *Workers after the Workers' State: Labor and Politics in Postcommunist Eastern Europe,* edited by David Ost and Stephen Crowley (Lanham, Md.: Rowman and Littlefield, 2001), 79–96. Stephen Crowley stresses workers' dependence on state-distributed social benefits to explain low levels of union militancy; see *Hot Coal, Cold Steel: Russian and Ukrainian Workers from the End of the Soviet Union to the Post-Communist Transformation* (Ann Arbor: University of Michigan Press, 1997). Debra Javeline points to workers' inability to assign blame for their hardships as a central explanation for low levels of protest; see *Protest and the Politics of Blame: The Russian Response to Unpaid Wages* (Ann Arbor: University of Michigan Press, 2003).

[4] See "III S"ezd Federatsii Nezavisimykh Profsoiuzov Rossii," *Profsoiuzy 1* (1997): 2; T. Chetvernina, P. Smirnov, and N. Dunaeva, "Mesto Profsoiuza na Predpriyatii," *Voprosy Ekonomiki* 6 (June 1995): 83–84.

organizational, financial, and other resources to offer potential political allies, and their demands concerning employment, wages, and other issues were popular.[5] During the 1990s both the FNPR and its constituent unions did make a range of alliances with political parties and other organizations that included efforts to preserve and defend the old welfare state. The analysis here focuses on the political factors that ultimately undermined union influence.

In the transitional context, labor unions must make strategic decisions about how to position themselves vis-à-vis liberalizing governments, whether to oppose reformers or support them in exchange for concessions to their members or organizations. A number of factors affect these strategic decisions, including the unions' past political alliances, the level of competition among them, and the mix of their upward (on government) and downward (on the rank-and-file) dependencies. Upward dependencies are measured by the degree to which unions' position, power, and privileges depend on the discretion of government leaders; downward dependencies are measured by the degree of reliance on their rank-and-file for income and other resources.[6] Unions in less competitive environments, and more autonomous of their rank-and-file, are freer to acquiesce to government pressures. Those that are heavily dependent on government discretion have strong incentives to acquiesce to liberalizing policies. The capacity of unions to deliver the votes, quiescence, or militancy of their members in turn affects the willingness of governments to grant concessions. Leaders of weak unions sometimes support liberalizing reform programs, despite damage to their members' interests, because such support allows them to at least bargain for concessions or for their corporate interests.[7]

For most of the 1990s, the FNPR represented a rather extreme case of upward dependence and acquiescence. The FNPR had been embedded in the structure of the communist party-state, and the Soviet collapse threatened its existence. The new Yeltsin administration held discretion over its rights, property, social security distribution functions, and access to bargaining structures. In the early reform period, the FNPR

---

[5]   See Stephen Crowley, "Comprehending the Weakness of Russia's Unions," *Demokratizatsiya* 10, no. 2 (2002): 230.

[6]   See M. Victoria Murillo, "From Populism to Neoliberalism: Labor Unions and Market Reforms in Latin America," *World Politics* 52, no. 2 (2000): 135–74.

[7]   See Steven Levitsky and Lucan A. Way, "Between a Shock and a Hard Place: The Dynamics of Labor-Backed Adjustment in Poland and Argentina," *Comparative Politics* 30, no. 2 (1998): 171–93.

did seriously challenge the restructuring program, siding with the anti-reform legislature that rebelled against the president in the October 1993 conflict and calling unsuccessfully for a general strike. In the aftermath of the legislature's defeat, the FNPR was labeled part of the Red-Brown (Communist-Fascist) opposition, the weakness of its mobilizing capacity was starkly revealed, and its leadership literally feared repression. Its property and rights to representation on the Pension Fund and other social security boards were threatened, and the executive's discretion over both became a source of ongoing control and manipulation. Committed first and foremost to preserving its corporate interests, that is, its organization and the inherited property that generated most if its income, the FNPR acquiesced in the government's policies without supporting them.

Through the remainder of the 1990s, the FNPR's activism was restrained and largely defensive, giving the government few incentives to make concessions or to bargain seriously. Affiliated unions sponsored strikes, but most were brief protests against wage arrears. Despite the hardships of transition, the overall level of strike and protest activity in Russia during the 1990s was low in comparative terms, involving only a small percentage of workers, remaining below strike levels in OECD states for the same period.[8] Many of the strikes that did take place were coordinated with enterprise managements or local authorities, so-called directors' strikes, that posed little threat.[9] The FNPR's membership declined despite a lack of competition in most sectors, and multiple surveys showed low levels of membership trust.[10] Yeltsin's government, which in the early 1990s had been deeply concerned about the prospect of a social explosion, had by 1994 ceased worrying that its economic and social policies would lead to significant social unrest.[11]

---

[8]   In 1992, a year of hyperinflation, for example, only twenty-seven strike days were lost per 1,000 workers, compared with an OECD average of 110 in that year. In 1993 and 1994, the incidence of strikes in Russia fell below this level; see *Russian Economic Trends* 3, no. 2 (1994): 97. Although strike levels rose in the later 1990s, they remained low; see Javeline, *Protest and the Politics of Blame*, 35–37.

[9]   Directors' strikes were intended to extract payments from the state, not to confront management with demands; see, for example, *Trud*, 21 Nov. 1996; Labor Ministry official, Russian Federation, interview with author, Moscow, July 5, 1992.

[10]   For reports on surveys showing low levels of trust, see, for example, *Delovoy Mir*, 10–16 May 1994, 14–15; *Rabochaia Tribuna*, 28 Oct., 2 Nov. , and 6 Nov. 1993.

[11]   Lilia Shevtsova (personal communication), senior associate, Carnegie Endowment for International Peace, Williams College, Oct. 4, 2003. This concern was promoted in part by large strike movements, mainly in the mining sector, in 1989–1991.

The FNPR and its branch and sectoral unions did enter into political alliances that contributed to blocking welfare state change. In the early 1990s, the FNPR's national leadership joined with the Russian Union of Industrialist and Entrepreneurs (RUIE), the dominant industrialists' lobby in Russia, to form the Civic Union alliance. The majority of Russia's industrialists remained resistant to market reform in this period, and, in an alliance pattern different from those generally seen in the West, the FNPR cooperated with the industrialists' lobby in pressing the state to preserve the old systems of production and social protection. The Civic Union played a key role in ousting Egor Gaidar and Russia's first liberalizing government, including the radical social ministers, at the end of 1992. At this point, Yeltsin briefly sought to compromise with opponents of the broader reform program, before moving to the more confrontational strategy of dissolving the Duma in fall 1993.

The FNPR had less influence in electoral politics. It established no stable alliance, mostly shopping around on the moderate left of Russia's shifting party spectrum, and then in 1995 running in a failed alliance with a managers' party. In the later 1990s, the FNPR split from the increasingly divided managers and formed its own political wing, Andrei Isaev's Union of Labor, which had social-democratic proclivities and joined the then center-left Fatherland Bloc.[12] Branch and regional unions made their own political alliances, often further to the statist left, providing support to parties that became key parts of the Duma majority seeking to restore the welfare state. Agroindustrial unions, the largest group in the FNPR, allied with the Agrarian Party of Russia (APR), which "[relied] on [collective farm] directors and trade unions bosses to get out their vote."[13] Forestry, health, and communication unions also supported the APR.[14] Although it was a small party in electoral terms, the APR played a significant role in the legislative majority bloc that resisted welfare state change. Some regional union organizations and the military-industrial branch union supported the Communist Party of the Russian Federation (CPRF), the key restorationist party. The large and predominantly female textile and educationalists' unions supported Women of Russia (WR).[15]

---

[12]   See *Trud*, 15 Oct. 1997; Simon Clarke, "Russian Trade Unions in the 1999 Duma Election," *Journal of Communist Studies and Transition Politics* 17, no. 2 (2001): 43–69.

[13]   Michael McFaul and Nilolai Petrov, eds., *Previewing Russia's 1995 Parliamentary Elections* (Washington, D.C.: Carnegie Endowment for International Peace, 1995), 63.

[14]   *Moskovskie Novosti*, no. 31, 11 Aug. 1995, available at afnet.integrum.ru.

[15]   On communist and WR ties to the trade unions, see Krasnikov, *Moskovskie Novosti*, 6–13 Aug. 1995, 4, available at afnet.integrum.ru.

The Metallurgists' Union, a breakaway from the FNPR, endorsed the moderately reformist Yabloko. In the 1999 legislative elections as well, the branch and regional unions supported a range of parties.[16] (For a list of party-union alliances, see table 3.2; for Russian political parties' orientations to welfare, see table 3.4.)

The political transition in Russia also spawned new, independent unions, particularly in the mining and transport sectors and among white-collar workers. The independents began as genuinely democratic organizations, with much stronger downward dependencies than the FNPR, and were much more militant. They were involved in some of the most dramatic labor protests of the 1990s, including the miners' rail wars.[17] But the independents relied on the executive for protection of their rights to organize and represent members, which were under constant threat from the FNPR. Small and resource-poor, they made a different set of strategic decisions, allying politically with the executive and small liberal parties. When the government's policies began imposing costs on their members, the Russian independents found themselves in the dilemma of Solidarity and other unions that have backed adjustment programs, adrift politically and with stagnant or declining memberships.[18] They remained too small and divided to play any significant political role at the national level.

Table 3.2 shows that an incipient alliance politics emerged between the unions and political parties in the 1990s. But the unions made their alliances in fragmentary and shifting patterns, dividing their limited resources. They had no united electoral strategy, and, outside the agrarian sector, it remains uncertain how much support unions delivered to their party allies.[19] The pattern of broad, stable, national-level union-party alliances that was, and to some extent remains, central to the political support of European

---

[16]   Clarke, "Russian Trade Unions."

[17]   The rail wars, which blocked major railroad lines, were to some extent wildcat actions led by the a third wave of union leadership; Professor Leonid Gordon, Institute of World Economy and International Relations, director, Department of Social and Labor Studies, interview with author, Moscow, June 24, 1998.

[18]   For a discussion of the independents, see Kubicek, *Organized Labor in Postcommunist States;* Simon Clarke, Peter Fairbrother, and Vadim Borisov, *The Workers' Movement in Russia* (Aldershot, UK: Edward Elgar,1995).

[19]   Survey evidence for the 1995 election shows that unions had minimal influence on members' votes; see Timothy J. Colton, *Transitional Citizens: Voters and What Influences Them in the New Russia* (Cambridge, Mass.: Harvard University Press, 2000), 56. Other sources indicate that agrarian unions did get out the vote and that public-sector, textile, and other groups of workers supported particular political parties. See, for example, McFaul and Petrov, *Previewing Russia's 1995 Parliamentary Elections,* 25.

welfare states was absent. Also, in contrast to the East Central European pattern (see chap. 5), no major Russian union formed a stable alliance with any political party. The most effectual alliances that did emerge—between the FNPR and the industrialists' lobby and between the agroindustrial unions and the APR—were more corporatist arrangements than democratic political ones, elite-dominated efforts at preserving the old system of production along with its social protections. Both had collapsed by the later 1990s. Simply put, Russian labor found no political home.

Public-Sector Workers: The Futility of Collective Action

Public-sector unions (along with the better-known coal miners) were a major exception to the pattern of labor quiescence. Aside from agricultural workers, those in the public sector formed the largest branch unions in the FNPR and showed the strongest membership retention through the 1990s (see table 3.3). Unions of educators and medical

TABLE 3.2
Union Party alliances in Russia, 1992–1999

Year	Unions	Party/bloc/organization
1992[a]	FNPR leadership	Russian Union of Industrialists and Entrepreneurs
1993	Agro-industrial unions	Agrarian Party of Russia
	Forestry, Construction, Materials union	Civic Union
	Educators', Researchers' and Textile Unions	Women of Russia
1995[b]	FNPR leadership	Russian Unified Industrialists' Party
	Agro-Industrial, Timber, and Communications Unions	Agrarian Party of Russia
	Military Industrial branch and regional unions	Communist Party of Russian Federation
	Metallurgists' union	Yabloko
1999	FNPR leadership	Fatherland-All-Russia
	Agro-Industrial unions	Communist Party
	Regional unions	Communist Party; Unity; Peace, Labor, May (regional labor party)

Sources: Linda J. Cook, "Trade Unions, Management, and the State in Contemporary Russia," in Peter Rutland, ed., *Business and the State in Contemporary Russia* (Boulder: Westview, 2001), 158 and sources cited in text.

[a] FNPR, Federation of Independent Trade Unions of Russia.

[b] Some regional unions also supported the short-lived Congress of Russian Communities.

TABLE 3.3
Largest FNPR branch unions[a]

	Branch members (millions)
Workers of the agroindustrial complex	9.6
Educational and research workers	4.8
Health-care workers	3.5
Local industry and communal services	2.7
State institutions and social services	2.0
Total	40 (approx.)

Source: "III S"ezd Federatsii nezavisimykh profsoiuzov Rossii," *Profsoiuzy* 1 (1997): 2.
[a] FNPR, Federation of Independent Trade Unions of Russia.

workers depended directly on the state for employment, professional status, and income. They were among the most exposed to public-sector adjustment, including decentralization and wage declines and arrears. Their unions, particularly the FNPR-affiliated Union of Educational and Scientific Workers, supported legislative parties that defended public education against privatization and cuts in state educational guarantees.

During the 1990s, educators were the most strike-prone sector of Russia's labor force. From 1992 to 1999 "fully 91 percent of all strikes in Russia, or 54 percent and 56 percent when measured by days not worked and workers involved respectively, took place in the education sector."[20] This was the largest collective mobilization in defense of public-sector interests. During 1997, more than one-half million educators at more than 16,000 of Russia's educational institutions engaged in strikes, outnumbering those in industry. In some regions, strikes in the educational sphere were chronic. Periodic strike actions were coordinated across the Russian Federation; according to the Education and Scientific Workers' Union, in January 1999 400,000 teachers participated across seventy-two regions.[21] Health-care workers also struck during this period, although on a smaller scale.

Nearly all strikes were directed against wage arrears, which accumulated at the local level after decentralization. Public-sector salary

[20] Crowley, "Comprehending the Weakness of Russia's Unions," 232, citing the *Yearbook of Labor Statistics,* 2000. For reports on the strikes, see, for example, *Sevodnia,* 2 Feb. and 24 March 1994, available at afnet.integrum.ru.
[21] *Russian Economy in 1997: Trends and Outlooks* (no. 18) (Moscow: Institute for the Economy in Transition, March 1998), 160–62; *Russian Economy in 1998: Trends and Perspectives* (no. 20) (Moscow: Institute for the Economy in Transition, March 1999).

arrears were concentrated in education, and arrears of two to four months were widespread across the Federation, in 1997–1998 excepting only Moscow, St. Petersburg, the oil-rich Yamalo-Nenets region, and the Jewish autonomous region. But strikes accomplished little beyond the temporary clearing of arrears. Some analysts argue that local governments withheld wages and risked teachers' strikes as a means of bargaining with the federal government for additional fiscal transfers. Others hold that municipal governments faced stark choices between heating housing and paying teachers every autumn in the mid- and late 1990s.[22] In any case, teachers' pay continued to decline in real terms, more sharply than wages in the broader economy. By 1999, salaries for the majority had fallen below the subsistence level (see table 3.6, later in the chapter). The educators' union tried to protect teachers' material position, resisting efficiency-oriented measures, helping to block lay-offs and school closings, and continuing defensive strike activism.[23] On the ground, failed efforts at collective action yielded to informal, sometimes corrupt individual and institutional strategies of defense and professional survival.

Women: Organizing a Pro-Welfare Party

Studies of democratic polities have shown that women, in independent movements, within political parties and in state agencies, can play an important role in defending the welfare state. Comparative studies provide evidence that women in politics give particular priority to social policy issues and that they may band together across party lines to promote shared interests and goals.[24] Politically organized women sometimes succeed in preserving and expanding women-friendly policies even during periods of retrenchment. Women had a major stake in the socialist welfare state, particularly in its employment, maternity, and family policies.

Russian women's organizations did mobilize politically during the 1990s. Three organizations that had origins in the Soviet and *perestroika*

[22]   For the first interpretation, see Vladimir Gimpelson and Daniel Triesman, "Fiscal Games and Public Employment: A Theory with Evidence from Russia," *World Politics* 54 (Jan. 2002), 145–83; for the second, see *Russian Economy in 1997*.

[23]   Stephen Webber, *School, Reform and Society in the New Russia* (New York: Palgrave, 2000), 176–79; Organisation for Economic Cooperation and Development [hereafter OECD], *Reviews of National Policies for Education* (Paris: OECD, 1998,) 156.

[24]   Iulia Shevchenko, "Who Cares about Women's Problems? Female Legislators in the 1995 and 1999 Russian State Dumas," *Europe-Asia Studies*, 54, no. 8 (2002): 1201–22.

periods, the Women's Union of Russia (successor to the official Soviet Women's Committee), the Union of Navy Women, and the Association of Women Entrepreneurs (formed in 1990), combined to create a successful legislative party, Women of Russia (WR). WR was dedicated to a women-friendly social policy agenda. The party gained significant policy influence in the mid-1990s and built a network of cross-party contacts and cooperation among women Duma deputies. The tenure of WR in the Duma from 1993 to 1995 proved to be the high point so far for the representation of women's interests in Russian legislative politics.

LEGISLATIVE PARTIES, WELFARE AGENDAS, AND ELECTORAL POLITICS

This chapter's main argument is that effective resistance to welfare state change was mobilized through electoral politics between 1993 and 1999. The smaller part of this resistance came from moderate-reformist pro-welfare parties that were linked to the organizations of women and public-sector workers discussed above. A much larger part came from a different political coalition of hard-line, antimarket communist successor parties that were supported by diffuse groups of older, poorer, less educated, and rural Russian voters. The coalition of interests that most effectively tried to preserve Russia's old welfare state was distinctive to the post-Soviet context. It was not a thickly organized societal constellation of service providers, beneficiary groups, unions, and organizations linked to national political parties, like those described in the literature on Western welfare states. Instead, it was a thinly organized, dispersed, predominantly electoral coalition of Russia's older, poorer, and more state-dependent. Its organizational base was largely confined to the half million mass membership of the Communist Party, the collective farms and agrarian trade unions, and some nationalist organizations. The hard left got limited support from trade unions or workers, and in the public sector it was favored mainly by a stratum of older academics. But within the political-institutional system created by the 1993 Russian constitution, this dispersed electoral coalition became a major obstacle to welfare state restructuring.

In order to explain the electoral and legislative politics of welfare during the 1990s, I begin by mapping the welfare programs and electoral constituencies of Russia's major legislative parties and blocs. *Major legislative parties/blocs* are defined as those that passed the 5 percent barrier for party list representation in at least one election or formed a Duma faction.[25] The discussion here concentrates on one central cleavage issue—the orientation of parties toward political distribution versus private provision of social goods and services, the boundary between state and market in welfare provision. The parties are categorized on the bases of their electoral programs, the policy and programmatic positions taken by leaders, legislative activism, and voting records on key welfare restructuring issues as:

- Restorationist (hard-left): supporting the basic preservation of the statist welfare system.
- Moderate-reformist: favoring a mixed system of welfare provision with state and market elements.
- Liberal: favoring a minimalist or residual state role in welfare with strong predominance of private and market provision.
- Nonprogrammatic: vague in principle and inconsistent in positions and voting on welfare issues.

Generally speaking, the parties' positions on welfare state restructuring paralleled their positions on market transition more broadly, and on monetary and fiscal issues. Restorationist parties favored a large state role in the economy, production subsidies and credits, protectionism, and price controls. They tended to be fiscal populists, in favor of high taxation, and relatively tolerant of inflation.[26] Liberal parties wanted open markets, elimination of subsidies, monetary stability, and fiscal austerity. The positions of moderate-reformist parties were more complicated, favoring some version of a socially oriented market economy that would retain a substantial public sector.[27]

---

[25]   One of the parties included, Popular Power (PP), did not pass the 5 percent barrier in any election, but managed with the aid of the Communists to form a faction in the 1995 Duma. Factional status gave PP access to representation on Duma committees and the Duma Council and, thus, a significant legislative role.

[26]   Gerald Easter, "Building Fiscal Capacity," in *The State after Communism: Governance in the New Russia*, edited by Timothy J. Colton and Stephen Holmes (Lanham, Md.: Rowman and Littlefield, 2006), 27–34.

[27]   For attempts to classify Russian parties, see M. Dmitriev, "Evoliutsiia Ekonomicheskikh Programm Vedyshchikh Politicheskikh Partii i Blokov Rossii," *Voprosy Ekonomiki* no. 1 (Jan. 2000); Sarah Oates, "Party Platforms: Towards a Definition of the Russian Political Spectrum," in *Party Politics in Post-Communist Russia*, edited by John Lowenhardt (London: Frank Cass, 1998), 76–97.

Restorationist Parties, Programs, and Electorate

Leading the hard left was the Communist Party of the Russian Federation (CPRF), a largely unreformed communist successor party with strong nationalist leanings. The CPRF favored full state responsibility for and control over social welfare provision.[28] Its electoral platforms defined state social guarantees as a citizenship right and called for a return to the social protections of the communist era—free education and medical services, subsidized housing and transport, guaranteed employment, and so forth.[29] The party favored the preservation of the broad subsidies and entitlements in inherited social security programs and advocated increased spending along traditional lines to halt the fall in public-sector wages and social benefits brought by the transition. Its basic position was an uncritical and unrealistic restoration of the Soviet-era welfare state. Although more diverse orientations toward social policy were present within the party, the dominant Zyuganov group bluntly rejected revision of communist-era social guarantees.

The Agrarian Party of Russia (APR), essentially a corporatist representative of collective farm interests, was concerned with protectionism and subsidies for the agricultural and agroindustrial sectors, including the preservation of social infrastructure such as schools and polyclinics. The APR strongly opposed privatization of social services, especially education. The party's election program demanded broad accessibility to medical services, the preservation of established social security programs, rights to employment, and state support for the poor.[30] Although willing to allow some market elements, the Agrarians were predominantly restorationist, allying with the CPRF through the 1990s and cooperating with it on social policy issues. The third member of the restorationist camp, Popular Power (PP), was a small nationalist party that formed a

[28] All sources for the 1993 programs are from Interlegal, *Politicheskie Partii i Bloki na Vyborakh (Teksty Izbiratel'nykh Platform)* (Moscow: International Foundation of Political-Legal Research, 1993). Although not in their original formats, the platforms are considered authentic by scholars. This document was generously provided to the author by Sarah Oates.

[29] For the 1993 program, see "Kommunisticheskaia Partiia Rossiiskoi Federatsii, Tsentral'nii Ispolnitel'nyi Komitet, Obrashchenie, k Kommunistam, Trudiashchimcia, Vsem Patriotam Rossii," in Interlegal, *Politicheskie Partii,* 39–41.

[30] "Izbiratel'noe Ob'edinenie 'Agrarnaia Partiia Rossii': Predvybornaia Platforma," in Interlegal, *Politicheskie Partii,* 8–11; "Predvybornaia Platforma Izbiratel'nogo Ob'edineniia 'Agrarnaia Partiia Rossii'" (1995), available at http://www.nns.ru/elects/documents/aprplat.html.

parliamentary faction only with substantial help (i.e., lending of deputies) from the CPRF and others. It echoed the communist program,
calling for "a strengthened social security system resembling the former
Soviet system."[31]

The societal groups that provided most of the political base for restorationist parties were, overall, strongly dependent on the state for transfer payments, benefits, and social privileges. By far the largest group was
pensioners, who provided the parties' only significant reach into the
better-educated urban strata. The core societal support of this legislative coalition, the CPRF's grassroots organization and activist base, comprised
mainly older party functionaries, academics, and veterans. The APR controlled a portion of the rural vote through patronage and bureaucratic
domination. The electoral support for all three parties was concentrated
among those with elementary or incomplete secondary education, the
low-skilled, and people living in the agricultural south of the Russian
Federation. Groups especially hurt in the early stages of reform—those
living in villages and small towns with the largest declines in employment
and family income and the highest levels of wage arrears—also voted
strongly for the left parties.[32] These parties were politically and programmatically oriented toward low-income strata. Consistent support from its
base made the CPRF the largest and most stable party in the electoral
system during the 1990s.[33] Electoral rules exaggerated the left parties'
strength in the Duma, particularly after the 1995 election, and the strategic use of resources allowed them to dominate legislative politics.

The electoral success of the APR, as well as of the CPRF in rural areas,
points to an interesting comparative dimension of neo-liberal politics.
The postcommunist context provided no possibilities for Latin American–
style neo-populist strategies, in which reformers use minimalist new
social benefits to mobilize those from the poor strata who had been

---

[31]   McFaul and Petrov, *Previewing Russia's 1995 Parliamentary Elections*, 84.

[32]   See Ralph Clem and Peter Craumer, "The Geography of the Russian 1995 Parliamentary Election: Continuity, Change, and Correlates," *Post-Soviet Geography*, 36, no. 10
(1995): 289–317; Matthew Wyman, "Elections and Voting Behavior," in *Developments in Russian Politics*, edited by Stephen White, Alex Pravda, and Zvi Gitelman, 104–27 (Durham,
N.C.: Duke University Press, 1997); Jerry F. Hough, Evelyn Davidheiser, and Susan
Goodrich Lehmann, *The 1996 Russian Presidential Election* (Washington, D.C.: Brookings
Institution, 1996).

[33]   This is not to imply that welfare concerns or economic discontent per se account
for the communist/left vote but, rather, to show the socioeconomic correlates of that vote.
Research by Colton and others has demonstrated the influence of other factors, particularly political values, on voter choice.

excluded from state provision in the past.[34] Russia's rural population had stood at the very bottom of the distribution chain in the old welfare state, but it had not been excluded. All had something to lose from the state's withdrawal, and the poorer were integrated into structures of patronage and dependence. In Russia, the least privileged tended to support backward-looking, socially protectionist parties that blocked welfare state adjustment.

Moderate-Reformist Parties, Programs, and Electorate

The moderate-reformist parties in the 1990s Dumas, Women of Russia (WR) and Yabloko, had the most carefully elaborated, extensive, and specific programs on welfare issues, although these seem inversely related to the parties' longer-term influence. WR, formed from a coalition of women's organizations and comprising women exclusively, represented gender-based and family interests. The party placed social welfare at the core of its programmatic concerns. Although self-described as centrist, it leaned toward the left on welfare issues, favoring the maintenance of a dominant state role in social provision. WR accepted a place for private, paid services in the social sphere, but argued that state control was "essential in areas such as education and health" and called for universally free and accessible social services.[35] It placed priority on meeting basic needs and advocated the expansion of pension rights for women as well as state support for families and children. Although critical of the Soviet welfare state, WR was committed to defending the gains achieved by Soviet women, especially by preserving labor protections. The party saw women's access to labor markets as threatened by both changing labor practices and cuts in state funding for child care and other services. It viewed continued social subsidies and protections as key to women's interests in the transitional economy.

Yabloko, the most significant moderate-reformist party, promoted an essentially social-democratic program of shared state and market responsibility for welfare. Yabloko was critical of stabilization policies, calling for increased state spending to stimulate production, fight poverty, and

---

[34] On neo-populist strategies in Latin America, see Kurt Weyland, "Neopopulism and Neoliberalism in Latin America: How Much Affinity?" *Third World Quarterly* 24, no. 6 (2003): 1095–115. See also Carol Graham, *Safety Nets, Politics, and the Poor: Transitions to Market Economies* (Washington, D.C.: Brookings Institution, 1994).

[35] "Izbiratel'noe Ob'edinenie Politicheskogo 'Zhenshchiny Rossii'; Predvybornaia Programma," in Interlegal, *Politicheskie Partii*, 55–57.

preserve the public sector. It favored the selective maintenance of state subsidies (i.e., affordable housing), universally accessible education, and basic health care. At the same time, the party endorsed important elements of the liberal restructuring program, including means testing of benefits and the introduction of supplementary paid social services and voluntary private social insurance. Yabloko's programs addressed the need to build institutional infrastructure for social-sector markets. Its leaders understood social spending as investment in human capital as well as a social right. The party defined its moderate position on social welfare: "unlike the Communists, we think reforms are necessary. Our support for a strong social policy is the main difference between us and the radical democrats, who look on the social sphere only as a system of [minimalist] social protection and an annoying obstacle on the path of macroeconomic stabilization." [36]

WR and Yabloko went further than any other Russian parties in constituting the kind of thick constellations committed to the defense of the welfare state that are seen in the Western contexts. WR was built from and cultivated ties with organized women. Its 1993 election campaign "relied heavily on grassroots organization and mobilization of women's groups at the local level, which gave the ZhR [Zhenshchiny Rossii, or WR] a solid political base." [37] It was endorsed by the large and predominantly female textile, retail, and educationalists' unions; the head of the Educationalists Union, V. F. Yakovlev, declared in a television interview that WR was the only party that had a serious policy on education. The party's vote was heavily female and was partly a protest against social and economic policies; WR won the unemployed vote in light industry. [38] Yabloko also built links with public-sector and progressive unions and "poll[ed] particularly well with educated employees dependent on the state for salaries, that is, teachers, doctors, academics at research institutes, engineers working for military enterprises, and government bureaucrats." [39] For a brief period, these parties

[36] McFaul and Petrov, eds., *Previewing Russia's 1995 Parliamentary Elections*, 24; "O Deatel'nosti Fraktsii 'Yabloko' v Parlamente" (1994–1995), available at www.yabloko.ru/Faction/act, citing, *Izvestiia*, part II, July 13, 1995, 2; "Predvybornaia Programma 'Iabloko'" na Vyborakh Deputatov Gos. Dumy 1999," available at www.yabloko.ru/Program/prog-99.

[37] John T. Ishiyama, "Women's Parties in Postcommunist Politics," *East European Politics and Society* 17, no. 2 (2003), 287.

[38] Webber, *School*, 174; Wilma Rule and Nadezhda Shvedova, "Women in Russia's First Multiparty Election," in *Russian Women in Politics and Society*, edited by Wilma Rule and Norma C. Noonan (Westport, Conn.: Greenwood Press, 1996), 54.

[39] McFaul and Petrov, *Previewing Russia's 1995 Parliamentary Elections*, 25; Yabloko was linked with Boris Misnik's market-oriented Metallurgical Union, which broke away from the FNPR to support a more reformist position.

promoted with some success a reformist welfare policy agenda, between the liberalism of the executive and the restorationism of the left.

Liberal Parties, Program, and Electorate

Russia's Choice/Russia's Democratic Choice (RC/RDC) a pro-presidential party of power with Gaider in its leadership, was the one clearly ideologically liberal party in the 1990s Dumas. It gave priority to financial stabilization and advocated extensive liberalization of welfare. RC/RDC favored "in the social sphere, liquidation of previous social guarantees, and transition to targeted aid for non-competitive strata of the population."[40] Its program, although containing few specifics, called for the comprehensive restructuring of the system of social provision, including growth of private services. RC/RDC was supported by more urban, better-educated, and younger voters. Our Home Is Russia (OHR), the successor to RC/RDC as the pro-presidential party of power in the 1995 Duma, proved considerably more moderate in its program and relatively undisciplined in legislative voting, but it retained a generally liberal orientation. OHR was also supported by more urban, better-educated, and younger voters.

Nonprogrammatic Parties

The Liberal Democratic Party (LDP), although quite significant in electoral politics during this period, had no clear social policy orientation. Commonly characterized as populist, the LDP shifted between support for and opposition to liberalizing government initiatives. Neither its programs nor its voting record is clear or consistent enough to allow classification.[41]

The December 1993 Duma election produced a mix of moderate-reformist and restorationist legislative parties that sought to bargain over welfare state liberalization. The December 1995 election produced a restorationist majority that polarized welfare politics (see table 3.4). As the economic slide continued, tax receipts fell, and fiscal pressures mounted, the executive tried to further retrench and restructure while the legislature resisted. The deadlock produced incoherent outcomes that defunded but failed to dismantle the welfare state.

[40] "Demokraticheskii vybor Rossii—ob"edininnye Demokraty," (1995), available at http://www.nns.ru.elects/izobyed/drv.html.
[41] "Predvybornaia Platforma LDPR," (1995), available at http://www.nns.ru/elects/documents/ldprpl.html.

TABLE 3.4

Russian political party orientations on welfare issues and factional strength, 1993–2003[a]

Orientation	Name of deputy group/party	Number of Duma deputies			
		1993[b]	1995[c]	1999[d]	2003[b]
Restorationist	Communist Party of the Russian Federation	48	138	85	52
	Agrarians' Deputy Group, Agro-Industrial Deputy Group (1999)	33	35	—	2
	"People's Power" deputy group	—	39	42	—
	Rodina	—	—	—	37
Moderate reformist/ centrist	Yabloko	23	46	19	4
	Women of Russia	23	—	—	—
Liberal/pro- presidential	Russia's Choice	70	—	—	—
	Our Home Is Russia	—	64	—	—
	Unity/United Russia	—	—	84	225
	Fatherland-All Russia	—	—	46	—
	Union of Right Forces	—	—	33	3
Nonprogrammatic	Liberal Democratic Party Fraction	64	51	14	37
Others	Non-party deputy groups, small parties with SMD deputies, and independents	183	71	121	90
Total		444	444	444	450

Sources: Informatsionno-analiticheskii biulleten', Pravovoe Upravlenie Apparata Gosudarstvenoi Dumy (Informational-Analytical Bulletin, Legal Administration of the Apparatus of the State Duma), no. 3, 20 Feb.–19 Mar. 2001, available at www.duma.gov.ru; Stephen White, Richard Rose, and Ian McAllister, *How Russia Votes* (Chatham: Chatham House, 1997), 123; William A. Clark, "Communist Devolution: The Electoral Decline of the KPRF," *Problems of Post-Communism* 53, no. 1 (2006), 17.

[a] SMD, single-member district.
[b] 1993 and 2003 data are postelection.
[c] 1995 data are for mid-Duma, March 17, 1997.
[d] 1999 data are for mid-Duma, March 19, 2001.

THE EXECUTIVE'S PROGRAM AND POWER

Throughout this period, the Russian executive sought to sustain and advance the liberalizing agenda that had been initiated in the early 1990s. The post-1993 Yeltsin administration did not produce an elaborated, coherent restructuring plan like that introduced at the outset of the Putin presidency (see chap. 4), but it did generate a steady stream of proposals and initiatives for welfare state change and, with the support of the World Bank, a broader reform program toward the end of the decade. The executive tried to streamline and rationalize social provision, to cut subsidies and entitlements in major benefit programs and replace them with a targeted system of poverty-linked benefits. The privatization of social assets was promoted, and user fees, tuition, student loans, and other cost-recovery mechanisms were proposed in health and education. Legislation was introduced to deregulate labor markets, to extend social insurance markets for health care, and to partially privatize the pension system. In sum, the executive's program called for the ongoing diminution of the state's role and the transfer of greater responsibility for social provision to individuals and markets.

One of this study's central questions is about the capacity of powerful executives to impose social costs, to cut welfare and restructure provision. In chapter 2 I described how in the early 1990s the executive and small groups of reformers were able to extensively restructure the Russian welfare state. From 1993 on, Yeltsin was subject to much greater political constraint by the newly elected legislature. The president failed—for much of the period did not try—to build a base of support for welfare liberalization in the legislature. He stood above parties, vaguely connected only to the parties of power, RC/RDC in the 1993 Duma and OHR in the 1995 Duma. Each of these parties, in turn, proved weak and relatively isolated in legislative politics.

The absence of a powerful presidential party in the Duma, and the appointment of ministers who (with a few exceptions) were not connected to any parliamentary party meant that there were no effective coordinating mechanisms between the legislature and either the president or the government. Power in the Russian system was effectively fragmented. This structure left the president able to retrench the welfare state—to cut spending. He could, and did, veto spending bills, sequester funds budgeted for the social sector, and abrogate social guarantees in an ad hoc fashion (as well as providing selective social subventions in an equally ad hoc fashion). But, in the face of an adversarial legislature, he could not make further structural changes in the welfare state.

The legislature created by the 1993 constitution was weak in comparative terms, but it could block legislation with a simple majority vote. The constitution required that policy in key areas of the welfare state, including social security, housing, wages, and labor, be determined by federal law.[42] Most of the old welfare state remained deeply embedded in a set of legal guarantees. The executive could not systematically eliminate established entitlements and institutionalize enforceable new obligations, regulations, and principles of distribution without a rewriting of the legislative base. He needed the legislature's cooperation both to dismantle statist structures and to construct the institutional and legal frameworks for new private social security markets. And while Yeltsin did have some support within the upper legislative house, the Federation Council, he had few allies in the Duma.[43] Especially after the 1995 election, polarization between the executive and the Duma blocked most governmental initiatives on restructuring. Power was fragmented between these two bodies. The Duma emerged as a key veto actor against welfare state liberalization.

CONSTELLATIONS OF POWER AND WELFARE STATE CHANGE

The First Duma: Defending Women and Public Education

The 1993 election did not produce a working majority in the legislature, but it created a significant moderate voting block that included Yabloko and WR. WR placed itself in a strategic position to influence social policies, chairing a parliamentary committee on Women, Family and Youth Affairs and gaining strong representation on the health and labor committees.[44] It successfully promoted legislation on child benefits (which increased modestly in 1994) and on the protection of women's employment rights, gaining support from all legislative parties except RC/RDC and LDP.[45] Yeltsin signed much of this legisla-

---

[42] It should be noted that a presidential decree in any area could be issued to "fill a legislative void until such time as a law is passed." Thomas F. Remington, Steven S. Smith, and Moshe Haspel, "Decrees, Laws, and Inter-Branch Relations in the Russian Federation," *Post Soviet Affairs* 14, no. 4 (1998): 291.

[43] The Federation Council, which at this point comprised governors and regional authorities, was more fiscally conservative than the Duma and often supported the president, including blocking attempted overrides of his vetoes by the Duma on social spending measures.

[44] Beth Richardson, "Gender-Based Behavior among Women in the Russian Duma, 1994–1995" (M.A. thesis, Carleton University, 1997), 84–85. Party leader Ekaterina Lakhova also chaired the Presidential Commission on Women, giving WR a voice in the executive.

[45] "Deputaty Fraktsii "Zhenshchiny Rossii" v Gos. Dumy Pervovo Sozyva" (1994), available at http://women.centro.ru./ustav.htm; Richardson, "Gender-Based Behavior." In a selection of social policy votes that restricted liberalization or increased social expenditures, only RC/RDC and LDP voted against the majority.

tion because WR acted strategically, taking a pro-government stance on most other issues. According to Michael McFaul, "pragmatism enabled the faction to introduce many pieces of legislation that were adopted by the Duma."[46]

WR and Yabloko also focused legislative attention on the privatization of schools and the erosion of federal educational guarantees that had resulted from the reforms of the early 1990s. They mobilized moderate-reformist and left deputies to pass a temporary moratorium on privatization of state and municipal educational institutions and to restore the constitutional guarantee to a full (to grade 11) secondary education. This measure slowed the loss of school facilities and the *otsev* of young adolescents from public schools that had begun with the passage of the 1992 Law on Education. Both the moratorium and the restored guarantee have stood, setting a limit on the state's dismantling of the secondary public education system.[47]

The parliamentary role of WR and Yabloko constituted the height of constructive state-society negotiation over welfare reform and the representation of moderate pro-welfare constituencies in Russian politics. Both were programmatic parties with substantial connections to organized groups in Russian society. Interviews with WR deputies, for example, show that they had a strong sense of accountability to voters, saw themselves as representing interests specific to women, and coordinated women deputies across party lines to support these interests.[48] According to one WR deputy, in the 1993 Duma there was, "a sort of informal club headed by [WR leader] Fedulova where the majority of women met once in a while. . . . Laws concerning women were supported by practically all women in the Duma irrespective of their party affiliation."[49] Although small numerically, WR succeeded in rallying women and a critical mass of other deputies around a moderate

---

[46]   McFaul and Petrov, *Previewing Russia's 1995 Parliamentary Elections*, 45.

[47]   "Deputaty frakstii 'Zhenshchiny Rossii.'" The original law imposed a three-year moratorium; in 1998 the Duma, charging "distortions in the use of the Law on Education by organs of executive power," extended the moratorium indefinitely; see *Informatsionno-Analiticheskii Biulleten'* [hereafter *Inform*], 16 Sept.–20 Oct. 1998 (7 Oct. 1998), available at www.duma.gov.ru.

[48]   This section draws on twenty-six in-depth interviews conducted for the author by the Levada Center in Moscow in spring 2004 with women deputies who served in the first three Dumas; see Linda J. Cook, "Women in the Russian Duma, 1993–2004" (paper prepared for the Conference on Women in East European Politics, Woodrow Wilson Center for Scholars, Washington, D.C., Apr. 23–24, 2004).

[49]   Interview with WR deputy (#25), cited in Cook, "Women in the Russian Duma."

pro-welfare political agenda. In the 1995 election, WR collapsed as an electoral force, reflecting the general instability of the Russian party system. Women deputies did not form gender-based factions in later Dumas, and the defense of women's issues progressively deteriorated. The small numbers of women who were elected did not vote cohesively on gender or social issues and did not coordinate or caucus on strategies to promote women's interests. The implications of major social policy changes for women often went undebated or unrecognized. As one former WR deputy put it, "In all Dumas except the first one women separated and could not be characterized as a united force."[50] The loose moderate-reformist coalition around WR and Yabloko did not reappear, and the defense of welfare moved to parties that eschewed negotiation for obstructive tactics.

The Second Duma: The Politics of Polarization

After the December 1995 election, the Duma was dominated by left-restorationist parties that opposed retrenchment and rejected liberalization. The CPRF vote translated into 35 percent of the seats, nearly three times the number of the pro-government OHR. The communists were tactical, delegating members to the APR and PP factions in order to maximize the left's representation in the Duma Council, committees, and commissions. Members of these three factions initially controlled nearly the simple majority of votes needed to pass or block legislation (220 of 226) and chaired nearly half of the Duma's committees. Their internal cohesion on social policy and overall voting was strong, whereas the members of the four remaining factions remained divided.[51] The left produced a working majority on a range of social policy issues, with Yabloko and the centrist parties supporting some initiatives. It pursued a legislative strategy that was driven by both ideological opposition to markets and constituency interests.

---

[50]   Interview with United Russia deputy (#4), elected to second term in 2003, cited in Cook, "Women in the Russian Duma." For a related analysis of women Duma deputies' support for women's issues, based on roll-call voting, see Shevchenko, "Who Cares about Women's Problems?"

[51]   The correlation of the communist faction's vote with the agrarian faction's on social policy issues from 1996 to 1999 was 89.9 percent, and with PP, 88.3 percent, based on an analysis of all major votes (excluding votes that were procedural, technical, etc.); Iu. I. Malov, "Analysis of Votes and Internal Cohesion of Factions, 1996–1999," *Inform* (results of the work of the state Duma, second session, 1996–1999), available at www.duma.gov.ru/infgd/99_12/9912_017.htm.

One of the 1995 Duma's major legislative efforts was to increase the three key sets of payments that were regulated by the state: minimum pensions, the first grade of the public-sector salary scale, and the minimum wage, which formed the basis for calculating benefits to families, student grants, and most other state social benefits. These three sets of payments formed the core of the state's social obligations, and by the mid-1990s all had fallen drastically because of uncompensated inflation. The left's focus on these issues responded both to its welfarist ideology and to the interests of its relatively poorer, older, and more state-dependent electorate. In February, March, April, July, November, and December 1996 and again in March, June, and September 1997 and later, the Duma passed modest increases (10–20 percent) in minimum wages, minimum pensions, and/or the first grade of the public-sector salary scale. In several cases, it mobilized the two-thirds majority needed to override a Federation Council veto. The Duma also voted to raise the subsistence minimum, to increase child benefits for single parents, and to index wages in education and health care. Many of these proposals were supported by both left and moderate reformist parties.[52] In sum, the election produced a legislative majority for increased social spending.

Yeltsin vetoed most of these measures, which government spokesmen condemned without exception as unaffordable, irresponsible, and populist. The left was almost never able to put together the two-thirds majority in the more fiscally conservative Federation Council to override the presidential veto. Yeltsin did show some response to election-cycle pressures, agreeing to increases in minimum wages and pensions during the spring 1996 presidential election campaign and decreeing large increases in minimum pensions (compensation payments) unilaterally and far above the levels proposed by the Duma, evidently to compete with the communists for their core constituency. In sum, electoral feedback mechanisms did introduce some selective constraints on expenditure decline. (See Table 3.6)

The legislature was responsible for approving the federal budget, arguably a strong source of pressure that might have been used to force up government social expenditures. But the executive managed to substantially undermine the Duma's "power of the purse." The

[52] The evidence is from a range of Russian press and documentary sources and *Informatsionno-Analiticheskii Biulleten'*, Pravovoe Upravlenie Apparata Gosudarstvenio Dumy, *(Informational-Analytical Bulletin,* Legal Administration of the Apparatus of the State Duma) (hereafter *Inform)* at www.duma.gov.ru, a regular official report of the Duma's discussions and decisions.

Finance Ministry effectively controlled federal spending, and it rather arbitrarily sequestered budgeted social expenditures at significant levels during this period. According to an OECD report, in the mid-1990s, "The government's main instrument for expenditure control . . . was sequestration. The Ministry of Finance simply refused to make some payments that had been authorized."[53] (However, it did provide large, unbudgeted credits to powerful claimants.) In 1996, for example, 6.5 percent of GDP was allocated but only 4.9 percent expended for the social and cultural sectors.[54] According to Eugene Huskey, "this power of sequestration gave the executive broad discretion in doling out . . . budgetary funds."[55] This corruption of executive authority undermined the legislature's formal power to influence the funding of the social sector.

As a result, real minimum wages, pensions, and public-sector salaries declined substantially in real terms, though pensions were slightly better maintained than the other categories. Public-sector salaries also fell against average economywide wages. Doctors' average wage fell from 1.3 times the Russia-wide average in 1995 to 0.8 times in 2000, while the average for teachers fell from 0.8 to 0.5 over the same period, showing that adjustment here was more wrenching than in the broader transitional economy.[56] Real public expenditures on health and education continued to decline, to about half of their 1990 level in education and two-thirds in health by 1998 (see figure 3.1). At the same time, the numbers of personnel employed in health care actually grew during 1991–1998, and the number of teachers per 1,000 schoolchildren increased from seventy-three to almost eighty-two.[57] Declining financial resources were spread across a growing labor force, pushing wages below subsistence level for the majority and producing pervasive incentives for informality and corruption. (It should be noted here that some experts argue that these personnel numbers are inflated, with many fictitious doctors and others kept on payrolls and their meager salaries distributed among the real personnel, although there are no estimates of the numbers involved.)[58]

[53]   OECD, *Economic Survey, Russian Federation, 1995* (Paris: OECD, 1995), 36.

[54]   *Russian Economy in 1997,* 158, citing R. F. Goskomstat.

[55]   Eugene Huskey, *Presidential Power in Russia* (Armonk, N.Y.: M. E. Sharpe, 1999), 208.

[56]   *Trud i Zaniatost' v Rossii: Ofitsial'noe izdanie* (Moscow: Goskomstat, 2001), 386.

[57]   *Trud i Zaniatost' v Rossii,* 187; Yegor Gaidar, *The Economics of Transition* (Cambridge, Mass.: MIT Press, 2003), 613.

[58]   See, for example, Ksenia Yudaeva and Maria Gorban, "Health and Health Care," *Russian Economic Trends* 8, no. 2 (1999): 34.

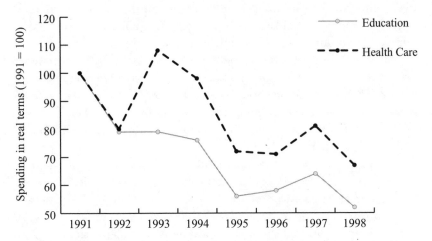

Figure 3.1 Real expenditures on health and education, Russian Federation, 1991–1998 (calculations based on Goskomstat data using GDP deflators)
Source: Yegor Gaidar, ed., *The Economics of Transition* (Cambridge, Mass.: MIT Press, 2003), 609 (table 18.6).

Legislative Obstacles to Restructuring

Though it largely failed to block the decline in real welfare expenditures, the 1995 Duma was much more effective in preventing further structural change in the welfare state and in diluting some of the reforms that had been introduced during the early 1990s. In housing, pension security, and labor relations, it rolled back, rejected, or kept off the table liberalizing executive initiatives. It blocked both the privatization and the closing of schools, and its legislative actions helped to undermine the medical insurance system. Overall, during its term the left-dominated Duma served as an effective veto actor against efforts both to dismantle the statist welfare system and to build new private markets for public goods.

The legislative majority viewed housing as a social right. Although they supported voluntary privatization of ownership (which was in fact popular with many older residents because it gave them, for the first time, rights to will their apartments to nonresident relatives), legislators resisted rent or utilities increases. In January 1996, as soon as the left had gained a dominant position in the Duma, it attacked and weakened the housing reform that had been legislated in 1992 by passing three key provisions which: (1) attenuated the pace of rent increases, extending the period of full cost recovery from five to ten years, then in 1998 to fifteen years; (2) placed a ceiling on the rent that could be charged to low-income households; and (3) made the annual cost recovery goals optional for municipalities.[59] The Duma also delayed legislation on the formation of condominiums, which was necessary in order to transfer privatized housing from municipal management to self-management. As a result of this legislation, housing reform slowed. A mosaic of reform practices emerged, with payment patterns highly variable. Housing subsidies remained very high, at 3–4 percent of GDP, on a par with health and education spending.[60]

The legislature rejected out of hand any diminution of pensioners' rights. As Pension Fund deficits and arrears became chronic, reformers floated various proposals to reduce entitlements. They proposed at various points to raise the retirement age, restrict rights to early retirement, cut or eliminate payments to Russia's 7 million working pensioners, eliminate privileged pensions, and suspend long-term service payments. The legislative left condemned these proposals at every opportunity, keeping the issues of pensioners' rights high on the political agenda.[61] Most proposals on pension reform were never even submitted to the Duma, where they would have faced inevitable defeat. Changes in basic pension eligibility rules came to be viewed by government officials as "not politically feasible."[62] The liberalization of the Labor Code to facilitate dismissals of workers and create more flexible contract rules was also placed on the executive's agenda in 1994 but was never approved by the legislature. In sum, the Duma blocked changes in the core legislative base of the old welfare state, keeping in place subsidies, entitlements, and protections and blocking adjustments to the conditions and constraints of the transitional economy.

As pointed out earlier, social-sector markets have to be both constructed and regulated, and this process began in the early 1990s (see chap. 2). The Duma now rejected most efforts to develop education and health-care markets. Deputies voted to extend indefinitely the moratorium

---

[59]   Nadezhda Kosareva and Raymond J. Struyk, "Reforming Russia," in *Restructuring Russia's Housing Sector: 1991–1997,* edited by Raymond J. Struyk (Washington, D.C.: Urban Institute, 1997); *Inform,* 21 Oct.-17 Nov., 1998.

[60]   OECD, *Social Crisis in the Russian Federation* (Paris: OECD, 2001), 37.

[61]   See Linda J. Cook, "State Capacity and Pension Provision," in Timothy J. Colton and Stephen Holmes, *The State after Communism: Governance in the New Russia* (Lanham, Md.: Rowman and Littlefield, 2006), 121–54.

[62]   This conclusion was expressed in interviews with a range of pension experts and political leaders involved with pension policy.

on the privatization of state educational institutions.[63] Other legislative measures reinforced political obstacles to the closing of public institutions, imposed onerous conditions for the formation of private schools, and rejected proposals to replace student stipends with means-tested assistance and loans (although tuition charges for a limited portion of university students were approved).[64] Partly in response to persistent pressure from the Ministry of Health, the Duma voted to rescind parts of the 1991 health-care restructuring package, undermining the health insurance companies that were supposed to make the system competitive. It also failed to pass legislation that would have regulated private medical practices, although deputies acknowledged the urgent need for such regulation in light of the extensive de facto private activity in the health sector.[65] These measures facilitated efforts at the regional and local levels to maintain inherited networks of schools, hospitals, and other social institutions. They, at the same time, frustrated efforts to establish controls over growing private and informal social-sector activity.

Patronage, Privileges, and Unfunded Mandates

The Soviet system of social provision was rife with privileges (*l'goty*), both benefits and exemptions, that extended to particular groups and categories in both the elite and the broader society. A major piece of the liberalizing program called for eliminating most privileges and replacing them with a streamlined, standardized system of means-tested social assistance. However, as incomes fell and costs for social goods (i.e., housing, utilities, transport, and medicines) rose through the 1990s, legislators were pressed to expand privileges, exemptions from payment, and special entitlements. The major vessel of this politics of privilege was the perennial Law on (Labor) Veterans, first passed in 1996. Through this legislation the Duma repeatedly tried to extend the pool of Russian citizens, especially pensioners, who were eligible for various privileges. Support for initial passage extended across the political spectrum, attesting to older citizens' electoral salience as well as empathy toward them. The Duma

---

[63] See *Inform,* 16 Sept–20 Oct. 1998.

[64] On the closing of institutions, the law required the agreement of the legislative organ of power for the elimination of educational institutions of corresponding jurisdiction and for all conditions of changing its status; see *Inform,* 16 Sept.—20 Oct. 1998. Private schools were still explicitly allowed to form, but were subject to extensive state supervision.

[65] The draft law, adopted on first reading in June 1999, annulled the requirement that regional CMI (Compulsory Medical Insurance) Funds operate through health insurance companies.

passed numerous amendments to this law, benefiting both mass and elite groups, demonstrating the left majority's commitment to a politics of patronage.[66] Yeltsin played a Janus-faced role here, vetoing some of the Duma's privilege-extending measures while introducing his own social welfare measures by decree, especially in the run-up to the 1996 presidential election.[67] The share of households receiving at least one subsidy or privilege increased from 31 percent in 1997 to more than 43 percent in 2001, effectively expanding the system of untargeted benefits.[68]

The proliferation of privileges and patronage further burdened and disorganized a system of social assistance that was already weakened by decentralization and funding declines. Measures that passed into law were sent out to the regions and municipalities as unfunded (or at best partially funded) federal mandates, contributing to conflicts and nontransparency in center-regional relations; local governments also added privileges and exemptions as part of their own social assistance measures. In 1997, for example, the implementation of the Law on Veterans was estimated to cost R63 trillion, but only about R13 trillion was included in the federal budget and center and regions disputed responsibility for the remainder.[69] Monetary benefits often simply went unpaid, while in-kind benefits added to the municipalities' de facto (implicit) subsidy burden. The distribution of privileges was badly skewed, with the poorest groups disproportionately excluded.

In sum, from the mid-1990s the legislature and executive were deadlocked over welfare state politics. Russia's political institutions produced a fragmentation of powers that permitted the president to retrench (reduce spending) while the legislature blocked restructuring. Yeltsin initially vetoed more than half of the social policy laws passed by the Duma in 1996–1997.[70] As Andrea Chandler concludes about this period,

[66]   Duma deputy, Committee on Labor and Social Policy, interview with author, Moscow, Feb. 3, 1999.

[67]   Remington et al., "Decrees," 304.

[68]   *Veterans* here meant not only war but also labor veterans, in effect a broad and ever-expanding category of older citizens and their households. For some of the legislation passed under the Law On Veterans, as well as presidential decrees and government resolutions expanding their social privileges, see *L'goty Veteranam: Dokumenty i kommentarii* (Moscow: Sotsial'naia Zashchita, 2000).

[69]   *Inform*, no. 1 (2000) at www.duma.gov.ru.

[70]   Remington et al., "Decrees," argue that the president did bargain with the Duma on social policy and eventually signed about half the vetoed legislation, that the two branches shared "the desirability of maintaining basic social programs. The President often favors smaller increases in social spending and negotiates with the parliament through several rounds before approving legislation" (307). But many of these compromises involved modest, long-delayed, one-time increases in social security payments that had been passed repeatedly by the Duma before they were finally approved by the president, often near elections, when the use of the veto declined dramatically; and there was much less compromise on institutional restructuring issues.

in welfare policy and in general "the use of the veto became 'normalized' in legislative-executive relations, and patterns of constructive consensus-building became less apparent than confrontation. The President was as capable of blocking legislation as the Duma was capable of blocking reform."[71] Russia's polarized constellations of power produced a stalemate that neither effectively preserved the statist system nor liberalized it.

STATIST STAKEHOLDERS AND DIVISIONS WITHIN THE GOVERNMENT

The government was also divided over the executive's program of welfare state retrenchment and restructuring. Support was predictably concentrated in the Finance and Economics Ministries[72] and in newly formed state committees, particularly Anatolii Chubais's Committee on State Property, which promoted privatization of social assets. Opposition emerged among statist stakeholders in the social ministries, which developed strategies to reverse reforms, to dilute them in the implementation stage, and to reconstruct and enhance ministerial roles in a semi-reformed system. The inconsistencies of presidential leadership facilitated their efforts. Yeltsin replaced the radical social ministers with a parade of others—five health and three education ministers between 1991 and 1999—most of whom were indifferent, and some who were openly hostile, to the reforms.[73] The president was never able to impose discipline on his shifting governments. Subject to neither clear presidential nor party control, the social ministers formed part of "an unwieldy coalition of ministers, most of whom are devoted first and foremost to their own institutional [departmental] interests."[74] The institutional weakness in the halls of the Russian government reached its height during this period.

The Health Ministry was the most aggressive in trying to reverse reforms. According to a well-placed observer, "At first, people at the Ministry of

[71] Andrea Chandler, "Presidential Veto Power in Post-Communist Russia, 1994–1998," *Canadian Journal of Political Science* 34, no. 3 (2001): 507.

[72] Although, even in these ministries, according to Huskey (referring to the broader reform project), "the reformist contingent ... was restricted to a small group at the top of each apparatus. Beneath them worked officials with largely unreconstructed views." *Presidential Power in Russia,* 115.

[73] The Health ministers were A. I. Vorob'ev (1992), E. A. Nachaev (1994), T. B. Dmitrieva (1997), O. V. Rutkovskii (1998), and V. I. Starodubov (1999); Ibid., 115–16. The Education ministers (after Dneprov) were E. V. Tkachenko and V. G. Kinelev (1996); Webber, *School,* 56.

[74] Huskey, *Presidential Power in Russia,* 103.

Health didn't seem to understand how much of their power and authority were being removed (by decentralization and the introduction of insurance in the early 1990s); [later] it fought against the plan. . . . civil servants in the Ministry of Health at all levels are against [reforming] through insurance."[75] E. A. Nachaev, minister 1994–1997, was "against the whole idea of insurance . . . and liked the administrative Soviet system."[76] The ministry launched a campaign to discredit and eliminate the medical insurance companies, so it could take back control over the money collected by the Health Insurance Funds. It lobbied through the press and in the Duma, turning the reformers' rationale back on them, claiming (with some justification) administrative waste and inefficiency in the new insurance system. From 1995, the Health Ministry promoted legislation that would have reconstituted government controls while health insurance companies and funds lobbied against it.[77]

This legislation did not pass, but attempts by health-care administrations in both center and regions to return to a state system had considerable de facto success. By 1997, medical insurance companies were being closed out of many regions.[78] Public authorities reasserted control over the spending of most health funds, which they used to keep existing facilities, personnel, and practices in place. The Health Ministry also tried to recentralize, that is, to establish more control over appointments of health administrators, approval of professional qualifications, and the setting of professional norms and standards for the health-care system.[79] Amid these struggles between reformers and statist bureaucratic stakeholders, the major health indicators of the Russian population continued to fall.

The Education Ministry also tried to obstruct and erode reforms, although less overtly and less successfully. It was the ministry most seriously undercut by the earlier reforms, suffering the serious erosion of its administrative capacity, budget resources, and political influence.

[75]   Interview with senior Health economist, May 21, 1997, with Judyth Twigg, in Trip Report (transcript), Moscow, May 1997, 39.

[76]   Interviews with deputy executive director, Federal Compulsory Medical Insurance Fund, and leader of Analytic Center, Federal Compulsory Medical Insurance Fund, with Judyth Twigg, in Trip Report (transcript), Moscow, June 1998, 15, 19.

[77]   Irina Rozhdestvenskaya and Sergei Shishkin, "Institutional Reforms in the Social-Cultural Sphere," in *The Economics of Transition*, edited by Yegor Gaidar (Cambridge, Mass.: MIT Press, 2003), 584–615.

[78]   *Russian Economy in 1997*, 162–67.

[79]   Interview with head of Department of Organization and Control of Medical Care for the Population, Russian Ministry of Health, with Judyth L. Twigg, in Trip Report (transcript), Moscow, June 1998, 23–24.

The ministers themselves struggled to protect funding while broadly supporting reform agendas, but overall the ministry "seem[ed] increasingly dominated by traditionalist and communist elements tied to the Duma and the Russian Academy of Education."[80] Ministerial officials opposed privatization or closure of schools which, according to one government advisor, was "almost impossible because the Ministry of Education uses the numbers to bargain with the Ministry of Finance."[81] The Education Ministry also tried to restore its role by recentralizing some control over educational standards. In response to the organizational chaos and inequities that had resulted from decentralization, the post-Dneprov leadership "stressed the urgency of developing compensatory mechanisms such as common national curricular standards and a unified system of examinations."[82] From 1997, education reform projects included versions of these proposals, effectively accommodating ministerial interests as they continued efforts to liberalize other elements of the system.

The reforms of social security also produced opposition within the government. The establishment of the off-budget social funds, particularly the Pension Fund, had removed a huge pool of tax revenues from the federal budget. The Finance Ministry from the outset wanted to reverse this reform, integrating social taxes back into the budget as well as moving toward partial privatization of pensions. Pension and other social fund managers, on the other hand, having gained control over large resource pools, dug in and defended their claims on tax revenues. In sum, Russia's social ministries as well as social fund administrators stood as a second set of veto actors against liberalization. The ministries often cooperated with the Duma in generating and supporting legislation to block change. A combination of administrative and legislative actors helped to maintain both personnel and institutional infrastructure.

THE FAILURES AND SUCCESSES OF WORLD BANK INTERVENTION

In early 1997, the World Bank stepped up its role in the Russian Federation, aiding a major governmental attempt to revive flagging

---

[80] Mark S. Johnson, "A Legacy at Risk: Russian Educational Policy and Politics in the Late 1990's" (Xerox, Dept. of History, Colorado College, Nov. 15, 1999), 4–5.

[81] Government advisor, interview with author, Moscow, Feb. 2, 1999.

[82] Mark S. Johnson, "Western Models and Russian Realities in Postcommunist Education," *Tertium Comparationis Journal für Internationale Bildungsforschung* 2, no. 2 (1996): 125.

social-sector reforms. The centerpiece of the Bank's intervention was an $800 million policy-linked Social Protection Adjustment Loan (SPAL), by far the largest social-sector loan of the Russian transition, complemented by social-sector conditionality in a larger Structural Adjustment Loan and coordinated with an International Monetary Fund (IMF) Extended Fund Facility.[83] The SPAL was negotiated with a new social-sector reform team, including Boris Nemtsov, Oleg Sysuyev, and Mikhail Dmitriev, whom Yeltsin placed in positions of control over Russia's social ministries.[84] This renewed reform drive came in response to both a fiscal crisis and the welfare state's growing crisis as real expenditures fell. The reformers proposed a broad package of entitlement reductions for both mass and elite groups, user fees in health and education, privatization of social security, liberalization of the labor code, and replacement of the existing system of social transfers with means-tested antipoverty measures. Overall, it represented a renewed attempt at wholesale streamlining and rationalization of the inherited social welfare system. The SPAL's policy conditionality focused on pension reform, unemployment assistance, and means-tested poverty benefits, forming part of a broader effort to promote these policy models throughout the postcommunist transition states.

The comparative literature is divided over the influence of international interventions on domestic social policy. One school contends that, while social-sector professionals are receptive to IFI influence, domestic political elites protect resource flows to their constituents against external pressures for re-allocation, frustrating interventions. The other school points especially to the World Bank's success in promoting social-sector reforms through interventions backed by loans and coincidental IMF dependence, particularly in the transitional context.[85] I am arguing, in contrast to both of these views, that IFIs may succeed or fail depending on the political influence of their domestic allies. In the early 1990s global policy networks played an important role in shaping Russian social

[83] Jonathan E. Sanford, "Russia and the International Financial Institutions: From Special Case to a Normal Country," *Russia's Uncertain Economic Future* (Washington, D.C.: Joint Economic Committee (JEC), Congress of the United States, Dec. 2001), 450–53.

[84] Nemtsov was appointed first deputy prime minister with responsibility for housing and communal services reform, Sysuev was appointed deputy prime minister, and Dmitriev was appointed first deputy minister of Labor with responsibility for pension reform; *Rosiiskaia Gazeta,* 17 July 1997, 6.

[85] See the discussion in the book's introduction.

reforms. (see chap. 2). In the Russia of the latter 1990s, the balance of political power leaned against reform, and the Bank's efforts largely failed. Legislative and ministerial elites did protect entitlements and resource flows against Bank-promoted reorganizations and re-allocations, despite Russia's strong dependence on Bank and IMF loans.

The World Bank's efforts to shape and hasten welfare reform in Russia entailed deep intrusions into the domestic policy process. Loan documents set as the goal a "major and far-reaching reform of the whole social protection system . . . establishment of a new legal framework." In pension reform, they called for "moving the system away from public financing and solidarity toward a funded, accumulative, individual market model."[86] The SPAL was negotiated solely with the government, and Bank officials placed great stock in the ability of the new high-level reformist appointees to provide momentum and energy.[87] Aside from some vague references to building consensus and educating the public about the need for reform, the formal documents (at least) show an almost complete disregard for the polarization over welfare that characterized Russian politics in this period or for any process of democratic deliberation.

To address the problems of the pension system, Bank officials advocated the expansion of pension insurance markets and the introduction of mandatory investment accounts. They pressed for re-orienting social assistance toward poverty-linked benefits, with eligibility to be determined by household-level means tests. The Bank devoted considerable intellectual and financial resources to promoting this core piece of the liberal model in Russia. A set of poverty pilots addressed the difficulty of collecting income data in Russia's large informal economy, developing model proxy means tests that could establish benefit eligibility even in a demonetized economy.[88] Information about these projects was broadly disseminated among governmental and professional specialists.

Reformist social policy specialists were receptive to the Bank's approach. Interviews showed that poverty experts in Russia had become deeply frustrated with the politics of privileges, the politically driven

---

[86]   "Report and Recommendation of the President of the International Bank for Reconstruction and Development to the Executive Directors on a Proposed Social Protection Adjustment Loan in the Amount of US$800 Million to the Russian Federation" [hereafter, SPAL], Washington, D.C., June 5, 1997, 9.

[87]   World Bank official, interview with author, Washington, D.C., Apr. 29, 1999.

[88]   On the poverty pilots, see Jeanine Braithwaite, "Targeting and the Longer-Term Poor in Russia" (draft, World Bank, February 1999).

dispersion of scarce social assistance resources, and had developed commitments to a rationalized system of poverty alleviation. One prominent expert, for example, agreed that "All attention should be focused on poverty relief, and other programs ended." Although critical of means testing because of its potentially high administrative costs and errors of exclusion, she nevertheless saw it as the only solution and focused on how to adapt it to Russian conditions. Other specialists similarly supported variants of targeted benefits.[89]

By contrast, officials from the Labor Ministry responded to the Bank's approach using a political logic, citing the need to continue benefits to established recipients. Referring to the poverty pilots, a deputy head of the Ministry of Labor said, "the analysis is good but the situation is complex. . . . [T]here is an accumulation of guarantees. . . . [O]ne can't say there will simply be no guarantees. . . . [T]here are laws on various groups—disabled, veterans."[90]

In the short term, the Bank did not affect policy outcomes. The governmental reform team did generate a pension reform program that included a funded pillar, as well as benefits reform legislation that would have targeted social assistance. But key bureaucratic stakeholders in the government as well as the Duma majority rejected these measures. Pension reform was opposed by both the Labor Ministry and the Pension Fund, defending their institutional interests in the existing system. In 1997, the Duma voted down twice, by large majorities, a broad package of legislation devoted to these reforms as well as other liberal restructuring measures.[91]

The government did not extend the poverty pilots. According to a well-informed source, "the (Labor) Ministry is just not willing to take on the issues. [They are] now circulating the reports in dialogue with the government. This is all that can be done."[92] Regional and local governments continued to allocate scarce social assistance resources according to their own priorities. Only token funds were re-allocated to unemployment assistance. In sum, bureaucracies and elected politicians protected their institutional interests and domestic constituencies against external pressures to re-allocate welfare

[89] Poverty and social policy expert, Institute for Social and Demographic Problems, Russian Academy of Sciences, interview with author, Moscow, Feb. 9, 1999; expert, Municipal Economic and Social Reform of TACIS, interview with author, Moscow, June 7, 2000.

[90] Deputy head, Department on Income, Wages, and Social Insurance, Ministry of Labor and Social Development, Russian Federation, interview with author, Moscow, Feb. 3, 1999.

[91] A single measure passed, introducing means testing of child benefits.

[92] World Bank economist, Poverty Reduction and Economic Management, Europe and Central Asian Region, World Bank, phone interview with author, Jan. 12, 2000.

resources. The onset of the 1998 financial crisis then derailed the Bank's assistance strategy, and Russia's ensuing economic recovery brought an end to large-scale adjustment lending. The Bank retrospectively judged its social-sector interventions in Russia during the 1990s as its worst performance anywhere during that period, ranking its influence as marginal. Its self-critical 2002 country assistance evaluation bluntly recognized the political sources of this failure: "apart from a handful of reformers in the government, commitment to the reform agendas of the . . . SPAL was negligible."[93]

Stages of Restructuring in Russia

Table 3.1 summarizes domestic political balances during this period and their effects on welfare state change in Russia. It shows that pro-reform institutions and actors—the executive, reformist social-sector elites, and policy specialists and liberal international institutions—were weakened in 1994–1999, whereas the antireform Duma and state-bureaucratic stakeholders vetoed changes in the welfare state. The consequences across policy areas are summarized in table 3.5, which shows the effects—stalled pension and housing reforms, dilution of earlier liberalizing changes in health and education, and increasing social privileges. The table also contrasts policy outcomes in this period with those of the initial liberalization in 1991–1993 and with the following period of renewed liberalization under Putin.

The outcome of this period was an incoherent policy of retrenchment without restructuring that had three major effects on the welfare state: (1) the inherited system of basic social guarantees remained in place while benefit payments and social-sector wages fell and were chronically in arrears; (2) the redirection of welfare spending from inherited patterns was minimal and the system largely failed to address transition-induced poverty and unemployment; (3) the collapse of state financing combined with the absence of formal privatization or effective regulation to produce pervasive informality, spontaneous privatization, and corruption in Russia's social sector.

At the beginning of 2000 the newly elected Duma surveyed social conditions in Russia in the aftermath of the 1998 financial crisis that had brought about the collapse of the ruble and pushed social indicators to their lowest levels in the transition. Fifty million people, more than one-third of the population, were poor; 10 million were unemployed. All basic

[93] World Bank, *Assisting Russia's Transition: An Unprecedented Challenge* (Washington, D.C.: World Bank, 2002), 8.

TABLE 3.5
Stages of welfare state restructuring in postcommunist Russia

	Initial liberalization (1991–1993)	Deadlock (1994–1999)	Breakthrough (2000–2003)
Pensions, social security	Moved to off-budget fund; wage tax base	Duma rejects cuts; reform stalls in government	Duma passes pension reform with funded tier
Education	Radical decentralization; private schools legal; reduced federal guarantee to secondary education	Duma passes moratorium on privatization; rejects replacing subsides with loans, most education fees	Per capita financing; national testing; university tuition; user fees proposed
Health care	Radical decentralization; insurance financing; private practice legalized; competitive contracting	Duma dilutes reform, rejects regulatory legislation; local and federal health bureaucracy oppose insurance system	Insurance, co-pays; separate state guarantees for poor
Benefits, social assistance	Radical decentralization to local level	Duma defends subsidies, privileges; rejects means-testing	Duma cuts privileges for mass and elite groups; extends means-testing
Housing	Voluntary privatization; cost-recovery rents	Duma attenuates rent increase schedule; retains subsidies	Duma passes gradual cost recovery
Labor Code	Limited reforms to facilitate enterprise closings	Duma rejects Labor Code revisions	Duma revises labor code; makes hiring and firing more flexible; cuts benefits and protections

social guarantees had fallen below the subsistence level. The Law on Veterans was fully funded in fewer than one-quarter of Russia's regions.[94] All state social-sector payments had significant levels of arrears. In the following sections, I discuss the effects on basic social guarantees and poverty.

RUSSIA'S WELFARE STATE IN THE LATE 1990S

Basic Social Guarantees and Social-Sector Wages

Retrenchment without restructuring meant that entitlements, institutions, and social-sector salaries were progressively defunded. Table 3.6

---

[94]   *Inform*, no. 1 (2000) reports that the law was fully funded in twenty regions.

TABLE 3.6
Basic social guarantees and social-sector wages, 1993–1999 (%)[a]

	1993	1994	1995	1996	1997	1998	1999
Minimum wage	39	28	10	16	19	18	10
Wage rate for first-grade public-sector wage scale	41	30	19	21	18	19	10
Monthly benefit for each child[b]	19	21	8	13	15	14	7
Minimum student stipend, higher education	39	28	10	16	38	36	19
Old age pensions:							
minimum[c]	63	79	43	47	79	79	42
average	138	129	101	116	113	115	70
Invalid's pensions group 1	105	73	54	52	50	57	30
Wages in health sector (average)	195 (1992)	—	—	150	149	134	99
Workers below subsistence (%)	—	—	—	48.7	47.8	—	67.2
Wages in education sector (average)	185 (1992)	—	—	141	143	127	93
Workers below subsistence (%)	—	—	—	49.7	49.4	—	70.5

Sources: Sotsial'noe Polozhenie i uroven zhizni naseleniia Rossii 2002: statistichiskii sbornik, 165 (table 6.10); 145 (table 5.19); 147 (table 5.21); 2001, 148 (table 5.22), 150 (table 5.24) (Moscow: Goskomstat Rossii, 2001, 2002); *Russia in Figures 2000* (Moscow: Goskomstat, 2000), 98.

[a] On January 1, percentage of subsistence level.
[b] To 6 years old, 1993–1995; to 16 years old, 1996–1999.
[c] With compensation payments.

summarizes the payment of basic social guarantees, including child benefits, university student stipends, worker and invalids' pensions, and social-sector wages in relation to the subsistence level from 1993 to 1999. In 1993 (the first year for which these measures are available), minimum wages, public-sector wage rates, and student stipends stood at about 40 percent of subsistence; average pensions and public-sector wages were well above. By 1999, most of these guarantees had declined by one-half, and some had declined by as much as three-quarters against subsistence. The minimum wage and the first grade of the public-sector salary scale, two key sets of payments regulated by the government, had declined to 10 percent of subsistence; average pensions and public-sector salaries had fallen below this. The average unemployment benefit (not shown in the table), the one program designed to deal with new social problems, stood at 30 percent of subsistence in 1995 and 20 percent in 1998, and take-up rates were extremely low because of administrative obstacles.[95] All social-sector payments were subject to episodic breakdowns and chronic arrears, which tended to concentrate in the poorest regions. Pension arrears in particular were experienced as a deep betrayal of expectations and entitlements by older Russians.

Ongoing economic decline and polarization meant that there was very little re-allocation to meet the social needs created by transition. Although existing benefits served as something of a hedge against poverty for traditional claimants, they excluded large categories of the unemployed and new poor or working poor, those in jobs with low or erratically paid wages. One-quarter to one-third of the population was officially poor through the 1990s. Russian statistics show that the two lowest income deciles received the fewest state subsidies and privileges, whereas the World Bank estimated that one-fifth of poor households received no public transfers.[96] In the 1990s, a much lower proportion of benefits was transferred to the poor in Russia than in OECD or East Central European countries, or even Latin American countries with large informal sectors. During the early years of reform, many moved into and out of poverty, but by the mid-1990s 10–17 percent had become chronically poor.[97] There was also a steady increase in the duration of unemployment and in the correlation between unemployment and poverty. Regional disparities served to create pockets of joblessness and persistent poverty.

The distributive costs fell most heavily on children, the unemployed, and their households. Over the decade, poverty increasingly concentrated in families, with the highest risk of poverty and deep poverty in the latter 1990s to multichild households and those headed by a single parent or unemployed adult. More than half of households with an unemployed member were poor, and more than 40 percent of those with children (see table 3.7). The effects were evident in the declining health and welfare of children: increases in the rates of wasting (low weight) and stunting (low height) due to chronic malnutrition, and increases in the number of children abandoned by their families and institutional-

---

[95] Specialist on unemployment and poverty, interview with author, Moscow, June 1999.
[96] See *Sotsial'noe Polozhenie I Uroven Zhizhni Naseleniia* (Moscow: Goskomstat, 2002), 172.
[97] Braithwaite, "Targeting."

TABLE 3.7
Level of poverty for all households and households with children, unemployed, and
pensioners, 1997–1999 (%)[a]

	Poverty rates for all households	Families with children to 16 years old	Number of children		Single-parent[b]	Unem-ployed member	Non-working pensioner
			1–2	3+			
1997	25.7	38.3	36.8	57.4	41.5	53.8	11.7
1998	30.4	45.1	43.5	69.2	46.5	58.4	14.5
1999[b]	41.9	57.8	—	—	62.7	—	—

Sources: Rossiiskii Statisticheskii Ezhegodnik. (Moscow: Goskomstat, 1999), 166 (table 7.31); 1999 data
from *Feminizatsiia bednost' v Rossii* (Moscow: Ves', 2000).

[a] Based on household surveys.
[b] Quarter 3. Data for single-parent households and for 1999 are for families with children under
18 years old.

ized. For the first time since the 1930s, Russia had significant numbers
of street children.[98]

Pensioners, by contrast, were relatively well-protected from poverty.
They benefited as the main object of political competition between
the communists and Yeltsin, of protection by the left and patronage
by the president.[99] Pensions were the only clearly redistributive social
transfer program in the 1990s.[100] Although Russia did not see the large
increases in pension expenditures that were evident, for example, in
Poland, and payment arrears were a serious problem in mid-decade,
Russian pension levels were compressed toward subsistence and kept
the majority of recipients out of poverty except during the 1998 crisis.

Health and Education: Informality, Exclusion,
and "Spontaneous Privatization"

In the health and education sectors, real spending fell while political resistance blocked both the dismantling of infrastructure and the
development of legal private markets. Private education remained very

[98] See Murray Feshbach, *Russia's Health and Demographic Crises: Policy Implications and
Consequences* (Washington, D.C: Chemical and Biological Arms Institute, 2003), 47–49; on
institutionalization and other aspects of child welfare, see Alexandre Zouev, *Generation in
Jeopardy: Children in Central and Eastern Europe and the Former Soviet Union* (Armonk, N.Y.:
M. E. Sharpe, 1998).

[99] Pensioners were protected in part by the Law on Veterans and nearly universal
housing privileges, as well as by Yeltsin's decree providing large compensation payments to
supplement minimum pensions.

[100] OECD, *Social Crisis in the Russian Federation.*

limited except at the university level; in 1999, 1 percent of general educational, less than 5 percent of early professional, and 40 percent of
higher educational institutions were private. The ownership of medical
facilities remained almost exclusively public. The overuse of hospitalization and overspecialization of doctors remained the norm, and comparative international measures of the health-care system's effectiveness
assigned Russia very low rankings. In 1997, the World Health Organization (WHO) ranked the Russian Federation 75th in expenditures, but
127th in health indicators and 130th in effectiveness of the health protection system, indicating a very wide disparity between expenditures
and effectiveness.[101]

Legally, most health care and education remained free, but the weakness of the state led to poor regulation. In both sectors, there developed processes of spontaneous privatization and commercialization
mimicking those in the broader economy, "an increasing tendency
to spontaneous and unofficial replacement of free services with paid
ones."[102] Public-sector employees and elites on a significant scale used
their control over access to social services and their existing skill sets to
craft combinations of formal, semi-formal, and informal or shadow payment requirements that became important means of survival and profit.
By the mid-1990s, payments played a significant role in access to health
services, and people at all income levels were paying for care. Survey data
show that the percentages making both formal and informal payments
in public facilities grew through the 1990s from about 25 percent in 1996
to 40 percent in 1998 and 80 percent in 1999–2000. A study by a group
of Russian health experts estimated conservatively that the informal
health-care market in 1997 captured 0.86 percent of GDP, equal to about
25 percent of reported public health expenditures.[103]

Health-care administrators and employees developed vested interests
in this system and opposed both formal privatization and regulation.
According to prominent Russian experts on the sector,

[101]   World Health Organization, *World Health Report: Health Systems: Improving Performance* (Geneva: WHO, 2000), 152–55.
[102]   F. G. Feeley, I. M. Sheiman, and S. V. Shishkin, "Health Sector Informal Payments in Russia," available at http://doc2.bu.edu/RussianLegalHealthReform/ProjectDocuments/n650.111B6.
[103]   See, Yudaeva and Gorban, "Health and Health Care," 32; "The Evaluation of the
Attitudes towards Reforms and the Directions for Change in the Financing and Delivery of
Health Care in Four Regions of The Russian Federation" (TACIS: May, 2000), 8; Feeley
et al., "Health Sector Informal Payments in Russia."

TABLE 3.8
Abstinence from medical treatment by household income, 1997[a]

	Income (in thousands of rubles)			
	< 400	401–800	801–2,000	> 2,001
Prescription drugs	50	36	21	20
Laboratory tests	36	26	18	18
Dental care	43	32	19	13
Hospital care	18	9	4	4

Source: V. Boikov, F. Fili, I. Sheiman, and S. Shishkin, "Household expenditures on health and pharmaceuticals," *Voprosy Ekonomiki*, no. 10 (1998), cited in OECD, *Social Crisis in the Russian Federation* (Paris: OECD, 2001), 35.

[a] Percentage of households within income category.

central and local sociocultural authorities and the heads and employees of institutions resist privatization and any reorganization of their institutions, in part because they have already privatized most of the ownership rights to the public assets. Keeping the services free serves the interests of both the bureaucrats and the employees of service-providing institutions, for it provides the former with grounds to have public funds placed at their disposal and the latter with the opportunity to receive fees for their services directly from their customers.[104]

In sum, social-sector elites and staffs were becoming stakeholders in spontaneous privatization and informality.

Payment requirements led to significant limits on access and exclusion. Studies show substantial levels of abstinence from some types of medical treatment, which increased as income levels declined. Table 3.8 shows evidence of an emergent underclass without access to medical care.

Increases in both formal and informal out-of-pocket health-care payments produced large changes in the structure of Russian health-care financing—the public-private expenditure ratio. By the end of the decade, some studies placed private health-care spending at levels nearly equaling public spending. No direct relationship between expenditure and health outcomes can be assumed because many factors in addition to spending affect health. However, poor health outcomes in Russia appear to be linked to the fall in public expenditures. According to a recent World Bank study, "although defining causality is difficult, (in Russia) the

[104] Rozhdestvenskaya and Shishkin, "Institutional Reforms in the Sociocultural Sphere," 606.

decline in health status roughly parallels the decreases in public-sector health care expenditures, in real terms."[105] By the end of the decade, Russia had comparatively large unaddressed public health problems, including levels of premature male mortality that are rarely seen in peacetime; rates of infectious diseases, such as tuberculosis, that have grown by multiples throughout the transition; and (along with Ukraine) the highest rate of growth of registered HIV infections in the world. This heavily privatized pattern of expenditure became institutionalized during the transition and remained in place after economic recovery.

A mix of legal and shadow payments also developed in education. The 1992 Education Law legalized payment for supplementary services at secondary and university levels, as well as commercialization. These provisions opened the door to a range of charges for classes, tutoring, and other educational services to supplement school and teacher incomes. By 1996, there had developed a mix of payment-based and free education in state schools. According to the best available estimate, secondary-level tutoring services systematically increased by 60–100 percent the salaries of the best teachers in larger cities, and by 30–50 percent the salaries of those in small cities and towns.[106] Some of the tutoring was legitimate, but there were also serious abuses, especially at the university level. Here faculty and administrators who were attached to the more prestigious schools and programs used institution-specific entry exams to craft systems of high-priced tutoring and preparatory courses for students seeking admission, and also outright bribes. As formal tuition charges were introduced gradually through the 1990s, students made shadow payments to schools or their staffs for acceptance to the remaining state-funded slots, in effect paying to be awarded a state subsidy.

The Union of Rectors, based at major state universities, emerged as a key source of stakeholder opposition to efforts at renewed state regulation of university entrance testing and admissions. According the Eduard Dneprov, the reformist minister of Education in the early 1990s, "Nowhere has there been such privatization of state property as in the higher schools. The country's 500 or so rectors have essentially become the proprietors of privatized state institutions."[107] The structure of educational spending

[105] World Bank, *Russian Federation: Reducing Poverty through Growth and Social Policy Reform* (Report no. 28923-RU) (Washington, D.C.: World Bank, February 24, 2005), 87, 129.

[106] Ia. I. Kuzminov et al., "The Condition and Prospects of Development of the Russian Educational System," available at www.imf.org/external/pubs/ft/seminar/2000/invest/pdf/kuzmin.pdf.

[107] Svetlana Kirillova, "A Time of Eminences Grises," *Moskovskiie Novosti*, no. 97, 28 Nov. – 4 Dec. 2000, 19, trans. in *Current Digest of the Post-Soviet Press 52*, no. 49 (2001): 14.

at the end of the decade looked much like that for health, with about 5 percent of total GDP spent, half of it outside the state budget. As much as 1.5 percent of GDP was spent by families for tutoring and other access related services.[108] Here also the balance between public and private expenditures had shifted spontaneously toward private and shadow payments.

Other sectors too underwent limited structural reform amidst spending cuts. Rent increases were slowed by the Duma and housing privatization stalled. In 1999, about 60 percent of housing was legally private, but only about 1 percent had been reorganized into commercial forms (condominiums), and much of this was new private construction.[109] The population paid about one-half the cost of housing, leaving a high level of dependence on budget subsidies. Housing provision had become a hodge-podge of residual tenancy rights, subsidies, means-tested benefits, and partial rent payments. In labor relations, no legal reforms had been accomplished. Wage arrears reached their height in 1997–1998, and both hidden unemployment and informal employment were pervasive.

In sum, Russia was producing an informalized welfare state, governed effectively neither by the state nor by market principles. The state sponsored systems of social security coverage and social protection, but payments were unreliable and often too low to matter. It subsidized most services at low levels, but could neither adequately finance nor regulate them. Informal payments mediated access, and providers parcelized control over social-sector institutions. The system was fragmented and informalized. The scale of private expenditures for major service categories was approaching public. As Guy Standing has suggested for contemporary welfare states more broadly, significant numbers of people at both the top and bottom of society were becoming detached from the formal welfare state structures.[110]

Conclusion

Despite Russia's deep and prolonged recession and its strongly presidential political regime, major aspects of the executive's liberal restructuring

---

[108]   German Gref, "Proekt Strategiia Rossiiskoi Federatsii do 2010 Goda. Fond 'Tsentr Strategicheskikh Razrabotok 2000g" (2006), available at www.kommersant.ru/documents/Strat1.ht.

[109]   T. D. Belkina, *Zhilishchnaya Reforma v Rossii: Problemy I Perspektivy* (Moscow: TACIS, 1999).

[110]   Guy Standing, "Globalisation: The Eight Crises of Social Protection" (draft) (Geneva: International Labor Office, November 2001), available at www.ilo.org.

program were blocked by political opposition for most of the 1990s. As a 2001 OECD study of Russia's social crisis notes, much of the inherited social protection system remained in place.[111] The constitutional system fragmented power, giving the legislature a veto over structural change. Constellations of moderate pro-welfare and hard-left restorationist legislative parties slowed or blocked reforms. To a limited extent, the defense of welfare entitlements by a left legislative majority with a largely state-dependent electorate parallels the welfare politics of Western states.

But in Russia the main pro-welfare coalition was thinly organized and ideologically dogmatic. The kind of thick constellations of political parties, trade unions, public-sector workers' associations, and benefit recipients that negotiate welfare state change in the West (and to a more limited extent in the East Central European transitional democracies) emerged only briefly and in an anemic form in mid-decade. The hard left that dominated legislative politics for most of the period lacked a strong base in labor or social movements and was backward-looking, committed to an uncritical restorationism that served mainly to freeze up allocations in a welfare structure that was no longer viable. The Russian welfare state was also defended by a set of bureaucratic institutions that was far stronger than its parallel in Western systems. Russian social ministries served as veto actors against dismantling and privatization and as obstacles to the policy influence of the World Bank. Their resistance split the government and shifted the balance against liberalization within state institutions.

As a result, a stagnant welfare structure was progressively defunded in a rapidly stratifying society. The weakness of the state allowed the wealthier to provide for themselves through private spending and social-sector professionals to craft strategies of individual and institutional survival and adaptation. The degradation of the old welfare state and the limits of access for the poor strengthened the case for liberalization. At the same time, these corrupted and semi-privatized welfare structures became institutionalized and developed their own stakeholders.

[111]   OECD, *Social Crisis in the Russian Federation.*

4

Welfare Reform in Putin's Russia

Negotiating Liberalization within the Elite

Under the Putin presidency, Russia experienced something of a breakthrough in welfare state liberalization. In spring 2000, a high-profile government commission (the Gref Team) articulated a comprehensive liberalizing program that incorporated many elements of the failed Yeltsin-era efforts. The program acknowledged the significant breakdown of the welfare state and the need to regulate the spontaneous privatization that had taken place in Russia's social sector during the 1990s. Between 2000 and 2003, the legislature passed major parts of this program, including reforms of the pension system and Labor and Housing Codes. Initiatives were taken to reorganize the education and health sectors in order to increase competition, bring private payments out of the shadows, and expand reliance on insurance mechanisms. In spring 2004 the newly reelected president made a radical move to dismantle the massive system of state-administered, untargeted social benefits and privileges to which more than a quarter of the population remained entitled. The benefits reform provoked substantial social protest and governmental backpedaling, effectively setting the limits to liberalization. Overall, however, most of the reformist program was put in place. The contrast with the preceding period of policy deadlock was stark (see table 3.5).

Several key political factors enabled this breakthrough. First and foremost was a shift in political power balances, including a change in both the programmatic orientations of the major legislative parties and in their relationships to the executive and the electorate. The December 1999 Duma election ended the left's dominance, placing a more pro-market coalition of parties in a leading position, "mak[ing] it possible, generally speaking, to transform the legislative branch from a constant opponent to an ally of the executive branch in the implementation of social reforms."[1] The coalition was led by recently formed parties of power that had shallow roots in the electorate and weak programmatic commitments. They regularly deferred to the executive on welfare as well as most other issues. The new dominance of pro-presidential parties of power and the consolidation of the system of presidential dominance under Putin (known as managed democracy) signaled a further decay in the representative function of the legislature, a weakening in potential influence of welfare constituencies and of the electoral constraint on welfare state change. The Duma ceased to play a veto role, becoming for the most part a compliant partner of the executive in the liberalizing project.

The second political factor was Putin's creation of a strong and stable governmental reform team. The new executive worked to consolidate support for restructuring within the presidential administration and the government, including the leadership of the social ministries that had earlier played a veto role. Whereas Yeltsin had been forced to remove his initial reform team, frequently replaced social ministers, and faced opposition even among top-level appointees (see chap. 3), Putin kept in place committed liberal ministers. Key figures from the future government were brought together even before the spring 2000 presidential election in an extended policy-planning process that was designed to forge a consensus on welfare reform. It succeeded in producing some agreement, although divisions within the government and ministerial or departmental interests in established practices and programs remained major sources of policy conflict.

The Russian government remained committed to welfare state restructuring despite the economic recovery that began in 1999, because social-sector reforms were bundled with a broader set of macroeconomic goals. Reformers saw the reduction of social and other subsidies as key to fiscal stabilization, completed market transformation, and modernization of the economy. Welfare reforms were part of a renewed effort to reorient the Russian economy away from its statist past to a competitive market

[1] S. N. Smirnov and N. I. Isaev, "Podgotovka Programmy Podderzhki Sotsial'nykh Reform" (Preparation of a Program for Support of Social Reforms), *Sotsial'noe Obespechenie Ekonomicheskikh Reform* (2002), 9, trans.in *Problems of Economic Transition* 46, no. 1 (2003): 9.

model, to improve the business environment, and to spur economic development. The prime movers of welfare liberalization remained in the Ministries of Finance and Economic Development and Trade. Their agenda included deregulating the economy and labor markets as well as reducing taxes, subsidies, and overall social expenditures.

These changes were understood as essential to improving the investment climate, a major goal of the new administration, as well as to paying off Russia's high foreign debt. Reformers had a clear sense that Russia's recovery remained fragile, heavily based on uncertain energy revenues, and that a sustainable macroeconomic development strategy required further integration into the international economy. They also viewed the redirection of social spending to those who had lost from the transition as important for social stability. According to reports presented at the First International Conference of the Higher School or Economics, a combined social science think tank and feeder school for the federal government, "An analysis of the situation reveals certain positive tendencies . . . . Transformations are not over . . . . [K]ey components of the proposed strategy include: . . . social policy which is oriented towards support of restructuring and lifts [the social] tensions it breeds."[2]

Direct intervention by IFIs was strictly limited during this period, and their exclusion smoothed and insulated domestic bargaining. After its conflicts with the World Bank at the end of the 1990s (see chap. 3), the Russian government declined further large adjustment loans and accepted only narrow technical assistance; lending fell to zero in 2000 and remained low.[3] Bank representatives were kept at a distance from major policy deliberations, removing a potential source of contention and allowing for a more autonomous domestic policy process. At the same time, policy models that had been promoted by the Bank and other international organizations in the Yeltsin period continued to set the reform agenda. The liberal discourse of privatization, means testing, competition, and choice in the social sector dominated almost completely.

Resistance to liberal restructuring now came not from the Duma or defenders of solidaristic values such as trade unions and the Labor Ministry but mainly from social-sector elites and state-bureaucratic stakeholders

[2] Ye. G. Yasin S. Aleksashenko, Ye. Gavrilenkov, and A. Dvorkovich, "Economic Strategy and Investment Climate," in *Investment Climate and Russia's Economic Strategy* (Moscow: Higher School of Economics, April 2000), 3.

[3] World Bank, *Assisting Russia's Transition: An Unprecedented Challenge* (Washington, D.C.: World Bank, Operations Evaluation Dept., 2002), 9.

who had vested interests in the system of social provision. Some of these interests, particularly in continued state allocations and public management of the social sector, were held over from the Soviet period. Others, particularly interests in spontaneous privatization and informal controls over access to social services (discussed in chap. 3), had been created during the 1990s. In a social-sector variant of "winner take all,"[4] state-based actors who had gained control over pools of social security funds and social-sector elites who extracted informal payments for access to health and education services emerged as the opponents of reform. These groups played a major role in bargaining over liberalization, gaining various types of concessions and compensation. Societal constituencies gained fewer concessions, although they did force the government to slow down or backtrack on broad subsidy and benefit cuts. The Russian polity under Putin, in sum, gave the main voice in moderating welfare state change to state-bureaucratic and social-sector elites, producing a reform strategy of liberalization negotiated within the elite.

The introduction identifies two major factors that facilitate liberalization of welfare states: political institutions that restrict the representation of welfare defenders and systems that privilege executive power.[5] With the emergence of managed democracy at the end of the 1990s, the Russian polity met both of those conditions. The hard-left and moderate-reformist parties, which had earlier resisted governmental pressures for restructuring, were marginalized politically or brought under the control of the state. The Russian political system now reconcentrated power in the executive. Remaining veto actors in the state and among social-sector elites had narrow departmental interests that could often be accommodated in a reformed system. The resulting shift in the political balance produced movement toward liberalization, even as economic growth resumed and fiscal surpluses accumulated. In sum, politics played a major part in shaping welfare state change (The main actors in Russia's welfare politics during this period are shown in table 4.1).

[4]   Joel S. Hellman, "Winners Take All: The Politics of Partial Reform in Postcommunist Transitions," *World Politics* 50 (January 1998): 203–34. Hellman argues (for market reforms in the transition economies generally) that the main interest groups opposing completion of reform are "winners" who arise out of early partial reforms, for example, those who gained ownership of valuable assets in the early stages of privatization.

[5]   See, especially, Duane Swank, *Global Capital, Political Institutions, and Policy Change in Developed Welfare States* (Cambridge, UK: Cambridge University Press, 2002); Evelyn Huber and John Stevens, *Development and Crisis of the Welfare State: Parties and Policies in Global Markets* (Chicago: University of Chicago Press, 2001).

TABLE 4.1
Politics of liberalization negotiated within elite in Russia, 2000–2003[a]

Pro-reform; liberalizers	Anti-reform; welfare state stakeholders
Executive	*Societal constituencies, representative institutions*
Strong	**Weak**
Unified liberalizing government	Decay in representative function of
Gref reform team	parties, legislature;
Pro-executive legislative majority	Pro-liberalization legislative majority
Reformist social-sector elites	*Statist social-sector elites*
Moderate	**Moderate**
Policy access through government	Negotiate for narrow institutional interests,
advisory roles	compensation
Global policy networks, IFIs	*State-bureaucratic stakeholders*
Moderate	**Moderate**
Limited intervention	Negotiate for compensation,
Strong residual influence	recentralization and expanded
	regulatory roles
Outcome	
Liberalization negotiated within elite	

[a] IFI, international financial institutions.

In this chapter I first set out the context of the Putin period, including economic recovery, welfare effort, and improved state delivery on basic welfare guarantees. I then focus on welfare politics within the government, the shift in legislative coalitions brought by the 1999 and 2003 Duma elections, and the politics of welfare state change across the social sector. I show the successes and limits of liberalization in Russia and look at the consequences for programmatic structures and welfare provision.

ECONOMIC RECOVERY AND IMPROVED WELFARE STATE PERFORMANCE

Putin's presidency coincided with a period of economic recovery and sustained growth. Two major factors account for this turnaround after the 1998 financial crisis. First, high prices on international markets for oil and gas, Russia's major exports, increased financial inflows. Second, the collapse of the ruble and the resulting increase in prices for imported goods produced an import-substituting boon to domestic production.

Domestic and foreign investment increased modestly, and capital flight declined. There remained serious problems, including a high debt burden that peaked in 2002–2003, lack of diversification, low investment, and vulnerability to price fluctuations in international energy markets. Government budgets were calculated on the basis of an assumed price per barrel of oil. But oil prices held and the economy grew at an average annual rate of 6.4 percent over the period 1999–2002.[6] The major misery indexes improved: unemployment fell to 8 percent in 2002 and poverty, which had peaked at one-third of the population in 1992, declined to 20 percent in 2003. Still, incomes recovered slowly, poverty was persistent, and inequality remained high (see table 2.2).

Economic recovery brought a reduction in fiscal pressures and improvement in welfare state performance. Tax evasion declined, the government's capacity to tap the resources in the system improved significantly, and tax receipts grew. For the first time since the early 1990s, the federal government fully executed its budget. Putin identified full payment of the state's social debts as a major priority and eliminated most arrears in pensions, social benefits, and public-sector wages by the end of 1999. Public-sector wage arrears declined from over R20 billion in 1998 to less than R4 billion in 2001, although they remained persistent in some regions.[7] Reforms consolidated and lowered payroll taxes, creating a unified social tax that regressed against wages and proved easier to collect. The revenues of the social funds grew, allowing steady increases in pensions and other payments. Real public social expenditures on health increased modestly during the first years of economic growth, to 71 percent of their 1990 level. Most teachers' and doctors' salaries as well as average pensions returned to levels above subsistence, and other social benefits grew modestly (see table 4.6 later in the chapter).

The Putin administration also made major efforts to recentralize political control and administration of the Russian Federation and to re-order fiscal federalist relations, with important implications for welfare. Efforts were made to redress some of the starkest effects of the early 1990s decentralization by increasing the transparency of federal-regional social transfers and poverty-targeting federal expenditures. From 2000, a larger share of the major federal redistribution fund, the Federal Fund for Financial Support of Regions, was directed to the

[6] For an overview of economic developments in this period, see World Bank, *Russia: Development Policy Review* (Report no. 26000-RU, June 9, 2003), available at www.worldbank.org.

[7] *Russian Economic Trends* 1 (2002): 89, 98.

poorest regions.[8] Nevertheless, regional differentials in poverty and health and education expenditures and outcomes increased during the economic recovery. According to a 2002 OECD study, "Other than the creation of a new transfer fund to back some federal mandates with financing, . . . reallocation has not yet been realized."[9]

Overall, although real social spending did increase during this period, the improvements were modest, sufficient to overcome the effects of the 1998 financial crisis but not to compensate for the retrenchment of the preceding years. State salaries and transfer payments stayed below their pretransition levels. Fiscal policy remained conservative, and total public expenditures on welfare remained comparatively modest. The standard measure of welfare effort—percentage of GDP expended—remained near 1990s levels, well below those in the East Central European transition states, despite the accumulation of problems in Russia. In 2002, well into the economic recovery, the Russian government spent less than 3 percent of GDP on health and, while effort did increase in education, expenditures remained less than 4 percent of GDP (see table 4.2).

Finally, although some priority areas experienced increases in expenditure, the government made it clear that increases would not be sustained, that households and the private sector would absorb more of the costs of social provision as the economy grew. Government initiatives would be directed to regulating the shadow systems of social provision, on which households were already spending considerable funds, and expanding legal social-sector markets to replace the old statist structures. In sum, even as it increased social spending, the government re-affirmed its commitment to liberalization and a constricted state role in welfare provision.

Rather than reducing pressures for liberalization, economic recovery provided more favorable conditions in several respects. As discussed in the introduction, compensation strategies are key to the acceptance of welfare state reform among groups that are in a position to block it.[10] Economic recovery allowed the Russian government to fund compensation strategies that lessened such resistance. Growing revenues made it possible, for example, to increase the salaries of civil servants

---

[8] OECD, *Russian Federation, Economic Survey, March 2000* (Paris: OECD, 2000), 29.

[9] OECD, *Economic Survey: Russian Federation 2001–2002* (Paris: OECD, 2002), 13.

[10] On the significance of compensation strategies in the East Central European context, see Janos Kornai, Stephan Haggard, and Robert Kaufman, eds., *Reforming the State: Fiscal and Welfare Reform in Post-Socialist Countries* (Cambridge, UK: Cambridge University Press, 2001) 13.

TABLE 4.2
Social expenditures of the budget system of the Russian Federation, 1996–2002 (% GDP)

Type of public expenditure	1996	1997	1998	1999	2000	2001	2002
Expenditures of the budget system as a whole							
Consolidated budget	32.5	35.9	28.1	26.1	27.7	26.8	31.5
Federal budget[a]	17.7	18.6	18.0	13.8	14.1	14.6	18.9
Regional and local budgets	17	19.9	16	13.6	14.1	14.7	15.5
Budget expenditures for social measures							
Consolidated budget	8.8	10.7	9.0	7.7	7.6	8.1	12.5[b]
Federal budget	1.3	2.4	2.3	1.8	1.9	2.3	5.7
Regional and local budgets	7.5	8.3	6.7	5.9	5.7	5.8	6.8
Health and physical culture							
Consolidated budget	2.6	3.1	2.5	2.2	2.2	2.0	2.3
Federal budget	0.2	0.4	0.3	0.2	0.2	0.3	0.3
Regional and local budgets	2.4	2.7	2.2	2.0	2.0	1.7	2.0
Education							
Consolidated budget	3.9	4.5	3.6	3.1	3.0	3.1	3.7
Federal budget	0.5	0.7	0.5	0.5	0.5	0.6	0.7
Regional and local budgets	3.4	3.8	3.1	2.6	2.5	2.5	3.0
Social policy							
Consolidated budget	1.7	2.5	2.4	1.9	1.8	2.4	5.8[b]
Federal budget	0.5	1.2	1.4	1.0	1.0	1.2	4.5
Local and regional budgets	1.2	1.3	1.0	0.9	0.8	1.2	1.3
Off-budget funds							
Pension Fund	5.8	7.5	6.4	5.6	4.7	5.7	7.3
Social Insurance Fund	1.2	1.3	1.2	0.9	1.0	1.0	1.2
Medical Insurance Fund	0.04	0.05	0.05	0.04	0.04	0.04	0.05

Sources: Sotsialnoe Polozhenie i Uroven Zhizni Naseleniia Rossii: Statisticheskii Sbornik (Moscow: Goskomstat), 1999, 20,24, 186–87; 2001, 27; 2002, 27; 2003, 28, 34, 170–71; *Rossiiskii Statisticheskii Ezhegodnik* (Moscow: Goskomstat, 2003), 281, 553; *Raschety Proizvodilis's Ispol'zovaniem Dannykh: Obzor Ekonomicheskoi Politiki Rossii za 2000 god* (Moscow: TEIS, 2001), 472. Off-budget funds based on calculations by Elena Vinogradova.

[a] Including financial aid to budgets of other levels.

[b] Most of the apparent increase in social policy expenditures in 2002 is the result of an accounting change in which part of the unified social tax was added to the revenue side of the budget and spending on social policy began to include part of the labor pension. See *Russian Economic Trends* 3(2002): 86; 4 (2002): 68.

as their social privileges were cut and to finance new administrative functions for social ministries even as state subsidies to client institutions and populations were reduced. Liberalization requires investments in new institutions, and such investments became more feasible with economic growth. Rising revenues also allowed Putin's government to deliver more consistently on its existing social security obligations, reestablishing the state's credibility as provider of social welfare and gaining political support from groups dependent on state transfer payments.[11] More consistent delivery helped to draw workers and wages back into the social security system so that their contributions could be transferred to new, insurance-based mechanisms.[12] Also, the gradually rising incomes that came with economic recovery made it feasible for the population to absorb subsidy cuts, to take on more of the costs of social provision without increasing poverty and distress. This was key to the calculations of liberal reformers, who projected a growing capacity for private expenditures on housing, health, and education (although the slow recovery of incomes and continuing high levels of poverty disappointed their expectations.)[13] In sum, liberalization was not driven by worsening economic and fiscal pressures. Rather, it was enabled by the weakening of political opposition and facilitated by the growth of economic resources.

THE GREF PROGRAM FOR WELFARE STATE REFORM

The new administration's welfare reform agenda was laid out in a set of major policy planning documents generated by Putin's designated think tank, German Gref's Center for Strategic Planning, and approved by the government in spring 2000.[14] The center produced a comprehensive plan to move Russia toward a social model in which markets and private actors would play the major role and the state a limited one. According to the government program based on the Gref Plan:

> Policy . . . supposes a transition to a model . . . which redistributes social
> expenditures to the most vulnerable groups and at the same time reduces
> social transfers to secure families. Under this approach citizens who have

[11]   In surveys made during 1999–2000, 51 percent of respondents rated Putin as the candidate with competence in the issue area of social security; 39 percent of respondents overall and 59 percent of those in their sixties and seventies ranked pension increases as one of his best decisions; see Timothy J. Colton and Michael McFaul, *Popular Choice and Managed Democracy: The Russian Elections of 1999 and 2000* (Washington, D.C.: Brookings Institution, 2003), 190–97.

[12]   This was especially critical in the area of pension reform, in which invested accounts had come to be seen as a source of domestic investment and a means of deepening capital markets.

[13]   On the slow recovery of average incomes, which remained at less than half of pre-reform (1990) levels in 2000, see E. H. Sobolev and S. V. Lomonosova, *Oplata Truda v Rossiiskoi Ekonomike: Dinamika, Faktory, Napravlenie, Preobrazovanii* (Moscow, 2003).

[14]   German Gref would become Putin's minister for Economic Development and Trade. The center's documents were to set the intended directions of social and economic development over the following decade.

independent sources for the financing of social needs, themselves . . . should
pay practically all of the costs for housing and utilities, and part of the expenditures for medical services, education, pension insurance . . . . A significant
part of social services for this category of citizens should be provided mainly
on a competitive basis through non-state enterprises. At the same time, the
state should not decrease efforts to provide social help and a restricted list of
free services in health and education for that part of the population which,
without the state's help, would not have access to basic social goods.[15]

The means-tested poor, those with incomes below subsistence, would
receive income transfers and a separate set of basic social services, much
as in the U.S. welfare system that provides the prototype for the liberal
model. The Russian government would once again attempt to phase
out most social subsidies and privileges and to expand market and public-private cofinancing mechanisms. It would seek to "develop various
forms of non-state commercial and non-commercial provision of social
services" that promised to provide competition and choice.[16] The plan
was based on principles of subsidiary, which hold that the state should
not do what individuals and markets can do independently.

Although it drew on them programmatically, the Gref Plan differed
from the Yeltsin administration's welfare reform efforts in important
respects. It incorporated an appreciation for the complexities of institutional welfare state reforms and the embeddedness social security
markets in broader market structures. It mapped in some detail a
reorientation of the state's role from directly providing social welfare
to constructing, overseeing, and in some cases subsidizing the institutional mechanisms for private and other non-state provision, including mortgage and health insurance markets and educational voucher
schemes. It promised to formalize payments for social services and
to regulate access. In the words of a governmental advisor who was
involved in social-sector reform planning during both the Yeltsin and
Putin administrations: "The Gref program involved . . . for the first
time in government really deep analysis. . . . In many cases in the 1990s

[15]   "Programma Pravitelstva Rossii: Osnovnyi Napravleniia Sotsial'no-Ekonomicheskoi
Politiki Pravitel'stva Rossiiskoi Federatsii na Dolgosrochnuiu Perspectivy," [hereafter Gref
Program] available at www.akm.ru/rus/gosinfo/progr_gov/1_1.stm. The program is
revised from a long draft generated by the Gref team, "Proekt Strategiia Razvitiia Rossiiskoe
Federatsii do 2010 g.," (Moscow: Tsentr Strategicheskikh Razrabotok, 2000) [hereafter
Proekt Strategiia], available at www.kommersant.ru/documents/Strat1.htm.
[16]   Proekt Strategiia.

nobody could implement plans because they were technically impossible; with the Gref Program there was much deeper analysis of substantive possibilities."[17]

The major provisions of the Gref Program are laid out in table 4.3. It portended changes in programmatic structures across all areas of the welfare state. Most financing responsibilities in housing, health, and pensions would be transferred to individuals, markets, and insurance mechanisms. State stipends for higher education would be largely limited to the poor and the academically talented, and at lower levels cofinancing would be required for educational services above a state minimum. Access to health services would be segmented by income group. Part of pension provision would be moved from solidaristic principles to individual investment accounts. Labor markets would be deregulated, and restrictive social protections would be eliminated. Large new costs, risks, choices, possibilities, and responsibilities would be transferred to society.

The Gref team consulted broadly with the expert community in its policy formulation process, attempting to systematize the accumulated knowledge of the reform years. According to one informant, "Four people created the Gref program, but they worked for several months and discussed it with many people. They sent letters to many research institutes asking for materials—executive summaries—of what researchers proposed for the national economy and for social programs. Most institutes got these letters."[18] The final plan was, however, written by a narrow group from or closely connected to the executive who continued to control the policy agenda in the social sphere. This was a more inclusive and consultative, but still narrowly dominated, technocratic policy process, one divorced from society.

Creating a Governmental Reform Team

The drafting of the Gref Program was intended to forge a consensus around reform and to ensure coordination between ministries and the presidential administration.[19] In May 2000, German Gref was made head of newly created Ministry for Economic Development and Trade and

---

[17]   Government advisor, interview with author, Moscow, June 6, 2001.

[18]   Social policy expert, Municipal Economic and Social Reform of TACIS (MERIT), interview with author, Moscow, June 7, 2000.

[19]   Thomas F. Remington, "Putin and the Duma," *Post-Soviet Affairs* 17, no. 4 (2001): 290.

TABLE 4.3
The Gref Program for social-sector reform

Sector	State responsibilities	Responsibilities of households above poverty level
Social assistance	Re-targets assistance to poor Provides means-tested poverty relief and child benefits	Social transfers and privileges cut No eligibility for income assistance
Housing	Creates institutions for housing, and utility markets Provides means-tested housing assistance	Pay most costs of housing and utilities Join self-managing condominiums Buy, sell, and rent housing in market
Education	Provides free, universal basic primary and secondary education Finances on per capita ("money follows the student") basis Provides means-tested assistance, competitive vouchers for higher education Sets national standards, single state exam Sets national wage scale for educators	Co-pays for services above basic standard, cofinancing Partial or full tuition payment for post-secondary, preschool Increasing level of family contribution
Health care	Provides limited list of free services to poor Establishes and regulates mandatory medical insurance Legalizes private medical insurance Regulates private medical practices	Covered by mandatory medical insurance Co-pays for some services Legal private alternatives in medical care and insurance
Pensions	Guarantees basic (subsistence) pension Regulates financial services for pension investment No defined benefit	Individual, differentiated main tier Individual invested accounts Defined contribution system
Labor	Sets minimum wage Provides unemployment benefit Creates flexible labor regime Enforces labor contracts	Rights to union membership collective bargaining, strike Rights to court appeals of contract violations

Source: "Programma Pravitelstva Rossii: Osnovnyi Napravleniia Sotsial'no-ekonomicheskoi Politiki Pravitel'stva Rossiiskoi Federatsii na Dolgosrochnuiu Perspectivy," available at www.akm.ru/rus/gosinfo/progr_gov/1_1.stm.

Mikhail Dmitriev was appointed his first deputy. Yevgennii Gontmakher, chief of the Social Development Department of the Government Apparatus, and Valentina Matvienko, placed in overall charge of social policy in the government, both had long-standing credentials as liberal social reformers. The new minister of Labor and Social Development, Alexander Pochinok, was a fiscal conservative with a background in taxation and finance.[20] Reformist Health and Education ministers, Yuri Shevchenko and Vladimir Filippov, were appointed in 1999 and remained in place. The top elite of the government and presidential administration was unified around the welfare state reform program. The Ministry of Economic Development and Trade was the governmental powerhouse, the main force pushing social-sector reform, "in charge of everything." The Labor Ministry, the usual defender of solidaristic values, was universally viewed as weak, as exercising little influence.[21]

State-bureaucratic interests served as a main source of resistance to these reforms. Ministries and other organizations that oversee programs based on central administration and public financing resist spending cuts and privatization that reduce their authority and resources. Social ministries and social fund administrators stood as major obstacles to change during the Yeltsin period (see chap. 3). Despite Putin's efforts at consensus-building, such resistance continued, leading one well-placed observer to argue that the consensus was "superficial—all still pursue departmental interests. The major obstacle to reform is conflict within the government. Pension reform, education reform, are completely feasible in the sense of technical constraints. In most cases, practically the executive branch can get the Duma to do as it wants. The question is of political feasibility—a lack of homogeneity of views and interests within the government."[22]

But resistance proved significantly weaker than earlier. The president-Duma alliance was one key; according to Thomas Remington, referring to oppositional officials in social welfare, "For the most part Putin's team succeeded in preventing them from blocking his policy initiatives by forming tacit alliances with sympathetic committees in the Duma . . . and due to careful preparatory work in minimizing opposition from within the state bureaucracy."[23] Of even greater importance, in almost every area the reforms included the creation of new, recentralizing and regulatory

[20] Pochinok was characterized by the president of the U.S. Chamber of Commerce as a man who "infused his leadership ... with deep understanding of the financial factor in the workings of government"; "Remarks by Labor and Social Development Minister Alexander Pochinok at a Breakfast of the American Chamber of Commerce in Russia," *Federal News Service, Kremlin Package*, 23 Jan. 2002, available at www.securities.com.

[21] Similar views of the two ministries were expressed by multiple interviewees in the Russian government and social policy expert community in 2000–2002.

[22] Government advisor, interview with author, Moscow, June 6, 2001. The interviewee did argue that the president could push through measures if he fully invested his authority in them.

[23] Thomas F. Remington, "Putin, the Duma, and Political Parties," in *Putin's Russia: Past Imperfect, Future Uncertain*, edited by Dale R. Herspring (New York: Rowman and Littlefield, 2003), 54–55.; Remington, "Putin and the Duma."

roles that compensated ministries and other state bodies, preserving and even expanding their functions within the reformed system.

Business, Labor, and Welfare Reform

During this period, business organizations began to play a more visible and institutionalized role in policy making, and the Putin administration used corporatist mechanisms of representation to better integrate them into the policy process. The Russian Union of Industrialists and Entrepreneurs (RUIE), the main business lobbying association, revived and broadened its membership to include many of Russia's most prominent businessmen (oligarchs), including leaders in banking, industry, and the energy sector.[24] It initiated a regularized, formal process of participation in governmental and legislative politics, supporting market-friendly laws. No longer resistant to market reform, as in the early and mid-90s, RUIE became a powerful force in support of liberalizing measures. It created a set of departments to prepare legislative initiatives for the president and Duma, taking positions on the Labor Code, pension, and tax reforms.[25] Gref cultivated ties with the RUIE, and it became an important source of influence and advice. Business and financial interests that had become established in the social sector during earlier stages of reform, including investment companies and medical insurers, pressed for further reforms that would expand their sphere of operations. In sum, business and financial interests that had earlier been oriented either toward getting subsidies from the state or toward escaping taxation now became integrated into a pro-market coalition that cooperated with the executive to influence policy outcomes.

The trade unions presented a weak and fading defense of solidaristic values. They accepted most of the Gref Plan, including a regressive social security tax reform which, their spokesperson offered, "is against solidaristic principles and . . . doesn't appeal to the majority."[26] The unions made wage increases their main issue but during negotiations over labor code reform, at their point of greatest leverage, settled for limited and vague promises on national wage policy. Weak from the outset, without a political home, and having lost their one powerful ally

[24]   For a list of the twenty-seven new members who joined the bureau of the RUIE, including United Energy Systems Chair Chubais, Interros Head Potanin, and Yukos Chair Khordorkovskii, see *Russian Political Weekly*, 5 Mar. 2001, available at www.rferl.org.

[25]   *Russian Political Weekly*, 5 Mar. 2001; *Kommersant*, 27 Aug. 2001; Andrew Barnes, "Russia's New Business Groups and State Power," *Post-Soviet Affairs* 19, no. 2 (2003): 154–86.

[26]   Secretary, Federation of Independent Trade Unions of Russia, interview with author, Moscow, June 21, 2002. The FNPR did oppose housing reform.

(i.e., the RUIE Red Directors; see chap. 3), the FNPR leadership acquiesced in welfare state liberalization in exchange for concessions that
benefited the narrow institutional interests of the FNPR at the expense
of its membership. Like other social-sector elites in a system with very
weak accountability to their rank and file, the unions bargained mainly
for themselves. By the end of the period, they had become semi-official
organizations, bound to the party-of-power and the Putin presidency.

Women's organizations and other NGOs proliferated during the 1990s,
but sources agree that they had virtually no influence on policy at the
federal level. Under Putin, the main access to the federal government
for NGOs was through a state-managed, quasi-corporatist process of institutionalized consultation with selected organizations. The government
bureaucracy remained largely impervious to the influence of women's
organizations, which were themselves divided between supporters and
critics of traditional, statist welfare protections such as those that had
been defended by Women of Russia (WR).[27]

WELFARE POLITICS AFTER THE 1999 ELECTION

The Decline of Pro-Welfare Parties and the Rise of Parties of Power

The central thesis of this book holds that politics shapes welfare state
change. The December 1999 legislative elections led to a major shift in
the political constellation that dominated the Duma. This was partly a
shift in programmatic orientations that ended the left's dominance. But
there was also a deeper change in the nature of the major legislative parties. The Duma came to be dominated by a coalition of new parties of
power—parties created in the months before the election by central and
regional political executives—and by non-party factions. This new coalition was first and foremost pro-presidential, deferring to the executive for
programmatic and legislative initiative. It played little role in the development of policy direction and a very limited one in the articulation of societal interests. The influence of the legislative parties became constricted
in comparison with their influence in past Dumas. These changes signified decay in the representative function of political parties, the rise of

---

[27] Janet Elise Johnson, "Violence against Women in Russia," in *Ruling Russia: Law,
Crime, and Justice in a Changing Society*, edited by William Alex Pridemore, (Lanham, Md.:
Rowman and Littlefield, 2005), 147–66.

executive dominance over the legislature, and a commensurate decline
in electoral feedback on policy change.

The 1999 election brought a major change in the balance of parties'
programmatic orientations. Of the three new parties/coalitions that rose
to prominence during the election, Unity, Fatherland-All Russia (FAR), and
the Union of Right Forces (URF), the first two were vaguely centrist and
the third rightist. Established left-leaning parties, in particular the Agrarians (APR) and one branch of WR, moderated their programs and shifted
toward the center in the preelection period. Overall, there was a significant
shift in the parties' programmatic orientations toward welfare. According to
Mikhail Dmitriev, a past (and future) liberal member of the government,

> In 1995 the majority of leading political parties and blocs supported an
> unrealistic Soviet approach to social policy . . . . at the present time the
> situation has shifted, and almost all parties and blocs (with the exception
> of the Communists) support [market models] : means-tested social assis-
> tance, strengthening insurance principles . . . developing the nonstate sec-
> tor in health and education.[28]

(For the orientations of the parties, refer to table 3.4.)

Unity and FAR, the two major parties of power in the new Duma,
had both been created as overt representatives of elite interests and as
electoral vehicles for their leaders. According to a recent study of these
parties, their "social constituencies were fuzzily demarcated, (voters')
partisanship shallow, and issue opinions relatively inconsequential."[29]
Unity, close to then-Acting President Putin and the Kremlin, was cobbled
together literally in the weeks before the election by central and regional
political elites, advanced a minimalist preelection program, and held
its first congress well after the election. It addressed only a few welfare
issues, with a liberal bent, endorsing increased housing costs and means
testing.[30] The presidential administration promoted Unity through a
heavy-handed manipulation of the media and an orchestrated campaign
to discredit its more welfare-oriented rival, FAR.

[28] Mikhail Dmitriev, "Evoliutsiia Ekonomicheskikh Programm Vedyshchikh Politicheskikh Partii i Blokov Rossii," *Voprosy Ekonomiki* 1 (January 2000): 27–38. This includes
Dmitriev's analysis of the positions of major parties on social policy and other issue areas,
comparing 1995 and 1999.
[29] Colton and McFaul, *Popular Choice and Managed Democracy*, 125.
[30] "Tezisy k Izbiratel'noi Programme Bloka "Medved"" (1999), available at www.
panorama.ru:8101/works/vybory/party/p-med.html.

FAR combined, in late summer 1999, Moscow Mayor Luzhkov's Fatherland movement and the All-Russia movement that represented regional interests. Fatherland, founded in 1998, originally presented a fairly substantive program, endorsing socially oriented market reforms and giving primacy to the social sector, advocating a more activist state role in social policy and a return to free education and health care. It did accept some market elements for supplementary social provision, including voluntary private pension accounts and private medical clinics. But the party's program was in many respects vague, seeming to skirt the issues that had come to define the struggle over welfare reform—the ending of social privileges and housing subsidies, the expansion of private medical insurance, and mandatory invested pensions.[31]

FAR ran in opposition to Unity and was broadly perceived as center-left. A number of parties and organizations that had in the past resisted welfare state liberalization, including the APR, FNPR and its associated Party of Labor led by Andrei Isaev, and Yakaterina Fedulova's WR, joined or endorsed the bloc.[32] The largest group of converts to FAR in the 1999 election had voted for left parties in 1995, and survey evidence indicates that its supporters broadly opposed liberalizing reforms. According to an analyst of political attitudes publishing in *Obshchaia Gazeta* in late 2000, "Fatherland's supporters . . . are harshly critical of the government's proposed tough liberal reforms in the social sphere (the "Gref program"), and they reject . . . a savings-based pension system, having households . . . pay 100 percent of the cost of utilities and municipal services, requiring payment for medical care and education."[33] FAR became, in sum, the (admittedly weak) repository of moderate political opposition to welfare state liberalization, a position that it would abandon within a year of the election to merge with Unity in the pro-presidential coalition.

The parties that reelected significant deputy groups—the CPRF, Yabloko, Liberal Democratic Party (the LDP)—had more clearly defined constituencies and, except the LDP, programmatic orientations as well as clear

---

[31]   "Otechestvo- Vsia Rossiia, Predvybornaia Programma" (1999), available at www. panorama.ru:8101/works/vybory/praty/p-ovr.html. Fatherland's program, for example, called for the "minimum necessary social privileges."

[32]   Colton and McFaul, *Popular Choice and Managed Democracy*, 83–85. However, WR quit the coalition before the election and ran independently, gaining 2 percent of the vote. The APR split in 1999, with the majority joining Fatherland and a rump one-third maintaining their alliance with the CPRF.

[33]   Leonty Byzov, "An Opening Left of Center—the Main Contender for This Vacancy Is Fatherland," *Obshchaia Gazeta*, no. 51, 21–27 Dec. 2000, 7, trans. in *Current Digest of the Soviet Press* [hereafter *CDSP*] 52 (January 17, 2001): 12. Twenty-nine percent of OVR converts had voted socialist in 1995; Colton and McFaul, *Popular Choice and Managed Democracy*, 99.

positions on welfare state reform. But they would play a marginal role in Duma politics, especially after spring 2001. The CPRF had softened its opposition to Russia's overall market transition, but maintained its programmatic commitment to restorationism in welfare policy. The party's 1999 electoral program repeated the call for full employment, subsidized housing, and free medical care and education from preschool through university. The CPRF maintained steady grassroots support in the election, but remained the only significant restorationist party in the 1999 Duma.[34] Yabloko again addressed the defining issues of the welfare state debate squarely and from a moderate-reformist position, giving qualified support to the liberal reform program.[35] On the market side, it favored means testing of benefits, pension reform, supplemental paid health services, and voluntary health insurance; on the state side, Yabloko demanded free education, a minimal level of universal free health care, and affordable housing. It advocated incentives to bring the informal economy out of the shadows and continued to stress that social policy was a motor of economic development. The party maintained a modest position in the 1999 Duma (see table 3.4), becoming the sole consistent voice for a reformist welfare policy.

One additional new party, the Union of Right Forces (URF), emerged in 1999 as the successor to Russia's Choice/Russia's Democratic Choice (RC/RDC), articulating a coherent liberal program. The URF's 1999 election manifesto called for personal responsibility, and declared, "excess tutelage . . . excess social guarantees are a source of unfreedom, a reason for passivity and stagnation, an obstacle to the full use of abilities . . . . the state should take responsibility only for those who cannot care for themselves."[36] It supported means-tested poverty assistance, increased housing payments, and the elimination of most social privileges. URF went further than any other party in supporting an extensive role for markets in the social sector. Ideologically and programmatically, its approach to welfare reform was close to that of the Putin administration. With a modest electoral showing, it became an independent liberal voice in the Duma, often supporting presidential initiatives on welfare reform.

The Unity and FAR parties formed the core of the Duma majority that legislated welfare state liberalization. The dominance of these new,

[34] "Programma Kommunisticheskoi Partii Rossiiskoi Federatsii" (1999), available at www.panorama.ru:8101/works/vybory/party/p-kprf.html. However, the communists reportedly did accept the right of wealthier citizens to pay for health and educational services; see Dmitriev, "Evoliutsiia Ekonomicheskikh Programm."

[35] "Yabloko, Predvybornaia Programma: Yabloko v Sovremennio Politike" (1999), available at www.panorama.ru:8108/works/vybory/party/p-yab.html.

[36] "Soiuz Pravykh Sil, Pravyi Manifest" (1999), available at www.panorama.ru:8101/works/vybory/party/p-sps.html.

elite-constructed parties of power in the third round of Russia's post-transition legislative elections signified the failure of parties rooted in society to consolidate and grow, the broad failure of Russian society to generate political organizations that could articulate and represent its interests. In the words of Colton and McFaul, "the flimsiness of most of the parties and of other associations autonomous of the state eased the way for state-based office seekers; . . . [the] parliamentary . . . election 'reflected the weakness and embryonic character of structures of civil society' in Russia."[37] These parties had few constraining commitments and weak accountability to societal-level organizations or mass groups. The electoral feedback mechanisms that constrain welfare state change in democratic systems, and that had played some role in Russia during the 1990s, were greatly weakened.

Women's Interests in Legislative Politics

The decay in representation of societal welfare constituencies is well illustrated by recent research on women Duma deputies' support and advocacy of women's interests.[38] In 2004, women from the first three Dumas were interviewed about their commitments to women's interests and their efforts to cooperate across party lines in order to promote those interests. Deputies from the first and second Dumas, mainly from WR and CPRF, shared the view that women had specific interests, relating to employment discrimination and low pay as well as a range of other social problems. They reported cooperation with other women deputies across party lines to advance policy goals related to women's interests. In the 1993 Duma, WR played a key role in coordinating support on women's issues among women deputies across parties.[39] Cooperation on a more limited basis to support particular decisions concerning women continued in the 1995 Duma. Evidence from the vote analysis confirms the interview results, showing that in the 1995 Duma women banded together to vote on a set of women's issues.[40]

Women deputies from United Russia, by contrast, responded with near-uniformity that there were no problems specific to women, that social problems were common to society as a whole, and they reported little or no cooperation across party lines in the 1999 Duma to address

---

[37]   Colton and McFaul, *Popular Choice and Managed Democracy*, 205.

[38]   These interviews, with twenty-six women deputies who served in all three Dumas, were conducted for the author by the All-Union Center for the study of Public Opinion (VTsIOM) and an independent interviewer in February–April 2004 in Moscow.

[39]   Women of Russia deputy in 1993 Duma (interview # 25), Moscow, March 26, 2004.

[40]   The vote analysis is reported in Ilia Shevchenko, "Who Cares about Women's Problems: Female Legislators in the 1995 and 1999 Russian Duma," *Europe-Asia Studies* 54, no. 8 (2002): 1201–22.

these issues. The interview results are confirmed by vote analysis, which shows that women deputies in the 1999 Duma did not vote together on either social policy issues or on a narrower range of women's issues. The author of the voting study concludes, "Women [did] not make a difference in the 1999 Duma . . . in contrast to the previous Duma, in the current (1999) legislature constituents' political preferences are disregarded by legislators when they vote on women's issue bills."[41]

In sum, in contrast to their predecessors from other parties, women deputies from Unity/United Russia showed little or no commitment to representing women constituents. The program of welfare state liberalization incorporated major changes that were detrimental to women, including a revision of the Labor Code that reduced maternity and other protections in employment and a pension reform that is projected to seriously disadvantage women in the longer term. These effects got little mention in the Duma despite the efforts of some women's groups to draw attention to them. The decline in representation of women's interests is a particular case of the general decay in representation of societal interests within the Russian legislature and broader political system, the further detachment of legislators from societal interests and constituencies.

Legislative-Executive Coordination and Cooperation

By early 2001, Unity led a stable majority coalition that included FAR and two pro-presidential nonparty factions, People's Deputy and Russian Regions.[42] The pro-presidential Alliance of Four, with the URF, eventually gave the president victories on every major welfare liberalization measure that went to the floor (see table 4.4, later in the chapter). The Communists initially gained significant leadership positions, including the chairmanship of the Labor and Social Policy Committee, but the left was progressively weakened by parliamentary maneuvers and internal divisions, and it was marginalized legislatively. Unity coordinated between the Duma and the presidential administration.[43] The use of the veto was greatly reduced, and, in contrast to Yeltsin, Putin relied

[41] Ibid., 1215–16.

[42] Thomas Remington argues that the factions were less disciplined and more constrained by constituency pressures than the parties, but, for the key social welfare legislation, both voted in majorities for liberalization; see Remington, "Putin, the Duma, and Political Parties."

[43] Regina Smyth, "Building State Capacity from the Inside Out: Parties of Power and the Success of the President's Reform Agenda in Russia" *Politics and Society* 30, no. 4 (December 2002): 555–78; Thomas Remington, *Russia Political Weekly*, 10 Dec. 2001.

very little on decrees to pass reforms.[44] A normalized legislative process developed, with Putin setting much of the agenda and his government presenting comprehensive legislative packages to the Duma. The system was brought to a better-institutionalized form of presidential dominance than that of the early 1990s, and welfare reforms were given a legislative and institutional depth that could not be accomplished by decree. But reforms were still resisted, and each involved a complex and often prolonged process of negotiation with state, legislative, and other groups.

NEGOTIATING THE BREAKTHROUGH TO LIBERALIZATION

The new Duma placed social welfare reform high on its agenda. Its first policy overview, in winter 2000, included commitments to rewrite the Labor Code and restructure the pension system, to move subsidy and benefits systems toward targeting, and to reform health care, education, and housing.[45] I next present several case studies that look at the politics of these reforms: the initial policy proposals; how they were negotiated among the government, the Duma, social-sector elite and statist stakeholders, and societal constituencies; and their outcomes. The focus is on patterns of influence, support, resistance, and compensation.

Labor Code Reform

The essence of Labor Code reform was to make the labor relationship more flexible and market-friendly through changes in rules about employment, dismissal, and other dimensions of the labor relationship. Soviet labor law included many restrictions on managers, protections for workers, and provisions for unions' involvement in dismissal and other decisions. The code virtually guaranteed job security, making it very difficult for employers to dismiss workers even for cause. Written in 1971, it had been amended but not fundamentally revised because of political resistance in the 1990s Dumas. The International Labour Organisation (ILO) judged it one of the most restrictive codes in Eastern or Western Europe, and it was seen as a major constraint on economic development,

---

[44]   Remington, "Putin and the Duma."
[45]   *Informatsionno-analiticheskii biulleten'* [hereafter *Inform*], Pravovoe upravlenie Apparata Gosudarstvenio Dumy, (Legal Administration of the Apparatus of the State Duma) no. 1, January 18–February 22, 2000, available at www.duma.gov.ru.

blocking the establishment of a clear set of rules that could work in a market economy and contributing to informality and illegality.[46]

Prime Minister Mikhail Kasyanov's government proposed a very liberal revised draft code, providing for virtually unrestricted rights to use fixed-term and temporary contracts that would end job security for most workers. It included a loosening of rules on dismissals; restrictions on the role of trade unions; and cuts in protections for single mothers, maternity, and other benefits.[47] The draft was compiled by the Labor Ministry and the government's labor team. Deputy Prime Minister Matvienko and Labor Minister Pochinok firmly backed this strong version, which was placed before the new Duma in early 2000.

The government's draft generated opposition from the FNPR and independent trade unions, the left parties, and others in the Duma. The unions initially pressed for limitations on the use of short-term contracts, restrictions on dismissals, and maintenance of social benefits. They also demanded measures that would compensate rank-and-file workers for the loss of job security, most significantly an increase of the minimum wage to at least one-half the subsistence level (it stood at less than 20 percent of subsistence, a major contributor to poverty.)[48] Another set of issues placed on the bargaining table had more to do with unions' corporate interests: their right of consent over dismissals and rules for union representation of workers in collective bargaining. This last issue divided the interests of the major holdover union FNPR and the newer, much smaller independents. Existing practice allowed all unions present in an enterprise to bargain for their members. The FNPR had long pressed for rules restricting bargaining rights to unions representing a majority of the plant's workers, which would effectively close out most independents.[49]

---

[46] For the ILO view, see Sandrine Cazes and Alena Nesporova, "Employment Protection Legislation and Its Effects on Labour Market Performance" (paper presented at the High-Level Tripartite Conference on Social Dialogue, Malta, Valetta, 28 February–1 March, 2003), 18–19. See also Tatyana Maleva, "The New Labor Code: Victory or Defeat?," Moscow Carnegie Center, *Briefing* 12 (December 2001), available at pubs.carnegie.ru/english/briefings/2001/issue01–12.asp.

[47] On the government draft, see V. Kosmarski, "Draft Labor Code of the Russian Federation," Russian-European Centre for Economic Policy (Policy paper series, April 2001), available at www.recep.org/pp/kosmarskie.pdf; "Skol'ko Stoit Trudovoi Kodeks?" Moscow Carnegie Center, no. 3 (2001), available at http://pubs.carnegie.ru/workpapers/2001/wp0301.pdf.

[48] For the unions' demands, mainly for larger compensatory wage increases, see the interview with Shmakov in "Peace. Labor, May," *Rossiiskaia Gazeta*, 28 Apr. 2001, trans. in *Foreign Broadcast Information Service* [hereafter *FBIS*].

[49] Linda J. Cook, *Labor and Liberalization: Trade Unions in the New Russia* (New York: Twentieth Century Fund, 1997).

In order to resolve the differences a special ad hoc conciliation commission was established, with representatives of all legislative parties, labor unions, management (RUIE), and government. The commission was formed just as Unity consolidated its hold over a voting majority in the Duma, and it was chaired by a leading Unity deputy, Lyubov Sliska. The left parties worked with trade union deputies to produce an alternative draft code, one more pro-labor, reflecting the capacity of the left still to articulate an authoritative alternative and play a bargaining role.[50] Employers generally lined up with the government, pressing especially for contract flexibility and unimpeded rights of dismissal. In the end, the commission crafted a compromise that was supported by government, industrialists, and the FNPR and opposed only by the left parties and independent unions.[51] (The Duma vote on the third reading is included in table 4.4.)

The outcome was on balance a victory for the government, although it did make concessions. The new code allowed broad but not unrestricted use of temporary contracts, expanded managers' rights to transfer and dismiss workers, and reduced the powers of trade unions in dismissals. Maternity and other benefits were pared back but retained. The major compensation for the rank and file, a minimum wage at one-half subsistence, was put off into the indefinite future. The government indicated that the minimum wage would not reach subsistence for years, and increased it gradually to about 22 percent of the subsistence level in 2002.

The FNPR took its major compensation in the form of rules requiring majoritarian representation in labor bargaining—directors could conclude collective agreements only with unions that incorporated at least half of an enterprise's employees.[52] The FNPR, in other words, used its bargaining position first and foremost to protect its corporate interests in dominating the representation of workers. It provided a weaker defense of rank-and-file interests, approving a set of rules for labor

---

[50]   This trade union draft was produced by Duma deputies led by T. Saikin, CPRF head of the Labor and Social Policy Committee, and A. Isaev, OVR, deputy chair of the committee and a leader of FNPR. Several competing drafts were produced, but the compromise was mainly between the government and trade union versions. See Kosmarksi, "Draft Labor Code."

[51]   The Duma passed the Labor Code in the first reading on July 5, 2000, with CPRF, APR, and LDP voting against.

[52]   For views on the code, including, Pochinok and Isaev on government concessions, see *Rossiskaia Gazeta*, 5 July 2001, trans. in *FBIS*; for the outcome see *Rossiskaia Gazeta*, 18 Aug. 2001, 2, trans. in *FBIS*.

TABLE 4.4
Key Duma votes on welfare state liberalization, 2000–2003[a]

	Unity	OVR	RR	PD	URF	Yab	CPRF	AGDP	LDPR	Others	Total	Source
Labor Code Reform (21.12.2001, 3rd reading)												1
For	80	50	36	50	34	16	3	—	12	8	289	
Against	—	—	5	3	—	—	79	42	—	2	131	
On State Pension Security (30.11.2001, 3rd reading)												2
For	81	47	30	57	16	—	1	3	12	9	256	
Against	—	—	3	1	7	2	52	16	—	—	81	
Law on Calculating Incomes and Determining Eligibility for State Social Help (Means Testing) (No. 121512-3, 07.03.2003, 3rd reading)												3
For	77	51	42	51	31	13	1	—	13	13	292	
Against	—	—	4	—	—	—	71	34	—	2	111	
Housing Reform Law (No. 210133-3, 09.04.2003, 2nd reading)												4
For	79	53	31	49	7	—	—	—	12	5	236	
Against	—	—	12	2	25	15	79	41	—	7	181	

Sources: All of the votes are taken from *Informatsionno-Analiticheskii Biulleten'* (*IAB*), available at http://wbase.duma.gov.ru:8080/law. Abstentions were negligible in all but the last vote. Full titles and sources:
1. *IAB*, no. 10, (osenniaia sessiia), 2001.
2. *IAB*, no. 10 (osenniaia sessiia), 2001.
3. *IAB*, no. 3, 13 Feb–12 March, 2003.
4. *IAB*, no. 4, 13 March–16 April, 2003.

[a] AGDP, Agro-industrial Deputy Group; CPRF, Communist Party of the Russian Federation; LDPR, Liberal-Democratic Party of Russia; OVR, Fatherland–All Russia; PD, People's Deputy; RR, Russian Regions; URF, Union of Right Forces; Yab, Yabloko.

relations that, although still more restrictive than some in the OECD, substantially increased the flexibility of the labor relationship.

Approval by both the Duma and major trade unions of a Labor Code reform that formally weakened the employment rights and protections of Russian workers, with little compensation, speaks to the weakness of popular pressure and representative functions to constrain welfare state change. It indicates the unions' low capacity for, or interest in, shaping reforms to gain benefits for members. The reform also had deeper implications for Russian unions and union-government relations. The FNPR, from the beginning dependent on the executive and nonmilitant, had none-the-less been moderate-left in its political orientation and affiliations (see chap. 3). Now the FNPR melded into the liberalizing state, endorsing United Russia and moving close to the Putin administration, while the government tended to "treat the FNPR as the official and single representative of Russia's working population."[53] At the same time, the FNPR had used the Labor Code negotiations to consolidate its position as the corporate representative of labor. The independent unions were big losers in the labor code negotiations. According to Irene Stevenson, an international labor representative who worked closely with the independents, "the compromise draft . . . undercut all unions formed in the past ten years . . . . the fundamental issue was of representation, [this was] the most important part of the labor code."[54] Weak in most sectors and now faced with a set of bargaining rules that were inimical to their survival, most independents would likely wither, further weakening Russia's embryonic civil society and undermining the potential for inter-union competition that could provide incentives for greater union assertiveness. Russia was left with a liberalized labor code and one major, weak, pro-government union federation.

Pension Reform

The Putin administration also revived pension reform, which had become a source of contention within the Yeltsin government and had been shelved with the approach of the 1998 financial crisis (see chap. 3). The existing state-run PAYG system relied mainly on an intergenerational exchange; the wages of current workers were taxed to pay current

[53] Stephen Crowley, "Comprehending the Weakness of Russia's Unions," *Demokratizatsiya* 10, no. 2 (2002): 239.

[54] Field representative, American Center for International Labor Solidarity, interview with author, Moscow, June 6, 2001.

pensioners. Reformers proposed partial privatization, the introduction of market-based, or funded (accumulative), schemes in which employees would save for their own retirement, partly through the investment of pension contributions, with payouts depending on accumulation in personal accounts. Individual funded pension schemes are broadly seen, and have been heavily promoted by IFIs, as a way to ease the growing demographic pressures on PAYG systems caused by aging populations.[55] They also have several important political and economic effects and implications.

The transition to funding limits the state's role and responsibility in pension provision, its potential for redistributing pension income, and pensioners' possibilities for bargaining politically over payouts.[56] Funding shifts responsibility and risk to individuals. In the economic sphere, funded schemes create social insurance markets, enhancing the role and opportunities of the private financial sector. In emerging markets, particularly those (such as the Russian one) that badly need investment, funding can serve as a source for deepening capital markets and financing economic development. Both the reduction of budgetary pressures and the potential for deepening capital markets motivated the Ministry of Economic Development to prioritize pension reform.

From the inception of the Gref Program, pension reform provoked deep conflicts within the Putin administration. The most prominent division emerged between the Ministry of Economic Development and Trade, represented by Deputy Minister (and former Yeltsin administration pension reform architect) Mikhail Dmitriev, and the head of the Pension Fund, Mikhail Zurabov. The Pension Fund had been created in 1991, as the system moved from budget-financing to wage-based financing, and it was broadly viewed as mismanaged or corrupt. Reform threatened the Pension Fund with the erosion of its role in pension provision and loss of control over the contributions that would go into private investment accounts. In a clear case of winner-take-all politics, Zurabov resisted privatization, pressing for continued state collection and distribution of contributions by the Pension Fund. Dmitriev, Gref, and the Economic Development Ministry favored a large funded component

---

[55] World Bank, *Averting the Old Age Crisis: Policies to Protect the Old and Promote Growth* (New York: Oxford University Press, 1994).

[56] It is essentially a transition from a defined-benefit system in which the payout is established (although, as we have seen for Russia, economic instability and inflation can undercut its value) to a defined-contribution system in which the payout depends on accumulations.

and reliance on private investment mechanisms to minimize pension pressures on the federal budget as well as to maximize prospects for the investment of funds in the economy. The Pension War between these two government agencies, driven largely by differing institutional interests in the outcome, dominated negotiations over the reform.[57] Business and financial interests, most prominently the RUIE and voluntary nonstate pension funds that had been legalized in the mid-1990s, supported the accumulative system.

In March 2001, Putin created an ad hoc consultative mechanism, the National Council on Pension Reform, to resolve this and other disputes. The council provided representation for a broad range of interests, including the FNPR, veterans' and invalids' groups, and business/financial groups, ostensibly giving a voice to labor, business, and social organizations.[58] Zurabov claimed that the council was designed to reach a consensus between the public and the executive on pension reform issues. But the council was heavily weighted toward governmental actors, created late in the policy deliberation process, and broadly seen as a mechanism for resolving the intragovernmental disputes rather than facilitating a social dialog. According to an expert attached to the Duma Committee on Social Policy, "(Duma) deputies are a minority on the Council; the tone of the discussion is set by the ministries and the Pension Fund."[59] The council managed to reach a compromise and produced several pieces of framework legislation which were quickly approved by the Duma, again with opposition only from the left parties (see table 4.4). It served as an effective intragovernmental conciliation mechanism for all but the most contentious elements of the reform— the size and management of invested pension accounts. Meetings of the council also gave voice to a concern among deputies, specialists, and others that Russian markets remained too unstable and poorly regulated to provide long-term pension security.

Conflict and negotiations over the investment mechanism continued for more than a year despite the government's strong promotion. Business and financial interests lobbied heavily to gain access to the

[57]   On pension reform and the Pension War, see *Rossiiskaia Gazeta*, 20 Mar. 2001; Yulia Ulyanova, "Pension War—between the Pension Fund and the Ministry of Economic Development," *Segodnia*, 6 Mar. 2001, 1, trans. in *CDSP* 53, no. 10 (2001), 11.

[58]   For the membership of the National Pension Council, see "Sostav natsional'nogo Soveta pri Prezidente Rossiiskoi Federatsii pri Pensionnoi Reforme" (mimeo, 2001).

[59]   Expert for the Committee on Social Policy of the State Duma, interview with author, Moscow, June 4, 2001.

financial opportunities that privatization promised, while Zurabov lobbied to exclude them.[60] The final legislation was a compromise. The new pension system retained a basic redistributive component, a guaranteed minimum pension that was slated to decline in real value over time. The reform initially redirected to investment accounts a portion of the pension contributions (2–3 percent of the total 28 percent wage tax), that was small by international standards but slated to increase over time.[61] Pensioners could choose to keep this money in a state-managed fund or invest it privately. Most chose the former option.

This major pension reform was passed with very little societal input. Pensioners, in any case, had no significant national organizations that could articulate their interests. According to a World Bank representative who followed the process, "Pensioners' organizations are small. The most noticeable things they provoke are court appeals; this is what they do most of the time. They are not capable of strategic planning . . . . Employers' organizations are more powerful, and participated in all the discussions."[62] The trade unions and Labor Ministry, institutions that typically defend distributive approaches in pension-reform negotiations, played minor roles, although the unions did support the Pension Fund's position. The Labor Ministry did not play an active role in providing ideas or substance. Legislators did resist the more radical proposals for investment funds, contributing to constraints on the executive's liberalizing agenda. But social implications gained limited attention. The reform is likely to impose future costs on large groups of pensioners, especially women and lower-paid workers, who will be disadvantaged in a system of individual savings accounts. Women will also lose because the new system no longer provides labor *stazh* credit for time spent in education and child care. Women's organizations did mobilize against the reform, but they gained a hearing in the Duma only from the Committee on Women's Affairs.[63]

The reform was designed to have no immediate costs for current pensioners. Real pensions increased slowly but steadily as it was debated and adopted, and the pension increases were seen as important for acceptance of reform by the older generation. The issue of raising the pension age was

---

[60]   *CDSP* 53, no. 10 (2001): 11, trans. from *Sevodnya*, March 6, 2001.

[61]   World Bank, *Pension Reform in Russia: Design and Implementation* (Washington, D.C.: World Bank, November 2002), available at www.worldbank.org.

[62]   Technical specialist, Pensions and Social Protection, Moscow Office of the World Bank, interview with author, Moscow, June 26, 2002. For one prominent example of such a court campaign, see Ilean Cashu and Mitchell Orenstein, "The Pensioners' Court Campaign: Making Law Matter in Russia," *East European Constitutional Review* 10, no. 4 (2001): 1–7.

[63]   Expert on women's movement in the Russian Federation, interview with author, Washington, D.C., Apr. 23, 2004.

debated within the government but kept off the table, despite the insistence of many experts that it is unavoidable if the Pension Fund is to remain solvent. To this extent, there was popular political constraint. Concessions were made mainly to the Pension Fund, the strongest vested interest in the social security system. It retained a major role and was compensated by new legislation that consolidated its control over pension distribution. Conflict and accommodation over the reform were heavily dominated by state and financial actors with their own agendas, in which the interests of pensioners and the state's social security function held at best a subsidiary place. In the words of one pension expert who was critical of the reform, "the aim here was not so much raising pensions but developing the economy."[64]

Education- and Health-Sector Reforms

Initiatives were taken to reorganize the education and health sectors in order to increase competition and create pressures for streamlining and modernizing the sectors. The Finance Ministry proposed that state financing should shift from the funding of institutions (i.e., according to the number of beds and the size of the staff) to the funding of services, a shift that intended to force out the inefficient. Reforms would legalize, regulate, and expand private expenditures and public-private cofinancing mechanisms, bringing payments out of the shadows and supplementing state financing with funds from households and businesses. The comprehensive guarantees of state provision that remained on the books would be replaced with a set of minimum guarantees that the state would finance for the poor. Ministries would effectively be compensated for reduced state expenditures by new, expanded roles in the administration and monitoring of national standards in health and education.

Because it remained under the auspices of the federal government when other levels were decentralized, higher education gained the most attention. Reformers proposed to move most state financing to a voucher system in which "money follows the student," with students being funded on the basis of their performance on a national exam and free to choose a school. Vouchers would introduce a market for educational services in the higher, postsecondary, schools. Schools or programs that could not attract sufficient enrollments risked closing. In the reformers' conception, vouchers would empower the best students to demand they be taught marketable skills,

---

[64] Pension expert, interview with author, Moscow, June 6, 2001; the reform process also subjected the Pension Fund to competition and scrutiny, contributing to improvement in its professionalism and performance.

forcing the adaptation of curricula. The introduction of a standardized exam administered by the Education Ministry would undermine the system of preparatory courses and tutoring for individual schools' exams, ending the pervasive shady operations in the higher schools. In sum, the proposed reforms directly threatened the interests of higher educational institutions in guaranteed state funding and shadow supplementary income while expanding the role of the Education Ministry in the reformed system.

The Economic Development and Finance Ministries strongly promoted the reform, and both standardized exams and vouchers were introduced on an experimental basis in 2001. They met resistance from two sources: the lower levels of the Education Ministry and the influential Union of Rectors of the state university system (the Red Rectors), led by the rector of the flagship Moscow State. At its 2001 congress, the Rectors' Union expressed fears that the new financing system would worsen their financial problems and called on the government, "not to place the educational system under the complete control of the invisible hand of the market."[65] The Rectors' Union organized regional universities to refuse to accept applicants based on the national test.

There ensued a "battle of ironclad university interest groups," with the Red Rectors opposing reform while prestigious new Moscow institutes supported it and with the Education Ministry caught "between the Finance Ministry and educators."[66] The government ultimately compromised with the rectors, conceding that a part of student recruitment would remain under the control of the schools while the system of vouchers and national testing controlled by the Education Ministry also moved forward. For both the rectors and the ministry, the outcome demonstrates once again the capacity of elite stakeholders to negotiate for concessions that serve their narrow institutional interests.

Health-care reform was also initiated. Its main goals were to complete the transition to insurance medicine that had faltered since the early 1990s, to eliminate budget funding of medical institutions, and to restrict the state's role to funding services for the poor. The financing basis for insurance would vary by population groups, with employers contributing for their employees, the Pension Fund for retirees, and regional and federal governments for the nonworking population and the poor. Separate legislation provided for voluntary private medical insurance. The government also revived legislation on regulation of private medical practices. The changes would move the system toward a public-private

[65]   *Moskovskie Novosti,* 28 Nov.–4 Dec. 2001. Other organizations, including the National Academy of Education, a conservative pedagogical institute, also opposed the reform.

[66]   Advisor to the Russian government, interview with author, Moscow, June 22, 2002.

mix with formally differentiated benefits, including a separate program of state-funded, basic services for the poor. Drafts of all three measures were submitted to the Duma in fall 2001.

These initiatives met resistance and failed to move the health-care system past its long-standing conflicts. Regional governments still refused to contribute to insurance and continued the direct funding of medical institutions under their jurisdiction. According to Dmitriev of the Ministry of Economic Development, "the government must act to support the role of insurance companies . . . . Keeping non-governmental insurance companies in the Mandatory Medical Insurance (MMI) network has become especially urgent . . . . There is a reluctance on the part of the government to take action; on the contrary, regional authorities oust insurance companies from the system."[67] Some health-care professionals resisted fragmentation of the system, fearing, according to one, that a differentiated system would worsen the health care accessible to the poor. Overall, however, negotiations were dominated by statist and elite actors, with little input from either the public or providers. According to close observers of Russian health-sector reform,

> As things stand now, there is a near equilibrium of forces in the health service between three special interest groups: health bureaucrats, CHI [Compulsory Health Insurance, or Mandatory Medical Insurance (MMI)] funds, and health insurance organizations. The future course of the reform will depend on the fighting and cooperation among these groups. Almost no one seems to care much about the interests of the population, or even those of medical workers.[68]

Liberalization Negotiated within the Elite

Putin-era negotiations over welfare state change across these four policy areas—labor code, pensions, health, and education—were largely confined within state and social-sector elites. The constriction of legislative politics largely closed out popular influence, while stakeholders within state bureaucracies and in elite social-sector organizations were able to limit change and gain compensation. Despite Putin's construction of a social policy team at the top of government, resistance came from

[67]   Mikhail Dmitriev et al., "Economic Problems of Health Services System Reform in Russia" (paper prepared for the Conference and Seminar on the Investment Climate and Russia's Economic Strategy, Moscow, April 5–7, 2000), available at www.imf.org.

[68]   Irina Rozhdestvenskaya and Sergei Shishkin, "Institutional Reforms in the Social-Cultural Sphere," in *The Economics of Transition*, edited by Yegor Gaidar, pp. 584–615 (Cambridge, Mass.: Massachusetts Institute of Technology, 2003), quotation from pp. 598–99.

social ministries and funds that administered programs based on pub-lic financing and administration. The Pension Fund chair and regional medical funds resisted the diversion of state-administered contributions to private insurance mechanisms. University rectors organized against changes that would subject their institutions to competition for state financing and undermine their access to informal incomes. These elites were often able to force the moderation of reform goals. The reforms also had built into them compensation for statist stakeholders, expanded roles in monitoring and regulation for ministries and other central orga-nizations that partly reversed the decentralization of the early 1990s. Recentralization was part and parcel of the effort to reestablish state social standards and control corruption, but it also served to expand the functions and resource claims of ministries in the reformed system.

Pro-welfare societal constituencies and electoral constraints played almost no role. In both the Labor Code and Pension Fund Reforms, the key compromises were worked out by ad hoc commissions that included token or ineffective popular representation. One well-informed observer, speaking about the National Pension Council, pointed to the weaknesses of both civil society and institutional linkages as causes of weak representa-tion: "the problem is not that the government resists the attempts of civil society [to have influence.] The problem is lack of demand . . . . with pen-sion reform, the existing instruments were used less effectively than, for example, if the trade unions were more concerned about membership. There are no organized groups to lobby for the interests of pensioners."[69] The case of the Labor Code negotiations, in which the unions gained significant compensation for their corporate interests and little for their membership, is most telling. Also in this period, economic and financial interests favoring liberalization became stronger and more engaged with state policy making. But, as the next two case studies show, the politics proved to be different for broad consumer subsidies and social privileges, areas in which cuts provoked popular protests and government retreats.

HOUSING AND BENEFITS REFORMS: CHIPPING AWAY AT SUBSIDIES AND PRIVILEGES

Reform of Housing and Utilities

At the beginning of the Putin presidency, the largest remaining subsi-dies in the social sector went to housing and utilities. Although residents'

---

[69] Russian government advisor, interview with author, Moscow, June 22, 2002.

payments had been raised to cover about half of these costs, the consolidated budget still allocated over 3 percent of GDP (approximately equal to total budget spending on education) to housing and utility payments. Housing accounted, on average, for about 40 percent of municipal budgets, a huge burden, crowding out expenditures on health, education, and other municipal obligations.[70] Housing reform, however, carried a high political load, because cuts would have a direct and tangible effect on living costs for almost all strata of Russia's population. The sector also continued to suffer from major structural problems. Public utilities and services remained monopolistic in most areas. Years of underinvestment had led to severe decay of the infrastructure, chronic leaks, breakdowns, and winter heating crises. In the winter of 2002–2003, as the reform was debated in the Duma, thirty-eight regions suffered breakdowns in heating utility networks.[71]

Initial reform proposals based on the Gref Plan called for transferring 100 percent of costs to the public within two years, with housing assistance provided for the poor, but intragovernment discussions about economic and political feasibility led to a softening of the plan. The housing reform program signed by Prime Minister Kasyanov in November 2001 was "a gradualist but market-minded plan, envisaging major rate increases in 2004–05." Subsidies would be eliminated and a free housing market established by 2010.[72]

The housing reform legislation faced strong resistance and repeated delays and rejections in the Duma. Deputies protested the social costs, the prospect of large-scale payment failures and evictions, and the removal of housing privileges. The pro-government Alliance of Four coalition split on some votes, United Russia held a serious internal debate about whether to support the legislation, and at one point the press announced that the coalition had deserted the government over the reform.[73] Public opinion data showed intense concern.[74] The government had launched pilot reform programs in some regions, and in spring 2002 the resulting

---

[70]   Housing expert, department head, Institute of National Economic Forecasting, Russian Academy of Sciences, interview with author, Moscow, June 8, 2000.

[71]   *St. Petersburg Times*, 31 Jan. 2003, in ISI Emerging Markets Database, available at www.securities.com.

[72]   *Rossiiskaia Gazeta*, 9 Jan. 2002, trans. in *FBIS*.

[73]   *Nezavisimaia Gazeta*, 18 Nov. 2002 (trans. in ISI Emerging Markets Russia, Nov. 19, 2002, available at www.securities.com), reported that centrist parties had ended their support for the government over housing reform and that a pro-government majority had ceased to exist.

[74]   According to Yuri Levada, VTsIOM head, polls showed that, of all Putin's reforms, the population was interested only in pension and housing reforms and were afraid of housing reforms; in *Vremya MN*, 13 July 2001, trans. in FBIS.

increases in housing costs led to a large demonstration and public boy-
cott of utility and housing payments in Voronezh. Although the Voronezh
protest was an isolated incident, it held symbolic importance, prompting
federal authorities to promise compensation for households struggling
with reform-related cost increases. The FNPR staged demonstrations
against the reform, which were reportedly joined by many deputies; the
communists and unions called unsuccessfully for a referendum to limit
housing costs to 10 percent of household income.

In the end, the government gained its majority (see table 4.4) only by
making multiple concessions. The chair of United Russia stated the party's conditions succinctly: "the party supports the reform but it must not
make the life of the people worse."[75] Housing privileges for labor and
war veterans, rural doctors, and teachers were preserved.[76] Eviction was
made more difficult, and the mandated payment from poor households
was halved. The requirement for even eventual 100 percent payment
was dropped. Even with these concessions, it proved difficult to rally a
majority. Housing reform, in sum, faced substantial popular political
and electoral constraints. Commentary from diverse sources pointed to
the legislature's concern about the popular response to price increases,
especially given the proximity of elections (in December 2003) by the
time the reform was debated in the Duma.

Several features distinguish this reform and explain its comparative
difficulty. First, the breadth of its impact, which would affect all households as soon as the changes went into effect, touching everyone,
meant that there was no way to obscure the costs or keep negotiations
within the elite. Second, although conditions and state performance
were improving in other areas of the social sector as reforms were
passed—pensions, employment, and wages, for example, were increasing at least modestly—in the housing-sector costs were rising and conditions were tangibly worsening. Third, there were real constraints on
the increased costs the population could absorb without pushing up
both poverty and pressures for expanded assistance programs. This
was a story of progressive erosion of reform goals both within the
government and in the legislature because of considerations of the
popular effects. Still, the final legislation included commitments to

---

[75]   *FBIS*, 17 Oct. 2002, citing ITAR-TASS, 2 Oct. 2002.
[76]   But housing privileges for some groups, including the military and categories of
government employees, were eliminated under separate legislation; see the discussion of
benefits reform later in the chapter.

liberalize the housing sector, and subsidies continued their slow but steady decline.

Benefits Reform and the Outburst of Popular Protest: Monetization and the Limits of Liberalization

In spring 2004, the Putin administration stood at the height of its power and popularity. President Putin had won a landslide reelection victory in March 2004, and after the December 2003 legislative elections United Russia commanded a two-thirds super-majority in the Duma. From this position of strength, the administration moved to dismantle the massive system of in-kind social benefits and privileges that had been inherited from the Soviet period and expanded by the patronage politics of 1994–1999. Earlier efforts to monetize state employees' privileges and to void unfunded federal mandates had achieved limited success. Now the government proposed a comprehensive legislative package that would affect about one-quarter of the population, mainly veterans, pensioners, the disabled, orphans, single parents, and members of other vulnerable groups, and would eliminate a range of benefits, services, subsidies, discounts, and protections.[77] The centerpiece of the reform was monetization, the replacement of state-administered in-kind benefits with cash payments. Conversion to cash would standardize social payments, make the system of transfers more transparent, and compensate recipients. It was to be a major step toward Putin's goal of a national poverty reduction strategy based on a standardized system of means-tested state social assistance. Putin personally promised that no one's life would be made worse by the reforms, although poverty experts estimated that full compensation for lost benefits would cost several times the amount allocated by the government.

The major benefits affected by the reform included free or subsidized access to public transport, medicines, housing and utilities, phone, and other basic goods and services. The administration justified this profound shake-up of the benefits system on several grounds. It stressed that the existing system was unfair, favoring urban households over rural areas where access to privileged goods and services was often unavailable, and providing more to nonpoor than to poor households (see table 4.5).

[77] L. N. Ovcharova, ed., *Dokhody i Sotsial'nye Uslugi: Neravenstvo, Uiazvimost' i Bednost'* (Kollektivnaia monographiia) (Moscow: GU-VShE, 2005), 5, available at http://www.socpol.ru/publications/.

TABLE 4.5
Distribution of housing, medical, and transport privileges by household type (%)

Type of privilege	Proportion of households receiving benefit				
	Capital city	Medium city	Village	Poor household	Nonpoor household
Housing, utilities	45.7	40.8	38.8	28.2	49.5
Medical services and medicines	22.3	22	17.9	11.7	21.3
Transport	52.8	37.4	27.4	24.4	47.5

Source: L. N. Ovcharova, ed., *Dokhody i Sotsial'nye Uslugi: Neravenstvo, Uiazvimost' i Bednost'* : Kollektiv-naia Monographiia (Moscow: GU-VShE, 2005), chap. 2, available at http://www.socpol.ru/publications.inc&ben/ch.

Poverty experts pointed to poor targeting, showing that although a large majority of pensioners received privileges, most of the single-parent and multichild families that were at maximum risk of poverty did not. The system of privileges also constituted an obstacle to marketization in housing, utilities, and other areas; providers were often not compensated for in-kind benefits, leaving these sectors underfinanced and deteriorating and making it impossible to run them on a profit-and-loss basis. Poverty experts supported the reform in principle, but criticized it for still failing to introduce means testing.[78]

The legislative package that was submitted to the Duma, Federal Law #122 (FZ #122) ran to several hundred pages, annulled fifty-five laws and amended almost two hundred more to end the Soviet-era benefits system.[79] Although it had long been part of the government's program, the reform was hastily prepared and pushed through with minimal legislative bargaining. Experts claimed that no serious calculations were made of the numbers who would be affected or would become eligible for compensation, that there were widely varying estimates of the numbers of beneficiaries at different ministries.[80] Responsibility for compensation payments was divided between the federal and regional governments, about one-third remaining federal and two-thirds becoming regional, with little regard for individual regions' varying ability to finance them; it was estimated that up to one-third of regional governments lacked the resources to provide the mandated payments.[81] The schedule of

[78] Ibid.
[79] *Moscow Times,* 4 Aug. 2004.
[80] *Moscow Times,* 9 February, 2005.
[81] Ovcharova, *Dokhody i Sotsial'nye Uslugi,* 14.

compensation payments, differentiated by beneficiary category, could take little account of individuals' needs and costs. Some privileges, such as job preferences for disabled, could not be monetized.

This was a massive reform that would tangibly and immediately affect the day-to-day lives and costs of more than one-quarter of the population, most of them state-dependent because of old age or poor health. It was passed in a period of fiscal surpluses, driven not by austerity but by the desire or perceived need to rationalize welfare. An underlying element of liberal fundamentalism informed the project.

FZ #122 was sharply contested from the outset, rallying diverse sources of opposition—leftists, moderate-reformists, governors, trade unions, NGOs, and beneficiaries. Pensioners broadly distrusted and opposed monetization, fearing that compensation would be inadequate to cover the real cost of cancelled benefits, that inflation or other sources of financial instability would undercut the value of payments, and that promised payments would in any case prove unreliable. Most preferred the certainty of accustomed free access and discounts. Governors, generally loyal to the Putin administration, protested that compensation payments constituted new unfunded federal mandates, and petitioned against the bill. Legislative deliberation of FZ #122 generated the first nationwide protests since Putin took office in 2000, including daily demonstrations in Moscow running into the thousands and rallies in dozens of regions. The legislative sessions that passed it required the Duma to be cordoned off by police. More than one-third of the deputies, including large majorities of all parties except United Russia, voted against the legislative package. Amid strong popular opposition, United Russia passed it.

The societal response to the reform's implementation in January 2005 was surprisingly robust. The introduction of mass transport charges for pensioners and other privileged groups was met with large street demonstrations and protests that blocked roads and public transit routes in cities across the Russian Federation. Political parties, trade unions, and NGOs joined and helped coordinate demonstrations, but most were the spontaneous outpourings of outraged pensioners. The wave of public unrest continued for weeks, affecting more than seventy cities and ultimately involving many thousands in protests and demonstrations, precipitating a rare Putin-era governmental crisis.[82] Antigovernment and anti-Putin political slogans were commonly displayed, along with

---

[82] See, for example, reports in *Nezavisimaia Gazeta*, no. 17, 2005, 9.

hyperbolic rhetoric about state genocide to ease the burden on the pension and social welfare systems. Interior Ministry (OMON) troops were called up in a number of cases. Individual regions and cities began to restore privileges.[83] At the height of the crisis, the communists called a vote of no confidence, and although the government survived, UR deputies abstained en masse in order to distance itself from the reform.

The administration recognized that it had taken back too much too fast. Although standing by the reform in principle, it made multiple concessions, substantially raising pensions, increasing federal allocations for compensation payments, and allowing so many exceptions and exemptions to FZ #122 that the basic rationalizing thrust of monetization was undermined.[84] Some regions abandoned the reform and others increased payments or created a mixed system; federal beneficiaries were offered a choice between money and a social package. Some benefits were monetized, but the resulting system remained fragmented and opaque, characterized by divergent regional practices and a continuing predominance of inherited, untargeted subsidies.

The monetization episode defined the limits of liberalization in the Russian polity, even by an insulated elite with a compliant legislature. A generally quiescent society mobilized against the wholesale imposition of immediate, tangible costs on a very large societal constituency. The strength of the economy, the existence of a government surplus, and a large Stabilization Fund from oil profits undermined the rationale of the reform. Only repression on a substantial scale against socially vulnerable strata would have quashed the protests. Instead the reform was rolled back and changed into a more gradual process of chipping away at the old system. Russia's fragmented bureaucratic environment, particularly in federal-regional relations, as well as popular resistance, blocked any serious rationalization of social assistance policy.

POLITICAL BALANCES AND PATTERNS OF INFLUENCE

I return to the key questions of this book: How did politics mediate welfare state change in Russia's weak transitional democracy? Who influenced decisions to cut, preserve, or reshape the system during the period of economic recovery? Table 4.1 summarizes domestic political balances

---

[83] *Kommersant,* 16 Jan. 2005, 3
[84] *Vremnya Novosti,* July 8, 2005, 4.

and patterns of influence over liberal restructuring during the Putin years, 2000–2003. As table 4.1 shows, pro-reform forces were strengthened during this period, which featured a unified liberalizing government and a pro-executive legislative majority. Reformist social-sector elites exercised moderate influence as advisors to the government, although the policy process was more centralized than it had been during the initial period of radical liberalization in 1991–1993. IFIs had little direct role but a strong residual influence on reform policies. Societal welfare state interests were weak because of the decay in the legislature's representative function. Statist stakeholders, both social-sector elites and bureaucracies, were moderately influential in negotiating for their narrow institutional interests, producing a pattern of liberalization negotiated mainly within the elite.

As the case studies discussed here show, in this period the Russian government was able to gain approval for liberalizing measures across major areas of the welfare state. Between 2000 and 2004, the legislature weakened formal claims to job security, trade unions' prerogatives, and women's employment protections. It reduced the state's responsibility for future pension provision and introduced market investment accounts. Reforms that expanded cofinancing and insurance mechanisms, privatization, and competition in health care and education were initiated. Less successful efforts were made to end subsidies and privileges. The government, in sum, succeeded in reorienting the Russian welfare state, in shifting its direction from the inherited statist model toward a more market-conforming model.[85] (See table 3.5 for a summary of the outcomes across policy areas.)

These reforms were the project of the executive, designed by a narrow committee with expert consultation, passed by a largely compliant Duma. Discussions about reform policies revolved mainly around elite and state interests, or (at best) an expert-technocratic conception of societal interests. According to a man who was deeply involved in the reforms:

> the basic weakness of Russian political life is that the suppliers of options are a narrow group of experts and top-level officials; social policy [should be] a set of responses to various challenges, interests articulated by society. In Russia it is the ideas of a few people. Most of society is out of the picture.

[85] It is important to remember that the old welfare state had been defunded and corrupted during the years of economic decline and political deadlock, and that liberalization was in part an effort to legalize and regulate changes that had already taken place spontaneously. Nevertheless, both the formal reorganization of the state's role in welfare provision and the construction of social security markets depended on a supporting political constellation.

The main problem is the demand side—people are not prepared. In the Yeltsin period there were some social pressures on the government, because there was a powerful opposition in parliament, so a primitive but strong articulation. Now it is marginalized.[86]

In most areas reform politics was dominated by elite stakeholders, and their interests were accommodated. Defense of solidaristic values and broader societal interests in the welfare state were very weak.

It is important to note, however, that both the legislature and government did rely on strategies of delay, obfuscation, and avoidance of responsibility that are familiar from studies of welfare state retrenchment in democratic systems. The direction of change toward a liberal model that would do less in the welfare realm and impose costs on most societal groups was somewhat obscured by the government's constant announcements of small but steady increases in pensions, minimum wages, and other state social payments after the 1998 trough. The popular constraint on housing and especially benefits cuts that could not be obscured was much stronger. In short, a version of the Paul Pierson argument holds—there seems to be some feedback constraint on welfare state change that imposes immediate and tangible costs on broad groups even in Russia's semi-authoritarian polity.[87]

The World Bank's active role was, as already noted, muted in this period, but its earlier interventions shaped much of what was done. The Bank's own assessment of its impact in Russia over the 1991–2001 decade seems to capture the reality quite well:

The CEA (Country Assistance Evaluation) judges the outcome of most Bank-supported operations which were closed and evaluated during 1991–2001 unsatisfactory, but notes that sustainability ratings are higher than outcome ratings as many of the lessons from the Bank's operations and analytical advice were applied after 1998 . . . . The Bank has become the main external interlocutor on the . . social reform agenda, and the government has adopted many of the policies that the Bank had recommended.[88]

[86]   Russian government advisor, interview with author, Moscow, June 22, 2002.

[87]   Paul Pierson, *Dismantling the Welfare State: Reagan, Thatcher, and the Politics of Retrenchment* (Cambridge, UK: Cambridge University Press, 1994).

[88]   World Bank, "Lessons from the Country Assistance Evaluation (CAE) and the Country Impact Review (CIR)" (2002), available at www.worldbank.org.ru/ECD/Russia.nsf/ECADDocByUnid/.

The experience of Russia shows that compliance is driven not primarily by financial dependence on IFIs but by domestic political interests and power balances. The model of the liberal welfare state, carried by the IFIs, had profound effects on Russian welfare state reform, but these effects were processed through domestic politics in complex ways.

The agendas and priorities of social welfare reform were set by the Ministry of Economic Development and Trade and, to a lesser extent, the Finance Ministry, state actors whose central concerns are investment and the business environment. Reforms were pushed first that mattered most for the developmental model: Labor Code liberalization; pension reform that provided potential investment funds; housing and benefit reforms that were designed to relieve pressures on the state budget. Education and health sectors were assigned lower priority. Although there was been much discussion in the Russian government about health and demographic crises and the importance of education for the development of human capital, reforms in both areas have lagged. Throughout the social sector, organizations that generally defend welfare functions in their own right—trade unions, labor and social ministries, beneficiaries' organizations, and pro-welfare political parties—played limited roles or defended institutional and bureaucratic interests rather than solidaristic or societal ones. Except for demanding the retention of benefits and subsidies, Russian society had little voice in welfare state change.

OUTCOMES: RUSSIA'S WELFARE STATE IN 2002–2003

By 2003, Russia had experienced five years of steady economic growth and a coherent program of liberalizing welfare reforms. The government increased social spending modestly in real terms, built some social security markets, and made efforts to regulate private social spending and service provision. In this section, I discuss the outcomes (paralleling the discussion of outcomes in chap. 3), looking at the effects on major dimensions of welfare provision: basic social guarantees, poverty and social assistance, and access to health care and education. I draw on a World Bank study that uses the National Survey of Household Welfare and Program Participation (NOBUS), a survey of Russian households' access to social services. Carried out by the Russian Federation State Statistical Committee (Goskomstat) in 2003, NOBUS provides the most comprehensive available picture. The discussion shows the sustained effects of the sharp regional disparities that were stressed in chapter 2 and provides an overall assessment of welfare state liberalization and welfare provision in Russia.

Basic Social Guarantees

Basic social guarantees improved in both amounts and reliability during the Putin years. As noted earlier, most benefit and public-sector salary arrears had been cleared by the end of 1999. Table 4.6 (paralleling
table 3.6) shows the levels of basic social guarantees, including child
benefits, university student stipends, workers' and invalids' pensions,
and social-sector wages, in relation to the subsistence level from 1999
to 2002 (with 1993 included for comparison). As table 4.6 shows, the
key sets of payments regulated by the government—the minimum wage,
the first grade of the public-sector salary scale, and pensions—increased
gradually. The effects were most marked for average pensions and
public-sector wages, which rose above subsistence level by 2001. The
proportion of public-sector workers with poverty wages had declined
by one-third by 2002, although the sector continued to have the highest share of workers with below-subsistence wages economywide, except
for agricultural.[89] Other payments—invalid pensions and student stipends—remained very low in terms of contribution to income, and all
remained substantially below their 1993 levels.

In terms of coverage and adequacy of social security, pension coverage for the current generation of retirees remains nearly universal and
payouts are sufficient to keep most pensioners out of poverty, although
benefit levels remain compressed and wage-replacement levels are very
low. However, high levels of informality and minimal compliance (i.e.,
employers making contributions based on the minimum rather than real
wages) are likely to leave a substantial number of future retirees outside
the system or eligible for only subsistence pensions. In 2001, when tax
administration had improved considerably from the levels of the mid-
1990s, the head of the Pension Fund estimated that the majority of contributions would qualify employees only for minimum benefits.

Social Assistance and Poverty Relief

Poverty declined progressively and significantly during this period, to
20.3 percent in 2003, mainly as a result of economic recovery, increased
employment, productivity, and wages. However, the patterns of poverty
across regions and social strata that were shown in chapters 2 and 3 have
persisted. More than 30 percent of unemployed and rural, almost 27 percent of children to age sixteen, and almost 50 percent of all households

---

[89] World Bank, *Russian Federation: Reducing Poverty through Growth and Social Policy
Reform* (Report no. 28923-RU) (Washington, D.C.: World Bank, February 8, 2005), 26.

TABLE 4.6
Basic social guarantees and social-sector wages, 1999–2002 (%)[a]

	1993	1999	2000	2001	2002[b]
Minimum wage	39	10	6.8	13.2	22
Wage rate for first-grade public-sector wage scale	41	10	10.7	13.2	22
Monthly benefit for each child to 16 years	19	7	5.0	5.0	3.7
Minimum student stipend, VUZ	39	19	13.6	13.2	10
Old-age pensions:					
minimum[c]	63	42	48.2	44.0	36.5
average	138	70	76.4	89.5	100.0
Invalid's pensions, Group 1	105	30	30.6	31.7	—
Health-care sector wages					
(average)	195[d]	99	107	126	166
Workers below subsistence (%)	—	67.2	65.7	61.0	38.8
Education-sector wages					
(average)	185[d]	93	99	117	153
Workers below subsistence (%)	—	70.5	67.5	61.3	41.4

Sources: Sotsial'noe polozhenie i uroven zhizni naseleniya Rossii statistichiskii sbornik (Moscow: Goskomstat), 2000, 167, 145, 147; 2001, 148; 2002, 150, 152, 194.

[a] On 1 January or first quarter, percentage of subsistence level.
[b] Quarter 4.
[c] With compensation payments.
[d] 1992.

with three or more children were poor in 2002. As in the 1990s, the elderly had the lowest risk of poverty. Moreover, the patterns of regional differentiation that emerged from the decentralization of the early 1900s have largely been sustained. The highest concentrations of poor are in European Russia and the north Caucasus, where the incidence of regional poverty in many cases exceeds 40 percent of the population. The official poverty count across regions varied from 7 to 87 percent in 2003.[90] Families with children constituted the majority among the poor in all regions.

The Putin administration did make some efforts to reestablish federal control over social assistance as part of its recentralization and reorganization of fiscal federalist relations. Selected benefit programs were taken over by the federal government and covered under a Regional Equalization Fund, guaranteeing financing and freeing these programs from the vagaries of regional financing. Most important here are child

[90] Ibid., 19, 39.

benefits, which have become standardized and means-tested. Coverage, levels, and targeting have improved measurably.[91] According to Russian poverty specialists, in 2001, "For the first time in years, all the money was sent to regions to finance child allowances . . . . there was a real, federally financed guarantee for child benefits for those below subsistence."[92] The program is broad in coverage, reaching two-thirds of households with children. It is a standard liberal program, the first major initiative in targeting the poor for spending. But the child benefit remains seriously underfunded, at only about 5 percent of the subsistence level, contributing only 1.6 percent of the consumption of an average household, although it is most significant to the incomes of the bottom 20 percent. It is also poorly administered, with low efficacy at targeting the poorest. Its impact on poverty reduction is relatively low. Except for a small program of housing allowances, it remains the only federally funded program targeting poverty. Most poverty-relief programs remain decentralized. The World Bank has called on the Russian government to take over the patchwork of local and regional programs, to "transform . . . the decentralized social assistance programs into one core program that is federally funded and monitored but locally implemented . . . so that it reaches the poorest households."[93] Overall, state assistance to the eligible poor remains fragmentary and benefits extremely inadequate.

Health Care and Education

Real public expenditures on health care and education increased modestly with economic recovery. Levels of welfare effort remained relatively low, and the legacies of decentralization and de facto privatization remained major obstacles to addressing problems of access. Per capita public as well as private spending variations across regions increased during the recovery. Interregional variations in health status are sharply evident in statistics on the rates of tuberculosis, infant mortality, and life expectancy, variations that have increased since 1999 (see table 4.7). According to a recent World Bank study, "the health financing reforms and the decentralization policies of the last decade have had unintended consequences . . . . There are . . . clear signals of failures in efficiency and

[91] World Bank, *Russia: Development Policy Review* (Report no. 26000-RU) (Washington, D.C., World Bank, June 9, 2003).

[92] Poverty expert, project coordinator, International Labour Organisation, interview with author, Moscow, May 31, 2001; social protection expert, operations officer, Social Protection, Moscow Office, World Bank, interview with author, June 5, 2001.

[93] World Bank, *Russian Federation*, v, 93.

TABLE 4.7
Health outcomes in the Russian Federation by region, 2000–2001

	Tuberculosis (per 100,000 population)	Infant mortality (per 1,000 live births)	Life expectancy		
			Total	Male	Female
Maximum (worst region)	80.3	42.1	56.4	51.1	62.8
Minimum (best region)	2.3	8.1	74.6	70.0	79.1

Source: World Bank, *Russian Federation: Reducing Poverty through Growth and Social Policy Reform* (Washington, D.C.: 2005), 126–27, citing Goskomstat.

in equity and in protecting the poor."[94] Fragmentation of governance and weak management remained endemic in both sectors.

The private health-care sector continued to expand, with state regulation remaining weak. Private medical practices remained largely unregulated and out-of pocket expenditures continued to grow as the economy recovered. Private expenditures were variously estimated at 30 percent to 55 percent of total health expenditures, with more reliable Russian surveys tending toward the higher estimate. The need for out-of-pocket payments has worsened access to health care for Russia's poor. A 2001 World Bank study found "a burgeoning underclass" with no or limited access to services.[95] Fifty to sixty percent of respondents in the 2003 NOBUS survey across all income groups reported paying for some medical services because there were no free providers or specialists available. About 20 percent of those not seeking care for medical problems reported that they were deterred by inability to pay, with percentages higher in lower-income quintiles. Ten percent could not follow prescribed treatments, especially purchase of pharmaceuticals, for financial reasons. Availability of needed care was especially problematic for the rural poor. [96]

The education sector has become less rigid and centralized and more diverse. The completion of compulsory education remains nearly universal. However, the NOBUS survey showed that income-linked and regional disparities in access to both preschool and postcompulsory levels have increased during the recovery. The steep rise in inequality in per capita education spending that resulted from decentralization has persisted. The federal contribution has remained very limited below the university level,

[94] World Bank, *Russian Federation,* 133.
[95] World Bank, "Public Information Document," (2001), 5.
[96] World Bank, *Russian Federation,* 130–33.

with 63 percent of total education financing coming from municipal budgets in 2001. Inequalities are compounded by the increase in legal, privately financed education and a growing incidence of informal payments.[97] Drop-out rates in the lower secondary stage and poor graduation rates remain substantial. In terms of measured access and exclusion, about 22 percent of 16–17-year-olds were not in school, and the numbers of 15–18-year-olds out of both school and work grew during the early years of recovery.[98] In higher education, 54 percent of students paid fees in 2002, up from 10 percent in 1995, while budgets at all levels paid a little less than half the cost.[99]

In education and, especially, health care a system of low public expenditure, high private expenditure, and official tolerance of informality has de facto flourished. Although the evolution of this system was unintended, it works tolerably well for most actors, effectively reducing the pressures for further reform. It allows the state to restrict spending without forcing large-scale staff cuts, the wealthy in Russia's highly inegalitarian society to purchase services, and public-sector workers to supplement their incomes with informal payments. It is, in the terms of one recent study, a system of welfare patronage in which political authorities tolerate ubiquitous informal payments to gain professionals' acquiescence to low official salaries while clients and providers collude to evade state regulation and taxation.[100] But the system fails to provide either access for the poor or adequate public health expenditures. Despite an estimated overall level of public and private health expenditure that approaches the lower range of OECD levels, Russia's general and public health outcomes remain comparatively very poor.

How Much Liberalization?

By 2002–2003, the Russian welfare state was partially liberalized, with a greatly reduced role for the state in social provision, some social security markets, competition, user fees, private alternatives in health and education sectors, a substantially deregulated labor market, and a few poverty-targeted social assistance programs. Of the main measures of

[97] Ibid., 113–20.

[98] World Bank, *Russia: Development.*

[99] Mary Canning, "Modernization of Education in Russia," (Washington, D.C.: World Bank, 2004).

[100] Conor O'Dwyer, *Runaway State-Building: Patronage Politics and Democratic Development* (Baltimore: Johns Hopkins University Press, 2006).

liberalization employed in this study—public versus private pension pro-vision, public versus private health care expenditure, and the proportion of means-tested social assistance—substantial movement had been made on the first two.

1. An invested pension tier was established; benefits for future pensioners depend in part on contributions to individual ac-counts and accumulation in invested accounts.

2. The proportion of private health-care expenditure including both formal and informal payments is commonly estimated at 40–50 percent of the total, heavily skewed toward private expen-diture in comparative terms.

3. Only a small fraction of social assistance, an estimated 7 per-cent of total transfers, was means-tested or explicitly poverty-tar-geted in 2002. Although subsidies have been reduced, the bulk of social transfers continued to go to untargeted subsidies and privileges, equaling about 4.3 percent of GDP while only about 0.4 percent of GDP was targeted. The effectiveness of social transfers in poverty relief remained low.

The liberalization program has been more effective in privatizing than in building market and regulatory institutions for the social sec-tor. These limitations reflect both continued limits on state capacity and resistance from welfare state constituents and stakeholders. Overall, as the discussion has shown, unregulated costs (shadow payments), infor-mality, and institutional deficits in the social sector remain very high. Substantial numbers of the wealthiest and poorest stand effectively out-side the system of public social provision.

CONCLUSION

The comparative literature identifies two major factors that facilitate lib-eralization of welfare states: political institutions that restrict representa-tion of pro-welfare state interests and constitutional systems that enhance the power of liberalizing executives.[101] Russia's weak transitional democ-racy constricted societal representation comparatively, but in the mid-1990s it allowed representation through the legislature of moderate and hard-left pro-welfare interests, effectively blocking liberalization. With

[101]   See, especially, Swank, *Global Capital;* Huber and Stevens, *Development and Crisis.*

the emergence of managed democracy under Putin, representatives of pro-welfare societal constituencies were weakened. Except for social subsidies, influence on welfare state change was largely confined to state-bureaucratic actors and social-sector elites who held narrowly conceived commitments to preserving their roles in welfare administration. Strategies of compensation and concessions were used by the executive to gain the compliance of these groups with the liberalizing project.

The comparison of the Yeltsin and Putin periods confirms the centrality of domestic political institutions for liberalization. These institutions mediated the effects of economic, fiscal, and international pressures on the welfare state, first blocking and then facilitating change. In the mid-1990s, they resisted pressures for restructuring even in the face of Russia's severe economic downturn. The political institutions that represented pro-welfare societal constituencies in Russia were much weaker than their Western counterparts, but, in de facto cooperation with state-bureaucratic welfare state stakeholders, they kept most programmatic features of the old welfare state in place for a decade. The shift in control over political institutions then permitted liberalization under conditions of economic growth and fiscal surpluses. After 1999, power was concentrated in the presidency and potential statist veto actors were compensated. Societal interests did continue to matter for welfare policy but mainly as veto actors on subsidy cuts. In sum, politics critically shaped welfare state change.

In the next chapter, I place the Russian welfare state within a comparative framework and examine patterns of welfare state change—expenditures, programmatic structures, and outcomes—across two sets of cases, one with liberal democratic political institutions (Poland and Hungary), the other with electoral-authoritarian regimes (Belarus and Kazakhstan). I compare patterns of welfare state change and ask whether these patterns can be explained by differing structures of political representation and executive power across the three sets of cases. I also consider differences in state capacity, concluding that liberalization in the context of weak state taxing and regulatory capacities produces a distinctive welfare state type that is substantially shaped by informal relations and processes.

5

Comparing Postcommunist Welfare State Politics

Poland, Hungary, Kazakhstan, and Belarus

I now add a comparative dimension to the book and ask who influenced decisions to cut, preserve, or reshape welfare provision in four additional postcommunist cases: Poland, Hungary, Kazakhstan, and Belarus. As explained in the introduction, these two pairs of cases were chosen because their political systems stand at opposite ends of the postcommunist spectrum in both representativeness and concentration of power. Poland and Hungary are competitive multiparty democracies with effective legislative institutions and active trade union movements. Kazakhstan and Belarus are electoral authoritarian regimes dominated by strong executives that have marginalized political parties and legislatures and repressed unions. In this chapter, I map comparative patterns of change across all areas of the welfare state and look at the politics of key decisions about pensions and health care for the four cases. As I did for the Russian Federation, I focus on political power balances between the supporters and opponents of liberalization in party, governmental, and state structures to explain the differences in welfare outcomes. As with Russia, I also pay attention to state capacities and consider briefly the influence of international interventions.

The economic trajectories of the four cases are broadly similar. All experienced transitional recessions in the early to mid-1990s and then substantially recovered by 2002 (see figure 1.1). The length and depth of these recessions varied. They were comparatively mild in Poland and Hungary but much deeper and more prolonged in Belarus and

Kazakhstan, producing much stronger pressures on welfare provision. At the same time, these latter two states were among the three experiencing the most modest declines and strongest recoveries in the post-Soviet region.[1] Like Russia, three of these four carried out policies of domestic and foreign trade liberalization, macroeconomic stabilization, and privatization of most of their economies. Belarus is an outlier here, retaining 80 percent of its economy under state control in 2000, continuing subsidies and protectionism. It nevertheless recovered economically in parallel with the others. By the late 1990s, all the economies were growing, and by 2002 Poland's GDP stood at 138 percent of its 1990 level, Hungary's at 113 percent, Belarus's at 103 percent, Kazakhstan's at 90 percent, and Russia's at 83 percent with recovery continuing.[2] Table 5.1 shows the effects of transition on two key indicators of welfare: unemployment and inequality. Unemployment increased in all cases, to double digits in Poland, Russia, and Kazakhstan, and remained especially high in Poland. Inequality also grew significantly across the cases from the comparatively low levels of the communist period.

As shown in chapter 1, all the postcommunist countries had mature welfare states, broadly similar in structure to the Russian one. Welfare standards were somewhat higher in Eastern Europe, especially in Hungary. Belarus had among the highest indicators of social well-being in the Soviet Union, and Kazakhstan had a full range of social security and social assistance programs as well as universal state-run education and health care. In all four cases, latent societal constituencies, social-sector elites, and bureaucratic stakeholders had interests in defending the established systems of public financing and provision. And although the recessions produced strong pressures for welfare state retrenchment and restructuring, the hardships of transition also produced counterpressures for expanded state assistance and compensation, especially in cases in which the welfare state constituents had somewhat effective political representation.

The politics matters theory predicts that societal defense of welfare programs and entitlements should be stronger in Poland and Hungary than in the other cases because executive power was weaker and more constrained and welfare constituencies had more possibilities for

---

[1]   World Bank, *Transition: The First Ten Years, Analysis and Lessons for Eastern Europe and the Former Soviet Union* (Washington, D.C.: World Bank, 2002), 5. The third is Uzbekistan, which is not a good comparator because it is low income.

[2]   My own calculations, based on data from the International Monetary Fund World Economic Outlook Database, 2004, 2006, available at www.imf.org.

TABLE 5.1
Social indicators for Poland, Hungary, Russian Federation, Kazakhstan, and Belarus,
1990–2002

Country	Indicators[a]	1990/1991	1994	1998	2000	2002
Poland	Unemployment (%)	3.4	14.0	10.5	16.6	19.9
	Inequality (Gini)	0.28	0.28	0.33	0.31	0.32
	Poverty rate	—	—	23	26	27
Hungary	Unemployment (%)	0.8	10.7	7.8	6.6	5.1
	Inequality (Gini)	0.21	0.23	0.25	0.25	0.25
	Poverty rate	—	—	20	18	12
Russian	Unemployment (%)	0.1	8.1	13.3	9.8	7.9
Federation	Inequality (Gini)	0.26	0.40	0.40	0.35	0.34
	Poverty rate	—	—	46	54	41
Kazakhstan	Unemployment (%)	0.4	7.5	13.7	12.8	9.3
	Inequality (Gini)	0.30	0.33	0.35	0.35	0.33
	Poverty rate	—	—	—	73[b]	71
Belarus	Unemployment (%)[c]	0.1	4.0[d]	2.3	2.1	3.0
	Inequality (Gini)	0.23	0.28	0.26	0.29	0.29
	Poverty rate	—	—	48	38	21

Sources: Sandrine Cazes and Alena Nesporova, *Labor Markets in Transition* (Geneva: International Labour Organizstion, 2003), 16; World Bank, *Balancing Protection and Opportunity: A Strategy for Social Protection in Transition Countries* (Washington, D.C.: World Bank, 2000), 56–90; Asad Alam et al., *Growth, Poverty, and Inequality: Eastern Europe and the Former Soviet Union* (Washington, D.C.: World Bank, 2005), 238–41. Inequality measures (Gini coefficients) from World Bank, *Transition: The First Ten Years, Analysis and Lessons for Eastern Europe and the Former Soviet Union* (Washington, D.C.: World Bank, 2002), 9. Unemployment data for the Republic of Belarus from International Monetary Fund, *Selected Issues* (IMF Country Report no. 04/139) (Washington, D.C.: IMF, , May 2004), 4.

[a] Inequality measures are Gini coefficient per capita; the figures are averages for 1987–1990, 1993–1994, and 1996–1998. Poverty rate measures are percentage below dollars purchasing-power parity ($PPP) 4.30/day. The Gini coefficients and poverty indicators are based on different calculations that those for Russia in table 2.2, which are from Goskomstat.

[b] 2001.

[c] Figures for Belarus are based on official registered unemployment only and are not comparable with those for other countries.

[d] 1996.

representation. In democratic polities, societal constituents can build pro-welfare political alliances to contest retrenchment and restructuring. But, although democratic institutions in these states look like their counterparts in the older European democracies, there are serious questions about their effectiveness in representing broad societal interests and influencing political outcomes (see the introduction). Various studies argue that the postcommunist states of East Central Europe have passive publics that are disengaged from politics or that they have very weak civil societies resulting in hollow democracy.[3] The prevailing view of trade

[3]   On passive publics and disengagement, see Maryjane Osa, "Contention and Democracy: Labor Protest in Poland, 1989–1993," *Communist and Post-Communist Studies* 31, no. 1

unions in these countries likewise holds that they are ineffective, either co-opted by the liberal reform project or undermined by structural economic constraints.[4] These conclusions are applied to both the democratic and semi-authoritarian regimes. According to Stephen Crowley, for example, "unions are quite weak throughout the postcommunist space. This is true despite wide variations in . . . levels of economic growth and unemployment, political opportunities, union configurations, candidacy for EU membership, hardness of budget constraints."[5]

To an extent, the evidence in this book confirms the analysis of Crowley and others. Welfare states in the East Central European democracies underwent broad liberalization and periods of sharp retrenchment during the 1990s. Labor unions and other welfare state constituencies were much less able to constrain change than their counterparts in most older industrial democracies. But the liberalization projects in these states differed in important respects from that carried out in Russia. First, during the transitional recessions some societal constituencies in Poland and Hungary were compensated for welfare losses. Second, the bargaining over programmatic change included representatives of broad societal interests and solidaristic values, unlike in Russia where bargaining became dominated mainly by the interests of state actors. Third, with economic recovery, welfare state effort stabilized at moderate levels and the predominance of public over private expenditure was institutionalized in the social sectors, in contrast to the Russian case. Bureaucratic welfare stakeholders played some role in resisting reforms in these cases, but the dispersion of power away from the state in the democratic transitions meant that their influence was limited. Representative political institutions, electoral feedback, and active labor movements played a major role in accounting for these differences.

Political institutions had another important effect on welfare state liberalization in East Central Europe. The coordination between executives and legislatures that is built into parliamentary systems and the need to form

(1998): 29–30. On weak civil societies, see Marc Morje Howard, *The Weakness of Civil Society in Post-Communist Europe* (Cambridge, UK: Cambridge University Press, 2003).

[4] See, for example Stephen Crowley and David Ost, eds., *Workers after Workers' States: Labor and Politics in Postcommunist Eastern Europe* (New York: Rowman and Littlefield, 2001); Paul Kubicek, "Organized Labor in Postcommunist States: Will the Western Sun Set on It, Too?" *Comparative Politics* 32, no. 1 (1999): 83–102.

[5] Stephen Crowley, "Comprehending the Weakness of Russia's Unions," *Demokratizatsia* 10, no. 2 (2002): 247.

political coalitions facilitated compromise and helped produce a gradual, negotiated restructuring process through the 1990s. This was more the case in Poland than in Hungary, but both stand in sharp contrast to Russia. As Mitchell Orenstein has argued, the alternation in power of center-left and center-right parties moderated reform policies in East Central Europe.[6] Political compromise, along with compensation for key societal welfare constituencies, permitted the partial dismantling of old social programs and protections and some adaptation of welfare states to markets and pressing new welfare needs. New democratic institutions provided less influence for welfare constituencies than in Western Europe, but helped to avoid both deadlock and radical retrenchment and restructuring.

In Kazakhstan and Belarus, executive power dominated. Presidents were accountable to their populations only through the blunt instruments of referenda and plebiscitary elections, and they confronted little effective societal constraint or demand making. The economies of the two states followed similar trajectories (see figure 1.1). Yet welfare state structures and outcomes diverged sharply. Kazakhstan's welfare state was radically restructured by a liberalizing executive in a manner reminiscent of the Chilean experience under Augusto Pinochet. Belarus retained most of its Soviet-era structures and programs. How can these divergent outcomes be explained?

The balance of power within the executive coalitions was key. The Belarussian state remained largely intact during the transition, retaining control over economic resources as well as capacities to tax and redistribute. Statist elites, especially the managerial bureaucracies that continued to administer industry and collective agriculture, formed the core of the postcommunist executive's power. State-based welfare bureaucracies were able to retain their roles and defend their claims to resources even when the economy fell into deep recession. In Kazakhstan, by contrast, privatization deprived state actors of both resources and capacities, whereas executive power came to depend mainly on a narrow oligarchic elite based in the private energy economy. Welfare and other state bureaucracies were subject to frequent reorganizations and streamlining, and proved unable to defend against the executive's liberalizing project. Welfare also played a different role in the popular appeals of the two executives. The Belarussian president promised to preserve the old social contract, whereas the Kazakh president appealed to ethnic pride

---

[6] Mitchell A. Orenstein, *Out of the Red: Building Capitalism and Democracy in Postcommunist Europe* (Ann Arbor: University of Michigan Press, 2001).

TABLE 5.2
Welfare state politics in Poland, Hungary, Kazakhstan, and Belarus

Country	Executive	Welfare stakeholders	Policy process	Outcome
Poland and Hungary	Moderate liberalizing executives	Representation of societal interests (political parties, trade unions)	Liberalization negotiated with society	Gradual, moderate policy change
Kazakhstan	Strong liberalizing executive	No effective representation of statist or societal interests	Non-negotiated liberalization	Unconstrained policy change
Belarus	Strong statist executive	Representation of statist interests	No liberalization	Policy stasis

and promised future prosperity. But the electorate had little voice in either case; differences in the power and political access of state elites mattered more for welfare outcomes.

The politics of welfare state restructuring in the four cases is shown in table 5.2.

THE DEMOCRATIC CASES: POLAND AND HUNGARY

Poland

Poland began the transition with a constitutional system somewhat like Russia's, a mixed presidential-parliamentary regime with polarization and conflict between the executive and legislature. In the early 1990s, political parties were highly unstable, the legislature was too fragmented to sustain a government, and a liberal technocratic reform team dominated policy making.[7] From the 1993 legislative election, however, parties stabilized, presidential power diminished, and a normal parliamentary system emerged. Centrist parties dominated the political spectrum, and a modified proportional representation electoral system produced coalition governments. Parliamentary victories translated directly into control of the government and public

---

[7] Voytek Zybek, "The Fragmentation of Poland's Political Party System," *Communist and Post-Communist Studies* 26 (1993): 47–71; Frances Millard, *The Anatomy of the New Poland: Post-Communist Politics in Its First Phase* (Aldershot, UK: Edward Elgar, 1994).

policy, institutionalizing the mechanisms for societal representation and feedback.

During the postcommunist decade, center-left and center-right coalitions alternated in power. The core of the left coalition, the Democratic Left Alliance (DLA), was a communist successor party that (unlike its Russian counterpart) had abandoned hard-left politics and identified itself with European social democracy. It was supported by a cross-class constituency that included a large component of workers and socially weak groups as well as middle-class strata. The DLA favored the continuation of economic reforms and at the same time "articulated a desire to guard some of the most important social guarantees of communism" and reaffirmed the social responsibility of the state against the ideology of liberal minimalism.[8] Its victory in the 1993 legislative election is commonly seen as a powerful electoral protest against technocratic liberalism and the social costs of the early shock therapy reform. Once in power, the DLA moderated social policy, raised public-sector wages, and increased spending, even as it initiated liberalizing structural changes. The antireform electoral protest that brought polarization and deadlock to the Russian polity in mid-decade instead brought moderation and gradual change to Poland.

The center-right coalition, Solidarity Electoral Action (SEA), that won the 1997 election accelerated programmatic welfare state liberalization, including pension, health, and education reforms, in a period of ongoing economic recovery. But it sustained expenditure levels and was forced to build broad alliances in order to make structural changes. In sum, the political power balance between the supporters and opponents of liberalization in the Polish party and government structures shifted around a centrist consensus, slowing and then accelerating restructuring. Programmatic change was gradual, negotiated, and weakly correlated with economic and fiscal pressures.

Poland's three major trade union federations, the famous Solidarity, Solidarity 80, and the Communist-successor National Confederation of Trade Unions (OPZZ), played significant roles in politics. The OPZZ formed a stable alliance with the communist successor party in 1990, providing a working-class base for the future DLA and a source of pressure on the center-right coalition that governed from 1990 to 1994. Solidarity fragmented and split into the radical Solidarity 80 and a political wing

---

[8] Linda J. Cook and Mitchell A. Orenstein, "The Return of the Left and Its Impact on the Welfare State in Russia, Poland, and Hungary," in *Left Parties and Social Policy in Postcommunist Europe*, edited by Linda J. Cook, Mitchell A. Orenstein, and Marilyn Rueschemeyer (Boulder: Westview Press, 1999), 74–75.

that formed the core of the center-right SEA. Levels of trade union activism and strikes were comparatively high in Poland during the early 1990s; 1992 saw large-scale strikes against wage arrears, and in 1993 a public-sector strike effectively brought down the Suchocka government.[9]

Critics charge that the apparent political access of Polish unions did not translate into a defense of labor interests, that the unions backed adjustment, acquiescing in policies that led to the rapid growth of unemployment, declining wages, and the impoverishment of workers.[10] But union activism and labor mobilization, although they did not attempt to block market transition, did affect social provision and welfare state change. As later discussion in this chapter will show, activism contributed to pressures for compensatory welfare policies, especially in the early shock therapy period.[11] Labor protests kept workers' grievances high on the political agenda, and organized labor formed part of the social base for the center-left alliance that moderated the reform program and shored up the state's commitment to public social provision.[12] Polish unions did not, however, produce a European-style institutionalized system of social partnership or tripartite bargaining.

Hungary

Hungary's founding election in 1990 produced a stable parliamentary system. Although the initial parties splintered and regrouped, as in Poland the political spectrum focused around moderate left and moderate right parties, and parliamentary victories gave control of the government alternately to center-right and center-left coalitions. Two features of Hun-

---

[9]   On strike activity in Poland, see Gregorz Ekiert and Jan Kubic, "Collective Protest in Post-Communist Poland: A Research Report," *Communist and Post-Communist Studies* 31, no. 2 (1998): 91–117; levels of protest were high in comparison to other Eastern European states, but low in comparison to the industrial democracies.

[10]   See David Ost, "The Weakness of Symbolic Strength: Labor and Union Identity in Poland, 1989–2000," in Crowely and Ost, *Workers after Workers' States*, 79–96; Steven Levitsky and Lucan Way, "Between a Shock and a Hard Place: The Dynamics of Labor-Backed Adjustment in Poland and Argentina," *Comparative Politics* 30, no. 2 (1998), 171–92.

[11]   Tomasz Inglot, "The Politics of Social Policy Reform in Post-Communist Poland: Government Responses to the Social Insurance Crisis during 1989–1993," *Communist and Post-Communist Studies* 28, no. 3 (1995): 361–73.

[12]   Osa makes a parallel argument, showing on the basis of protest-data analysis that workers' strikes and strike threats in Poland were effective in gaining concessions from employers and governments, and maintained pressure on government to take workers' interests into account, although she explicitly distinguishes strikes from efforts to work through political institutions; see Maryjane Osa, "Contention and Democracy: Labor Protest in Poland, 1989–1993," *Communist and Post-Communist Studies* 31, no. 1 (1998): 29–42.

gary's political system are distinctive and significant for the present analysis. First, Hungary has a mixed single-member district (SMD)– proportional representation (PR) electoral system that tends to concentrate power in a dominant parliamentary party and a "positive vote of no confidence" rule that functions to insulate the government from parliamentary opposition.[13] These features tend to limit representativeness and accountability. On the other hand, the Constitutional Court has played an unusually prominent activist role in welfare policy as "the principal guardian of the old regime's social safety net and a sharp critic of government attempts to curtail the same."[14] It has at several points nullified governmental efforts to retrench and restructure the welfare state.

Hungary's initial conservative government implemented moderate economic reform and restructured social services. But despite a sharp decline in GDP it did not cut other social expenditures; rather, it increased them to cushion the effects of reform. A large protest vote nevertheless materialized in 1994, giving a parliamentary majority to the Socialists, who promised to moderate the social impacts of the transition. Here the Hungarian story diverges from the Polish.

Confronting a serious financial crisis, the Socialists reversed course, implementing in 1995 an austerity plan (the Bokros Plan) that entailed deep retrenchment as well as restructuring of the welfare state.[15] The Bokros Plan was a betrayal of the Socialists' electoral promises as well as the expectations of their trade union allies and electorate. It highlights the limits of electoral accountability in the face of strong financial pressures in Hungary's transitional democracy. But the Bokros Plan was modified, in response to both Constitutional Court rulings that reinstated some benefits and public-sector strikes that brought a softening of wage cuts. And later expenditure increases under both the Socialists and their more conservative successors partially restored welfare state effort.

Hungarian trade unions exercised influence on welfare politics through both strikes and political alliances. In 1991 and again in 1995, union-led strikes brought the government to the bargaining table and forced concessions. The 1991 strikes were a factor in the maintenance of

[13]   David Stark and Leszlo Bruszt, *Postsocialist Pathways: Transforming Politics and Property in East Central Europe* (Cambridge, UK: Cambridge University Press, 1998), 170–75. Parliament can vote no confidence only if it can simultaneously propose a new government.
[14]   Rudolf L. Tokes, "Party Politics and Political Participation in Postcommunist Hungary," in Karen Dawisha and Bruce Parrott, *The Consolidation of Democracy in East-Central Europe*, (Cambridge, UK: Cambridge University Press, 1997), 122.
[15]   Cook and Orenstein, "Return."

social expenditure levels by the first elected government, which, "fearing a disruption similar to the [earlier] taxi blockade, ceded and reshuffled the state budget to cover certain social policy measures."[16] From 1991 to 1993, unions participated in co-decision-making bodies that gave them some policy influence. Several union federations made alliances with political parties, most prominently the communist successor union confederation, the National Council of Trade Unions (SZOT), with the Socialists. The Socialists began to develop a web of neo-corporatist institutions, but effective tripartite bargaining was not institutionalized. The center-right government that was elected in 1997 marginalized organized labor. Then in 2002 the Socialists reestablished cooperation and brought union leaders into government.

Andras Toth captures the situation in Hungary at the end of the 1990s: "Each of the major union confederations had moments of strength due to the mobilization of workers and moments of political influence due to links with political parties. However, . . . momentum for the construction of a social-democratic type of industrial relations . . . broke down, and the Hungarian industrial relations system is again in transition, this time seemingly away from the practices of Continental Europe."[17] In sum, the alliance of socialists and unions produced a weaker defense of the welfare state in Hungary than in Poland, and neither state institutionalized the neo-corporatist arrangements that have provided unions with regularized participation in labor, fiscal, and welfare policy making in Western Europe.

THE ELECTORAL-AUTHORITARIAN CASES:
KAZAKHSTAN AND BELARUS

Kazakhstan

Kazakhstan began the transition with an elected legislature and incipient political parties. By mid-decade, however, the initial process of democratic institution building had all but ceased and power was concentrated in the presidency of Nursultan Nazarbaev. Nazarbaev twice dissolved parliament before the 1995 constitution formally expanded presidential power and rendered the legislature a largely consultative body. Under

---

[16]   Andras Toth, "The Failure of Social-Democratic Unionism in Hungary," in Crowley and Ost, *Workers after Workers' States,* 46.

[17]   Toth, "Failure," in Crowley and Ost, *Workers* (2001), 54.

the constitution, the president appoints the cabinet and all government officials, initiates legislation, has broad decree and veto powers, dominates the judiciary, and heads a centralized unitary state. Political parties remain legal, but their leaders are subject to arbitrary restrictions and intimidation and electoral outcomes are often fraudulent. In sum, political institutions retain almost no autonomy and the president's power is virtually unconstrained.[18] Kazakhstan, nevertheless, falls short of full-blown authoritarianism. Throughout the 1990s, independent political parties continued to elect small numbers of deputies to the legislature, which has rights to enact legislation. Pockets of opposition and the potential for challenge persist.[19]

The executive pursued a consistent policy of privatization, stabilization, and liberalization of both the macroeconomy and the welfare state, relying mainly on presidential decree powers to pass reforms.[20] Until it was dissolved, the first legislature resisted the economic privatization program, and small parties rooted in the communist past have continued to protest against welfare state reform. In the mid-1990s, the legislature threatened to block austerity budgets and initially rejected pension reform, but deputies gave in to presidential intimidation.[21] Trade unions that stage strikes and protests have been overtly repressed. Representative institutions play marginal roles. Plebiscitary elections provide some possibility for societal feedback and protest, and they constitute a forum in which Nazarbaev must make an appeal for popular support. Here he offered mainly national pride for Kazakhs, political stability in the ethnically divided state, and the promise to distribute postreform proceeds from the country's vast oil and mineral wealth. In sum, the balance of political power in party and governmental organizations has fallen heavily on the side of retrenchment and liberalization.

In Russia, with the weakening of institutions that represented societal interests, bargaining over welfare resources became concentrated mainly within the state. Similarly for Kazakhstan, according to Martha Brill Olcott, "with the muscle taken out of parliament, the cabinet and

---

[18]   Martha Brill Olcott, *Kazakhstan: Unfulfilled Promise* (Washington, D.C.: Carnegie Endowment, 2002); Michael Fergus and Janar Jandosova, *Kazakhastan: Coming of Age* (London: Stacey International, 2003).

[19]   Stephen Levitsky and Lucan A. Way, "The Rise of Competitive Authoritarianism," *Journal of Democracy* 13, no. 2 (April 2002), 51–65.

[20]   In 1995, for example, more than 150 presidential decrees were issued to promote market reforms.

[21]   Olcott, *Kazakhstan*, 113–14.

ministry system [became] one of the few potential arenas for political contestation."[22] But state-based welfare stakeholders proved much weaker in Kazakhstan than in Russia, and IFI advisors had much greater access and influence. Within the governmental apparatus, power was increasingly concentrated in the presidential administration. There were "repeated attacks on the institutional framework [of government] through repeated opening and closing of agencies," and the influence of ministries fell over the decade.[23] The executive dismantled and transformed both inherited welfare programs and the ministerial structures that administered them. In 1997, responding in part to IFI pressures to downsize the bureaucracy, Nazarbaev precipitously eliminated one-third of the national government's personnel and ministries, with heavy turnover and appointment of presidential loyalists at the top levels. In 1999, he again reorganized the social-sector institutions. Health, Education, and other ministries were merged into a single ministry, with some functions transferred to nongovernmental agencies.[24] Between 1991 and 2001, central governmental institutions were subject to "an extraordinary degree of reshuffling . . . and slow deprofessionalization."[25] In sum, Nazarbaev's power was not strongly vested in state institutions, and they were unable to defend their resource claims.

Belarus

Belarus had the weakest democratic moment of these transition states. The first democratically elected parliament began sitting in 1995 and was dissolved by President Alexandr Lukashenka in 1996. A constitution, passed by referendum in that year, established a presidentialist system similar to that in Kazakhstan. A broad spectrum of small, intelligentsia-based political parties persists in the capital, but they are too weak and internally divided to challenge the president. The largest, an unreformed communist-cum-agrarian successor party with a substantial mass base and parliamentary corps, has expended most of its energy in futile power struggles with the executive. Political challengers are subject to arbitrary violence, imprisonment, and disappearance. Independent trade

---

[22]   Olcott, *Kazakhstan*, 114.

[23]   Sally N. Cummings, *Kazakhstan: Power and the Elite* (New York: I. B. Taurus, 2005), 53.

[24]   Sally Cummings, *Kazakhstan: Center-Periphery Relations* (London: Royal Institute of International Affairs, 2000).

[25]   Cummings, *Kazakhstan: Power*, 49, 53.

unions were declared illegal in 1995 after a transit workers' strike over wage arrears was repressed by security forces. In sum, "every effort has been consciously made since 1994 to inhibit the development of civil society."[26] The regime remains electoral-authoritarian; periodic elections and referenda are held in Belarus and President Lukashenka appears to retain substantial support, especially among older and rural strata.

The communist-era state was kept largely intact during the abortive Belarussian transition. Although the Stanislav Shushkevich–Viacheslav Kebich government of the First Republic (1991–1994) had some democratic leanings, it stifled market reforms and, with the support of the communist-dominated parliament and pressure from economic administrators, largely preserved the state monopoly on property and the command-administrative system.[27] While some spontaneous privatization took place, it was comparatively limited, and elites remained dependent on administrative positions and state subsidies. In sharp contrast to Kazakhstan, during the 1990s there was a "slow and often stagnant process of transformation within administrative structures [with] many of the patronage clientele of the 1980s still in office."[28] This stable state-bureaucratic elite formed the basis of Lukashenka's regime, providing "the two pillars on which the power of the presidency is based—collective farms and collective labor in state-run enterprises."[29] Lukashenka, in turn, relied on enterprise and collective farm managers to deliver the compliance and votes of their subordinates. The maintenance of the old social contract through budget financing and administrative planning and control of the social sector constituted a key part of this governing formula, in which state welfare bureaucracies maintained their positions and claims on resources.

[26] Steven M. Eke and Taras Kuzio, "Sultanism in Eastern Europe: The Socio-Political Roots of Authoritarian Populism in Belarus," *Europe-Asia Studies* 52, no. 3 (2000): 539.

[27] Kathleen J. Mihalisko, "Belarus: Retreat to Authoritarianism," in *Democratic Changes and Authoritarian Reactions in Ukraine, Belarus, and Moldova*, edited by Karen Dawisha and Bruce Parrott, pp. 223–81 (Cambridge, UK: Cambridge University Press, 1997); David R. Marples and Uladzimir Padhol, "The Opposition in Belarus: History, Potential, and Perspectives," in *Independent Belarus: Domestic Determinants, Regional Dynamics, and Implications for the West*, edited by Margarita M. Balmaceda, James I. Clem, and Lisbeth L. Tarlow (Cambridge, Mass.: Harvard University Press, 2002), 55–76.

[28] Rainer Linder, "The Lukashenka Phenomenon," in *Independent Belarus: Domestic Determinants, Regional Dynamics, and Implications for the West*, edited by Margarita M. Balmaceda, James I. Clem, and Lisbeth L. Tarlow (Cambridge, Mass.: Harvard University Press, 2002), 79.

[29] Hans-Georg Wieck, "The Role of International Organizations in Belarus," in *Independent Belarus*, 368.

The Lukashenko government did face significant levels of trade union activism from both inherited and new independent unions during the mid-1990s, including protests over wage arrears and other economic hardships brought by Belarus's deep recession and cuts in real social expenditures. Unlike the Polish and Hungarian governments, which responded with compensatory policies, Lukashenka repressed the protests and outlawed the unions. Although it did maintain an extensive welfare state, the Belarussian government did not negotiate with societal interests or adjust social expenditures in response to social needs.

In sum, the balance of power in government and state institutions fell heavily on the side of preserving old welfare structures. Although the severe economic decline of the early to mid-1990s forced reductions in real spending, social infrastructure and services were kept in place with minimal restructuring or privatization. Employment in Belarus's social sector increased more than in the other cases during the 1990s; health and education were the major areas for job creation and for political patronage[30] (see table 5.9 later in the chapter). Substantial, politically motivated subsidies to the Belarusian economy from Russia undergirded this strategy, and dependence on Russia was encouraged by the disproportionately ethnic-Russian provincial and local bureaucracies.[31] Belarus represents a distinctive postcommunist welfare state trajectory.

DIVERGENT PATTERNS OF WELFARE STATE CHANGE: EXPENDITURES AND RESTRUCTURING

Social conditions in all of the postcommunist states worsened dramatically as a result of output declines and subsidy cuts, but there were *three major differences* in the patterns of change across the cases.

1. *Compensation for welfare losses.* In the democratic states, societies were compensated for welfare losses by selective increases in welfare effort during the transitional recessions. Compensation took different forms in Poland and Hungary, but in both

[30] International Monetary Fund, *Republic of Belarus: Selected Issues* (IMF Country Report no. 04/139) (Washington, D.C.: IMF, 2004), 8. Health and education employment increased from 14 to 18 percent of total employment between 1990 and 2002.

[31] Eke and Kuzio, "Sultanism in Eastern Europe."

cases it constituted an effort by liberalizing governments to anticipate and respond to welfare losses. In Kazakhstan during the same period, the welfare state underwent deep retrenchment, whereas in Belarus there was little change in welfare effort during the prolonged recession.

2. *Pattern of liberalization.* In Poland, and to a lesser extent Hungary, liberalization was a gradual and negotiated process. By contrast, in Kazakhstan the executive dominated an early and radical change toward welfare state privatization and means testing, and in Belarus the old structures were largely kept in place.

3. *Level of post-recession welfare provision.* During economic recovery, the democratic states maintained a commitment to predominantly public expenditures for social provision, nearly universal access to services, and comparatively high levels of social insurance coverage. In Kazakhstan, although real social spending increased with economic growth, welfare effort remained comparatively low, private-public expenditure ratios for social services were high, and parts of the population were excluded from access to basic services and social insurance coverage. In Belarus, welfare spending recovered with the economy, and nearly universal access to a heavily centralized and bureaucratized welfare system remained the norm.

Welfare Expenditures and Compensation during Recession

In Poland, compensation was directed mainly toward workers who lost jobs or were pushed out of the labor force into early retirement, and it was provided in the depths of the recession. According to Augusto Lopez-Claros and Sergei Alexashenko of the IMF, "increases in social expenditure in Poland in 1990–1992 were particularly high (9 percentage points of GDP), mainly in the form of increases in pensions and unemployment benefits . . . intended to offset declines in real wages and in income from consumer subsidies following price liberalization."[32] When the center-right government passed the shock therapy program in 1989, it also instituted unemployment benefits with liberal eligibility rules and extended early retirement benefits. The result was a large expansion of social expenditure, a doubling of cash social security payments and a large increase in the number of the new pension-eligible. Total social

---

[32] Augusto Lopez-Claros and Sergei V. Alexashenko, *Fiscal Policy Issues during the Transition in Russia* (Washington, D.C.: IMF, March, 1998), 26.

spending increased from 25 percent of GDP in 1990 to 32 percent in 1991, mainly because of increases in pension expenditures. By 1993–1994, Poland was spending more than 15 percent of its GDP on pensions and employment policies alone, nearly equal to the total welfare effort in Russia during the same period.[33] These policies were largely the consequence of ad hoc decision making, and they resulted in accumulating fiscal problems and pressures for restructuring. But they did cushion the impacts of reform for the most mobilized constituencies in Poland during a period when economic and fiscal pressures for spending cuts were high.[34]

As Thomas Inglot's account of Poland's social politics in the early 1990s makes clear, these policies were sustained by a mobilized labor movement, opposition left parties, and a relatively strong labor ministry. The Minister of Labor, Jack Kuron, had a major influence on social policy decisions, and trade unions, opposition parties, and pensioners actively pressed to preserve social rights. Proposed reductions in benefits produced effective social and parliamentary opposition, with "Solidarity, the left-wing trade unions (the OPZZ), and most opposition parties in the Sejm united in their opposition. . . ."[35] Attempts to cut social spending produced strikes among public-sector workers in health and education that contributed to the government's collapse in 1993 and the election of the left-leaning DLA. The contrast with Russia, where public-sector unions found weak and temporary party allies and significant strike movements brought at best the temporary clearing of wage arrears, is striking. Starker fiscal pressures in Russia during this period are part of the explanation, but they combined with weaker societal constraints to produce sharp declines in public expenditures.

In Hungary, consumer subsidies were cut during the early reform years, but most other social expenditures stayed in place. There was a "(tacit) agreement [among the parties of the center-right governing coalition] on preserving, and subsequently gradually modifying, the basic institutions of the Kadarist welfare state."[36] Although pension spending did not increase, it remained high. The system of unemployment insurance that was already in place was expanded by the 1991 Employment Act into a

---

[33]   Jorge Garces, Francisco Rodenas, and Stephanie Carretero, "Observations on the Progress of Welfare-State Construction in Hungary, Poland, and the Czech Republic," *Post-Soviet Affairs* 19, no. 4 (2003): 344–45.

[34]   Claus Offe, "The Politics of Social Policy in East European Transitions: Antecedents, Agents, and Agendas of Reform," *Social Research* 60, no. 4 (1993): 649–84.

[35]   Inglot, "Politics," 371.

[36]   Tokes, "Party Politics," 118.

comparatively very generous system. Trade unions were actively involved in designing the legislation, which increased benefit amounts to 70 percent of previous income for up to one year.[37] Universal family allowances and other child benefits, which were quite generous in Hungary at the end of the communist period, were initially retained. In the early 1990s, family allowances reached virtually all households with children and unemployment benefits were received by 90 percent of households with an unemployed head. In 1993, while it was still in deep recession, Hungary spent more than 11 percent of its GDP on pensions and unemployment benefits, 19 percent on all cash transfers, and more than 27 percent on social expenditures—above the average for the European Union and the OECD.[38] The social safety net remained extensive and progressive until the introduction of the Bokros Plan in 1995, which reduced social spending for the first time in the transition.

Janos Kornai explains these policies as resulting from a combination of path dependence and political constraint. Although it carried out macroeconomic reforms that reduced wages and increased unemployment, the center-right Hungarian Democratic Forum that was elected in 1990 committed itself to maintaining social security. It was also influenced by a disruptive transport strike in 1990, after which "the government retreated. . . . The episode acted as a precedent. The Antall and Boross governments of 1990–1994 never again ventured an action that would elicit mass opposition. . . . while the country's economic situation steadily deteriorated, the system of transfers tended to expand."[39] Analysts agree that the Bokros Plan, the austerity package introduced by the Socialists in 1995, was a response to the financial crisis produced in part by these policies. Many criticize the social expenditure policies of the early 1990s in both Poland and Hungary as financially unsustainable and poorly targeted.[40] My point here is that they testify to the comparative political constraint on retrenchment in transitional democracies.

In Kazakhstan, by contrast, social expenditures across all categories were cut sharply during the early transition years. A thinning of the social

[37] Dana L. Brown, "The New Politics of Welfare in Post-Socialist Central Eastern Europe" (Ph.D. diss., Massachusetts Institute of Technology, 2005), 170–72.

[38] Christiaan Grootaert, *Poverty and Social Transfers in Hungary* (Washington, D.C.: World Bank, March 20, 1997), 2–5.

[39] Janos Kornai, "Paying the Bill for Goulash Communism: Hungarian Development and Macro Stabilization in a Political-Economy Perspective," in *Struggle and Hope: Essays on Stabilization and Reform in a Post-Socialist Economy*, edited by Janos Kornai (Northampton, MA: Edward Elgar, 1997), 127, 139.

[40] See, for example, Inglot, "Politics"; Kornai, "Paying the Bill for Goulash Communism"; Orenstein, *Out of the Red*.

safety net proceeded in tandem with the decline in GDP. Public expenditure on social protection declined from 11.2 percent of GDP in 1992 to 6.6 percent in 1996. Pensions, which constituted the bulk of transfers, fell from 8.2 to 4 percent of GDP. The number of pensioners was reduced by legislation that raised the age for eligibility, and the real value of pensions declined by more than two-thirds between 1993 and 1995. An unemployment benefit was established, but coverage remained limited, compensation levels remained well below subsistence, and arrears were common. Eligibility for social assistance was severely restricted, and public outlays for health and education plummeted.[41] Kazakhstan spent a smaller proportion of its GDP on social protection than Russia and, to an even greater extent, dealt with deficits through the accumulation of wage and pension arrears. In 1998, the government suspended its own minimum wage laws until 2004.[42] Although some small categorical benefits and privileges were preserved, this was a polity in which the executive faced virtually no constraints in retrenching the welfare state.

Belarus carried out very modest compensation in pension programs during its recession and generally maintained its welfare effort in other areas. Universal benefits and subsidies were kept in place, although real levels fell and problems such as poverty and health-care breakdowns were common. Like Russia, Belarus did not redirect significant resources to new transitional social problems such as unemployment. Although unemployment levels remained much lower than in the other cases, officially reaching about 4 percent of the labor force in the mid-1990s, no effective state assistance was provided to those affected.

Table 5.3 shows comparative welfare effort in three major areas of the welfare state—pensions, health, and education—across the five cases. (The table does not include all social expenditures because of limits of comparable data; in particular, the high levels of social benefits in Hungary are not evident here.) As the table shows, Poland, Hungary, and Belarus maintained comparatively high levels of expenditure in all three areas. Russia and, especially, Kazakhstan were at considerably lower levels of welfare state effort during the recession and retained these levels well into the economic recovery. In Kazakhstan, public spending on health care and pensions as a percentage of GDP stood at one-half its 1992 level

---

[41] World Bank, *Kazakhstan: Living Standards during the Transition* (Report no. 17520-KZ) (Washington, D.C.: World Bank, March 23, 1998), 31–33. Spending rose significantly, to over 7 percent of GDP in 1997, mainly to clear pension arrears.

[42] Olcott, *Kazakhstan.*

TABLE 5.3
Public expenditures on health, education, and pensions, 1990–2002 (% GDP)

Country	Sector	1989–1992	1993	1994	1995	1996	1997	1998	1999	2000	2001	2002
Poland	Health	4.8	4.6	4.6	4.6	—	4.2	4.2	4.6	—	4.6	4.7
	Education	5.4[a]	5.4	5.3	5.2	5.4	5.5	5.3	5.1	5.1	5.0	6
	Pensions	8.7	15.0	14.9	14.5	14.3	14.4	12.8	12.3	11.5	10.8	11.2
Hungary	Health	6.4	6.8	—	6.3	6.0	5.6	5.2	5.3	5	5.1	5.5
	Education	6.6[b]	6.5	6.4	5.5	4.9	4.3	4.8	5.1	5.3	5	6
	Pensions	10.5	10.4	11.4	10.5	9.7	7.1	7.5	7.9	7.8	7	7.6
Russian Federation	Health	2.5	3.6	4.0	3.4	2.6	3.1	2.5	2.2	2.2	2.0	2.3
	Education	3.6	4.0	4.4	3.4	3.9	4.5	3.6	3.1	3.0	3.1	3.7
	Pensions	5.0	6.0	5.9	5.3	5.8	7.5	6.4	5.6	4.7	5.7	7.3
Kazakhstan	Health	4.4[b]	2.5	2.0	2.0	2.7	3.2	3.5	2.0	2.1	2.0	2.0
	Education	4.0[b]	4.0	3.3	4.5	4.5	3.9	—	4	3	3	3
	Pensions	8.2[b]	4.1	3.8	4.3	5.0	7.1[c]	—	—	—	3.8	—
Belarus	Health	5.3	4.7	—	4.8	—	5.2	5.6	5.0	5.0	5.1	5[e]
	Education	4.7[d]	5.9	—	5.6	—	6.6	2	6.1	6.2	6.5	6.8
	Pensions	5.4	7.6	5.6	7.5	8.4	7.7	7.7	7.3	8.2	—	—

Sources: World Bank, *Balancing Protection and Opportunity: A Strategy for Social Protection in Transition Economies* (Washington, D.C.: World Bank, May 3, 2000), 56–97; World Bank, World Development Indicators, 1998, 2004, 2006, available at devdata.worldbank, org; International Monetary Fund, *Republic of Belarus: Statistical Appendix* (IMF Country Report no. 03/118) (Washington, D.C.: IMF, April 2003), 25; Natalia Murashkevich, "The Pension Scheme in Belarus: Situation Analysis and Perspectives," *International Social Security Review* 54, no. 2–3 (2001): 164; Maksut Kulzhanov and Judith Healy, *Health Care Systems in Transition: Kazakhstan* (Copenhagen: European Observatory on Health Systems and Policies, 1999), 22; Michael Keane and Eswar Prasad, "Poland: Inequity, Transfers, and Growth in Transition," *Finance and Development* 38, no. 1 (2001) 50–54; Martha Brill Olcott, *Kazakhstan: Unfulfilled Promise* (Washington, D.C.: Carnegie Endowment, 2002), 263; Elaine Fultz, ed., *Pension Reform in Central and Eastern Europe, vol. 1, Restructuring with Privatization: Case Studies of Hungary and Poland* (ILO, 2002), 64, 106. OECD Social Expenditures Database, available at: www.oecd. org/els/social/expenditures; "Republic of Kazakhstan: Statistical Appendix" (Washington, D.C.: IMF, July, November, 2004).

[a] 1990.
[b] 1991.
[c] Increase is because of payment of pension arrears.
[d] 1992.
[e] Preliminary.

in 2002, whereas in Russia it remained below the levels of the early 1990s. The table also shows the declines in pension expenditures as percentage of GDP in Poland and Hungary in the later 1990s from the very high levels during the period of compensation policies.

Patterns of Restructuring

During the 1990s, Poland, Hungary, and Kazakhstan, like Russia, made changes in the basic institutional features of their inherited welfare systems, adopting key components of the liberal model. State monopolies in welfare provision were eliminated, and public financing and administration of social services were restricted. Governments cut consumer subsidies and universal social benefits, and shifted toward means or income testing. In health care, privatization, competition, insurance mechanisms, and decentralization were introduced, and in education, markets and fees were introduced. Pension reforms reduced the redistributive aspects of the systems, tightened the links between contributions and benefits, and shifted part of contributions to mandatory individual investment accounts. Labor codes were revised to allow for greater flexibility in the hiring and firing of workers and to weaken dual-wage-earner accommodations. In all cases except Belarus, social insurance markets, individual responsibility and choice, and at least some degree of poverty-targeting of social benefits partially replaced the communist-era state welfare systems.

Virtually all of these changes affected welfare programs that had large political constituencies both in society and within postcommunist states. According to the comparative welfare state literature, these constituencies should have used the available political institutions to defend established entitlements. Indeed, they did so, and the differences in political institutions and power balances produced major variations in the patterns of liberal restructuring. Liberalizing welfare state change was more gradual, negotiated, and limited in the democratic states than in authoritarian Kazakhstan and semi-authoritarian Russia. Democratic institutions provided stronger representation of societal welfare constituencies through social democratic parties, trade unions, and labor ministries.

In the authoritarian cases, the strength of state-based stakeholders and their place in the executive's power base were key to welfare state maintenance or dismantling. Economic constraints mattered for these differences, but the cases varied independently of economic factors, and liberalization in both the democratic and authoritarian cases continued well into the period of economic recovery. Next, I look at the general patterns of welfare state restructuring across the cases and then focus on the politics of the pension and health-care reforms to illustrate the differences in policy processes(see table 5.4).

Poland liberalized its welfare state gradually as its economy recovered. In 1995–1996, income or means testing was introduced for family allowances and other benefits.[43] In 1999, after an extended period of negotiation, the government implemented a partial privatization of the pension system. Health and education reforms proceeded in a piecemeal fashion. The management of both sectors was decentralized and private schools and medical practices were legalized in the early 1990s, but budget financing of health care continued until 1999. At that point, the National Health Insurance Act introduced regional funds.[44] Budget subsidies have, however Insurance, remained significant. Labor Code restrictions on employment were progressively liberalized through the 1990s to increase flexibility in hiring and firing (e.g., part-time and fixed-term contracts) in the overall economy. By the end of the 1990s, Labor Code revisions had made Poland's legislation more liberal than that of the European Union, close to the OECD average for employment protection.[45]

The pension and health-care reform case studies later in the chapter show that changes in the welfare state were gradual and limited because of the process of political negotiation. The initial liberalizing proposals of government reformers and Finance Ministries were moderated through bargaining with representative institutions and concessions to pro-welfare interests. This pattern contrasts sharply with the rapid, radical, and largely failed reforms that were imposed by the Russian executive in the early 1990s. The more gradual process also provided several advantages. In Poland, pension and health insurance markets were introduced at the end of the 1990s, after several years of development of market institutions and regulatory frameworks. Later liberalization coincided with the growth of the economy, wages, and incomes, transferring costs to a population that had some capacity to absorb them. Negotiations meant that more interests were accommodated in the reforms and should have increased the likelihood that stakeholders would cooperate.

[43]   Michael F. Forster and Istvan Gyorgy Toth, "Child Poverty and Family Transfers in the Czech Republic, Hungary, and Poland," *Journal of European Social Policy* 11, no. 4 (2001), 324–41.

[44]   *OECD Economic Surveys: Poland, 1999–2000* (Paris: OECD 2000), 93–114.

[45]   Sandrine Cazes and Alena Nesporova, *Labor Markets in Transition: Balancing Flexibility and Security in Central and East Europe* (Geneva: ILO, 2003), 100.

TABLE 5.4
Patterns of welfare state restructuring in Russia, Poland, Hungary, Kazakhstan, and Belarus

Social Sector	Main Liberalizing Policies	Russia	Poland	Hungary	Kazakhstan	Belarus
Pension insurance	Privatization; Individual invested accounts	2001/02 Partial privatization	1999 Partial privatization	1998 Partial privatization	1998 Full privatization for new retirees (minimum guarantee)	No mandatory privatization
Education	Decentralization, Private schools legalized	Early 1990s	Early 1990s	Early 1990s	1996	Centralized, No private schools
	Fees in public schools	Some fees	Public finance	Public finance	Some fees, higher education private	Public finance
Health care	Decentralization, Private practices Insurance	1992 Dominant insurance financing	Early 1990s 1999, Partial insurance financing	Early 1990, Partial insurance financing	1996 Dominant insurance financing	Centralized, Publicly financed
Social subsidies and assistance	Replacement of subsidies with income-based eligibility requirements. Means testing	1998 Child benefit only	1995–96, Family benefits only	1995 Broad range of benefits, child, family, maternity (partly rescinded)	1994 Most benefits	Untargeted subsidies continue
Labor market, flexibilization Employment Laws Index[a]	Revisions of Labor Code to flexibilize hiring, firing and employment conditions	ELI=61	ELI=55	ELI=54	ELI=55	ELI=77

Sources: Jorge Garces, Francisco Rodenas, and Stephanie Carretero, "Observations on the Progress of Welfare-State Construction in Hungary, Poland, and the Czech Republic," *Post-Soviet Affairs* 19 no. 4 (2003): 365, and sources cited in text.

[a]The Employment Laws Index covers flexibility of hiring (part-time and fixed-term contracts), conditions of employment (minimum wage, hours per week, overtime), and flexibility of firing rules; Scale ranges from 0 = most flexible to 100 = most rigid; see World Bank, *Doing Business 2004: Understanding Regulation* (Washington: World Bank, 2004) at rru.worldbank.org/doingbusines

In Hungary the introduction of programmatic change was somewhat more radical than in Poland. At the beginning of the 1990s, the government implemented a health-care reform, including decentralization and the introduction of an insurance system, private practice, and patient co-pays.[46] Education was also decentralized, with financing and administration moved to the local level and private schools permitted. In 1995, as part of the Bokros Plan, the government introduced radical revisions (compared to Poland) in child, family, and maternity benefits, moving to strict income testing that produced a sharp decline in the number of eligible households. Pension reform paralleled that in Poland. Hungarian labor legislation was marginally more liberalized than the Polish legislation by the end of the 1990s.[47]

Welfare state restructuring proved somewhat more radical in Hungary than in Poland because societal welfare constituencies were weaker and less organized and a conjunction of political and economic factors favored liberalization. Restructuring was initiated by a center-right government that, even while it did maintain social expenditures, was able to implement structural welfare reforms because it faced a less active labor movement and less resistance from public-sector unions.[48] The levels of labor protest in Hungary during this period were considerably lower than in Poland. The Socialists came to govern in Hungary under much more intense fiscal pressures and less societal mobilization than the DLA in Poland, and had both pressures and opportunities to make considerably greater, more condensed changes.

But the real differences between Poland and Hungary were smaller than they at first appear. The medical insurance model proved largely formal in Hungary; in practice, the state continued to subsidize shortfalls and the population to receive effectively free services. Hungary's Constitutional Court reinstated many of the benefits that were cut during the Bokros period, and later governments reversed other changes. To the extent that they were implemented, Hungary's early social-sector reforms are generally considered to have failed. As in Russia, the health-care reform did not significantly improve efficiency and educational decentralization produced a wide variation in standards, financing, and

[46] Garces et al., "Observations."

[47] Forster and Toth, "Child Poverty." For measures of employment law liberalization or flexibilization, see table 5.4.

[48] See Grzegorz Ekiert and Jan Kubik, "Contentious Politics in New Democracies: East Germany, Hungary, Poland, and Slovakia, 1989–1993," *World Politics* 50, no. 4 (1998): 547–81.

administrative capabilities, leading to large interregional imbalances.[49] In the end, liberalization in both Poland and Hungary proved comparatively moderate, and in Hungry its more radical aspects were reversed by later decisions or largely ignored in implementation.

Structural reform in Kazakhstan, by contrast, was rapid and radical. Income tests for most types of social assistance were introduced in 1994, reducing the number of households eligible for the main program of child benefits by half. Targeting proved ineffective, with 60 percent of poor households receiving no public transfers. Private health-care services and user fees were introduced in the early 1990s, and a mandatory system of health insurance was introduced in 1996. Higher education was privatized, and although primary and secondary schools remained publicly financed, book charges and other fees were introduced in 1996.[50] Kazakhstan became the first postcommunist state to move to invested pension accounts and to legislate the nearly complete privatization of its pension system for new retirees. These changes were heavily influenced by IFIs and permitted by the weakness of both societal welfare constituencies and statist stakeholders.

In Belarus, structural welfare state change during the 1990s was minimal. The old systems of universal social subsidies, benefits, and services remained in place. The state continued to finance and administer pensions, health care, and education. Enterprises typically maintained their social facilities, providing clinics, kindergartens, housing, and so forth. Consumer and energy subsidies continued.[51] A limited number of nonstate universities were established, but these were later closed by the government because of perceived political challenge.[52] The rest of the educational system remained statist. The government did introduce unemployment benefits in 1999 but, as in Russia, financing was not redirected from existing programs, benefit levels remained below subsistence, and take-up rates were low. The Labor Code remained rigid, with

---

[49]   Garces et al., "Observations," 358–62. In Poland as well, the decentralization of the early 1990s had negative effects on social service provision; see Mitchell A. Orenstein, "The Failures of Neo-Liberal Social Policy in Central Europe," *Transition* 2, no. 13 (1996): 16–20.

[50]   World Bank, "Kazakhstan," 34–38.

[51]   World Bank, *Memorandum of the President of the IBRD and of the IFC to the Executive Directors on a Country Assistance Strategy for Belarus* (Report no. 23401-BY) (Washington, D.C.: World Bank, Feb. 16, 2002).

[52]   Irina Konchits, "Bilingual and Multilingual Universities in the Republic of Belarus," *Higher Education in Europe* 25, no. 4 (2000): 507–9. The major private university, the European Humanities University in Minsk, was closed by the Education Ministry in 2004.

employment legislation the most restrictive among Commonwealth of Independent States (CIS) and EU accession states[53] (see table 5.4).

CASE STUDIES: THE POLITICS OF PENSION AND HEALTH-CARE REFORM

Privatizing Pension Provision

Poland, Hungary, and Kazakhstan, like Russia, moved toward privatization of their pension systems in 1997–1999. Pension reform is the most studied aspect of welfare state change, and the discussion here focuses only on the political dimensions—the roles of institutions, societal and state constituencies, and international actors, in negotiating changes.[54] It draws especially on a 2000 World Bank report by Mitchell Orenstein, who interviewed participants and provides an excellent detailed mapping of the process in all three cases.[55] (Projections of comparative levels of privatization in the reformed pension systems are presented in figure 5.1, later in the chapter.)

In all postcommunist cases, pension reform was motivated by immediate fiscal pressures, as well as projections that PAYG systems would become unviable in the medium term because of demographic changes and declines in labor force participation. But the politics of reform in the democratic states differed from the politics in the authoritarian states in fundamental ways.

First, in Poland and Hungary, the Labor and Social Ministries played significant roles in defending aspects of the old redistributive system against the liberalizing agendas of Finance Ministries and World Bank emissaries. These welfare ministries served as advocates for solidaristic values, "stressing that a pension system should be designed not to bring about macroeconomic desiderata, but to serve the aged population."[56]

---

[53] International Monetary Fund, *Republic of Belarus*, 10.

[54] For studies of postcommunist pension reform that cover technical and financial aspects and differ in approach, see especially David Lindeman, Michal Rutkowski, and Olaksiy Sluchynskyy, *The Evolution of Pension Systems in Eastern Europe and Central Asia: Opportunities, Constraints, Dilemmas and Emerging Practices* (Washington, D.C.: World Bank, 2000); Elaine Fultz, *Pension Reform in Central and Eastern Europe*, vol. 1, *Restructuring with Privatization: Case Studies of Hungary and Poland* (Geneva: ILO, 2002).

[55] Mitchell A. Orenstein, *How Politics and Institutions Affect Pension Reform in Three Postcommunist Countries* (Policy Research Working Paper 2310) (Washington, D.C.: World Bank, March, 2000).

[56] Katharina Müller, "The Political Economy of Pension Reform in Eastern Europe," *International Social Security Review* 54, no. 2–3 (2001): 70.

Second, in Poland and Hungary political parties and trade unions engaged in extended debate and bargaining over the terms of reform. (Although, as in Russia, the unions and Pension Funds also bargained for their corporate interests and took side payments.) Third, concessions were made in response to the claims of societal constituencies, especially those that were strongly connected to political parties. The Finance Ministries played the larger role in shaping outcomes, but their initial proposals were significantly modified in political bargaining.

In Kazakhstan, by contrast, the initial intragovernmental negotiations over reform were held in secret, public and legislative opposition was largely ignored, and the executive dominated the process. The pension system was almost completely privatized, with little bargaining even among state-based actors. Belarus faced many of the same pressures as other transitional cases, but the public pension system remained in place.

The Cases

In 1994, Poland's Ministry of Finance proposed a fundamental pension reform featuring the introduction of a dominant funded pillar. A special governmental task force, with a World Bank official serving as plenipotentiary, generated a detailed reform plan. Initially the DLA Labor Minister tried to block the reform, and after his replacement in a government reshuffling, reform proposals were subject to extensive public discussion and tripartite bargaining with the major trade union federations. The Communist successor union (OPZZ) advocated continued dominance of the PAYG component, and the DLA pressed to maintain the redistributive elements of the old system. According to Orenstein, "Public deliberation with civil society interest groups produced . . . changes. . . . [G]overnment legislative drafts were deeply refined and revised in tripartite negotiations thanks in part to trade union representatives."[57] Solidarity, which supported the reform in principle, lobbied successfully for using the proceeds from industrial privatization to help finance the costs of pension fund transition and gained concessions for miners as well as other occupational groups. In the end, the reform was broadly supported by the public. It maintained a large redistributive PAYG component, with privatization to be phased in gradually. Political institutions empowered a range of actors to influence the outcome, although liberal actors exercised dominant influence. The Polish Pension Fund, like its Russian

[57]   Orenstein, *How Politics,* 47.

counterpart, resisted reform in an effort to preserve its own prerogatives, but it played a much more limited role in the overall process.[58]

In Hungary, the postcommunist center-left Socialist government initiated pension reform. The Finance Ministry pressed for a large funded pillar, and the World Bank financed a governmental working group to elaborate reform proposals. The main Socialist-affiliated trade union, the SZOT, proved influential in bargaining through the Interest Reconciliation Council, gaining a number of concessions on the generosity of benefits, state guarantees, and eligibility rules. The trade union also defended its corporate interests, gaining a promise that it would retain its seats on the Pension Insurance Fund (PIF) without election, thus guaranteeing its continued dominance of representation. The process was more closed and elite-dominated than in Poland, but parties and unions exercised significant influence, and the reform was phased in gradually. The list of more than twenty meetings on pension reform held in 1997 by political parties and civil society organizations stands in sharp contrast to the few constricted meetings of the National Pension Council in Russia (see chap. 4). These representative organizations clearly influenced the reform's outcome; again according to Orenstein, trade unions linked to the Socialist Party and the PIF "were able to substantially reduce the size of the new private pillar and gain other concessions."[59] The center-right coalition that won the 1997 parliamentary elections revised the reform, eliminating the PIF and curtailing the trade unions' role in pension administration, but the Socialist victory in the following parliamentary election brought the unions back in.

Kazakhstan privatized its pension system more rapidly and radically than the other cases. President Nazarbaev created an intergovernmental commission on pension reform in late 1996, and it drafted a proposal quickly and with little debate. Some government social security officials objected to the draft but, "With authoritarian political institutions and a centralized policy style, Kazakhstan was able to circumvent open disputes between different ministries and government agencies that broke out in the first stages of [reform] in Poland and Hungary."[60] Deliberations over the reform were secretive, and the government largely ignored criticism from pensioners' organizations, trade unions, and others once the draft was made public. The reform phased out the PAYG system over a

[58] Inglot, "Politics."
[59] Orenstein, *How Politics*, 38.
[60] Ibid., 20.

transition period. It was to be replaced by a minimum pension guarantee and mandatory private accounts—a significantly greater degree of privatization than in Poland, Hungary, or Russia. The government made few concessions to societal interests. Only the security forces succeeded in preserving their pension privileges. Workers in hazardous professions lost approximately half their previous pension entitlements.[61] The legislature was intimidated into passing the reform by threats of dissolution, although it did manage to insert some minor changes.

The Kazakh government did make two significant concessions, largely at the insistence of the IFIs. In 1997, it paid off pension arrears equaling 1.5 percent of GDP.[62] It also created a state pension investment fund as an alternative to private funds, which the population broadly distrusted. Both measures were motivated by a need to restore trust and generate compliance with the new pension system, which was seen as a means to deepen capital markets as well as to relieve fiscal pressures. The extent of public protest and legislative activism documented by Orenstein is unexpected, but it had little effect on the outcome. The active Kazakh labor force would be moved completely to mandatory private accounts, producing a much larger private to public ratio than in Hungary or Poland. The government made concessions to external financial institutions and to its own security forces. Otherwise, this was unconstrained liberalization.

Belarus, like Russia, moved away from direct budget financing of pensions in 1991 and created an off-budget Pension Fund that imposed high taxes on employers. Although the pension system confronted serious problems, including severe declines in the real value of pensions, the structure remained stable and expenditure levels comparatively high, above 7 percent of GDP through the 1990s. Real pension levels had recovered by 2001. At this point the Belarussian government was planning to introduce a system of individual (not invested) accounts within the state system, and other reforms were under discussion, but reforms met resistance within the government and from the incorporated trade unions. Accumulative principles were proposed only for supplementary pensions.[63]

Reforming Health Care

Scholars tend to agree that health and education are the most difficult parts of the social sector to reform successfully. First, these sectors involve

---

[61]   Ibid., 26–27.

[62]   World Bank, *Kazakhstan*, 5.

[63]   Natalia Murashkevich, "The Pension Scheme in Belarus: Situation Analysis and Perspectives," *International Social Security Review* 54, no. 2–3 (2001): 151–75.

a large number of constituencies in both society and state institutions, and here bureaucratic stakeholders have greater influence even in the democracies. Second, unlike with pensions, there exists no consensus model, no "broad vision of a better-functioning and sustainable health-care delivery system."[64] Poland, Hungary, and Kazakhstan, along with Russia, did nevertheless introduce reforms of their health-care systems during the 1990s, all informed by liberal principles of decentralization and the shift toward insurance mechanisms. They also legalized private medical practices, and mixes of formal and informal private payments grew as a proportion of health-care expenditures. I next discuss how politics affected comparative patterns of reform and show the resulting differentiation in public-private health-care expenditure ratios and access to health services across the cases.

Hungary's first postcommunist government, as previously noted, introduced reforms in health-care delivery during the early 1990s. The reforms decentralized financing and administration, created regional health insurance funds, introduced patient co-payments, and authorized private medical practices.[65] The policy process was largely technocratic, following recommendations from global policy networks (in this case particularly the OECD), with little negotiation or institutional preparation. The reforms produced institutional conflicts over resources between the inherited statist health bureaucracies and the new funds, similar to those in Russia, "constant power struggles [of the Health Insurance Fund] with the Ministry of Welfare and the Ministry of Finance."[66] Health-care unions had little say in the initial reform.[67] The reform did little to improve the health system's performance and, as previously noted, de facto supplementary state financing and universal access continued. At the end of the decade, most inherited infrastructure remained in place and the number of doctors had increased.

In Poland, major health reforms were adopted much later, in 1999, and they were less market-oriented than in Hungary. Political and technical experts from the government initiated reform proposals. Political bargaining over reform proved long and contentious, involving the World Bank, health-sector unions, and professional medical

---

[64]   Joan Nelson, "The Politics of Pension and Health-Care Reforms in Hungary and Poland," in *Reforming the State: Fiscal and Welfare Reform in Post-Socialist Countries*, edited by Janos Kornai, Stephan Haggard, and Robert R. Kaufman, (Cambridge, UK: Cambridge University Press, 2001), 260.

[65]   Garces et al., "Observations," 355.

[66]   Nelson, "Politics," 254.

[67]   Ost, "Weakness of Symbolic Strength," 53.

associations, but government reformers and political parties dominated. According to an exhaustive study of the process by Thomas Bossert
and Cesary Wlodarczyk, "medical associations in Poland, while strong
and influential, were countered by the active interest in health policy by
the political parties, the government bureaucracy and the international
donors."[68] Both liberal and more solidaristic alternatives were debated,
and in 1997 the DLA government managed to craft a political compromise around legislation that introduced an insurance mechanism and
competition but large state subsidies continued. It is significant that by
the later 1990s the problems with market reforms elsewhere, including
in Hungary, had entered the Polish debate; it had become "less clear
that market mechanisms would solve the problems that they were re-
puted to solve, adding a note of caution to the policy debates within
Poland."[69] The Health Ministry was largely bypassed in the reform process, and its subsequent refusal to cooperate in developing regulatory
mechanisms hurt the initial stages of implementation. Overall, however,
Poland displayed a more open and participatory process that produced
a more moderate reform.

In Kazakhstan, private health-care services were legalized in 1991
and a compulsory insurance scheme was introduced in 1996. The Finance Ministry led the reform, supported by the new Health Insurance
Fund that would have a major role in the reformed system. Health-care
workers' unions played a marginal role in the reform process, and their
professional associations in Kazakhstan had "no statutory standing or
formal representation in policy-making."[70] Nor did the Health Ministry
have significant influence. According to a close observer of the process,
"The Ministry of Health in Kazakhstan has experienced public-sector
re-organizations, initially being established as a health committee accountable to the Minister of Education, Culture and Health, then a state
health agency with autonomous status. Such internal restructuring dis-
tracted attention from its policy-making function."[71] Alone among the
cases studied here, Kazakhstan dismantled a significant part of its health
care infrastructure during the 1990s (see table 5.9 later in the chapter).

[68]   Thomas Bossert and Cesary Wlodarczyk, "Unpredictable Politics: Policy Process of
Health Reform in Poland" (Xerox, prefinal draft, January 4, 2000), 19.
[69]   Bossert, "Unpredictable," 21
[70]   Serdar Savas, Gülin Gedik, and Marian Craig, "The Reform Process," in *Health Care
in Central Asia*, edited by Martin McKee, Judith Healy, and Jane Falkingham (Philadelphia:
Open University Press, 2002), 84.
[71]   Savas, *Health Care*, 82.

Between 1990 and 1997, the number of hospitals was reduced by nearly half and the number of maternity and pediatric beds was reduced by one-third. Most of these closed facilities were small, poorly equipped rural district hospitals, and many larger specialized hospitals remained, but the closures often left rural populations with little access to health services.[72]

The insurance reform failed. The Health Insurance Fund ran large deficits because of inadequate tax and payment collections, defaulted on its contracts, and left an estimated one-quarter of the population without coverage. In the face of this crisis, the government abandoned the insurance system in 1998, returned to budget financing, and drafted a more gradual reform strategy.[73] At the end of the decade, the state continued to own most of the remaining health facilities, but welfare effort for health remained low as the economy recovered and access was restricted, especially in rural areas.

Belarus did not carry out significant reforms in its health sector. Long-standing problems of inefficiency, overstaffing, and low quality of services that were common to the communist successor states remained more severe here than elsewhere (see table 5.9, later in the chapter, for the comparatively high maintenance of infrastructure and staff in Belarus). At the same time, broad coverage was generally retained and corruption remained more limited than in Russia and Kazakhstan. In the early 2000s, the Belarussian government, in cooperation with the World Bank, launched pilot reforms, although as in Poland many informed observers were unimpressed with the results of reforms in neighboring states.[74]

Commitments to Public Expenditure

Finally, levels of public expenditures for welfare provision varied significantly across the cases through their periods of economic recovery. Limited available comparative data from the World Health Organization on real per capita public health expenditures from 1998 to 2004 illustrate this pattern. Table 5.5 shows that expenditures remained comparatively low relative to per capita GDP in Russia and Kazakhstan and higher in

[72] Olcott, *Kazakhstan,* 202; Maksut Kulzhanov and Judith Healey, "Profiles of Country Health Care Systems: Kazakhstan," in *Health Care in Central Asia,* edited by Martin McKee, Judith Healey, and Jane Falkingham (Philadelphia: Open University Press, 2002), 200.

[73] Maksut Kulzhanov and Judith Healy, *Health Care Systems in Transition: Kazakhstan* (Copenhagen: European Observatory on Health Systems and Policies, 1999), 53–57.

[74] World Bank, *Memorandum.*

the other cases, especially in Belarus. These expenditure levels correlate with a continued predominance of public over private expenditures in Poland, Hungary, and Belarus. In Russia and Kazakhstan, by contrast, private spending for health care nearly equaled public spending in 2002. (see figure 5.2, later in the chapter).

STATE CAPACITY

I turn now to a comparative examination of state capacity across the five cases, including the capacities of the postcommunist governments to extract revenue and regulate economic transactions as well as their effectiveness in formulating and implementing policy. Three comparative measures are presented: share of the informal economy as an indicator of the states' relative ability to regulate economic transactions; government expenditures as share of GDP as an indicator of taxing capacity; and the World Bank Governance index of government effectiveness as an indicator of comparative policy making and implementation capacities. Measures more specific to the welfare state are not available for all cases, but these general measures have direct implications for financing, regulation, and institutional change in the social sectors of postcommunist states.

TABLE 5.5
GDP and public expenditures on health, 1998–2004[a]

Country		1998	2000	2002	2004
Poland	GDP	8,839	9,914	10,719	12,293
	Health expenditure	364	411	521	567
Hungary	GDP	10,908	12,460	14,016	15,838
	Health expenditure	579	606	783	958
Russian Federation	GDP	5,891	7,205	8,338	10,150
	Health expenditure	239	252	317	341
Kazakhstan	GDP	3,955	4,654	6,043	7,464
	Health expenditure	108	128	151	245
Belarus	GDP	4,210	4,809	5,562	6,988
	Health expenditure	352	401	444	556

Sources: Data on health expenditure from WHO/Europe, European HFA Database, June 2006; data on GDP from International Monetary Fund, World Economic Outlook Database, September 2006.

[a] Dollars purchasing-power parity ($PPP) per capita.

TABLE 5.6
Share of unofficial economy in GDP, 1989–2001

Country	1989	1991	1993	1995	2000–2001
Poland	15.7	23.5	18.5	12.6	27.4
Hungary	27.0	32.9	28.5	29.0	24.4
Russian Federation	12.0	23.5	36.7	41.6	45.1
Kazakhstan	12.0	19.7	27.2	34.3	42.2
Belarus	12.0	16.6	11.0	19.3	47.1[a]

Sources: Data for 1989–1995 from Janos Kornai, Stephan Haggard, and Robert Kaufman, *Reforming the State: Fiscal and Welfare Reform in Post-Socialist Countries* (Cambridge, UK: Cambridge University Press, 2001), 276, based on EBRD *Transition Report, 1997.* Data for 2000–2001 average use the DYMIMIC method and are from Friedrich Schneider, "The Size and Development of the Shadow Economies and Shadow Lobor Force of 22 Transition and 21 OECD Countries," (Discussion Paper 514, Institute for the study of Labor, Bonn, Germany), 7.

[a] The 2000–2001 datum for Belarus is contradicted by other World Bank sources and the Transparency International Corruption Index.

Size of Informal Sectors

As table 5.6 shows, all five postcommunist states experienced significant increases in levels of informality as their economies diversified and old monitoring and control mechanisms broke down. High levels of taxes and social security levies also contributed to informality.[75] In Poland and Hungary, informality was relatively high in the early to mid-1990s and then declined as the states' economies recovered and they built effective market institutions. In Kazakhstan and especially Russia, informality proved deeper and more sustained, covering about 35–40 percent of their economies in the mid-1990s and remaining over 40 percent well into the periods of recovery. Belarus shows the smallest decline in this dimension of state capacity during the 1990s because here the state retained greater control over productive assets, limiting both privatization and the corruption and tax evasion that accompanied it elsewhere. The high level of corruption shown here for Belarus in 2000–2001 shows an unusual degree of discontinuity and is contradicted by other sources, including a 2002 World Bank report that asserts, "[T]he emergence of flagrant corruption and bad economic governance in Belarus has been largely avoided." The Transparency International Corruption Index also places measures for Belarus much lower and closer to those for Poland and Hungary.[76]

[75] Friedrich Schneider and Dominik H. Enste, "Shadow Economies: Size, Causes, and Consequences," *Journal of Economic Literature* 38 (March, 2000): 77–114.
[76] "Executive Summary," in *World Bank Memorandum,* n.p.; Transparency International Index, available at: www.transparency.org/policy_research/surveys_indices/cpi.

Government Expenditures

The data on government expenditures tell a broadly similar story about state capacities. General government expenditures declined for the transition states as their role in the economy lessened and privatization and informality put many activities beyond the reach of the tax authorities. Evasion of taxes and social security contributions was prevalent during the early transition period. By the late 1990s, enforcement and compliance had improved considerably in Poland and Hungary, with more than three-fourths of taxpayers reporting that they never evaded taxes, and only a small percentage admitting that they did so often. In Belarus, collections remained close to those of Soviet times. According to the IMF, "unlike many countries in the region, compliance is satisfactory in Belarus, tax administration and enforcement are adequate."[77] By 2001–2002, government expenditures as share of GDP varied significantly across the cases, almost 53 percent in Hungary, about 46 percent in Poland and Belarus, about 37 percent in Russia, and 21 percent in Kazakhstan.[78] Problems were especially severe in Kazakhstan, where, as previously explained, the government abandoned its effort to rely on tax-financed health insurance funds because collections were so low that basic health provision was collapsing.

The change in government expenditures might be seen as an adjustment to levels of economic development and recovery, but this is only part of the story. It is broadly assumed that communist states maintained levels of taxation and public expenditure that were too high relative to their income levels. Over the decade 1990–2000, public expenditure in the CIS on average fell to levels comparable to those in countries at similar levels of per capita income. In the East Central European states, by contrast, public expenditure in 2000 was almost one-third higher than the average for countries at similar per capita income levels.[79] In Belarus, expenditures remained considerably higher than for other CIS states. In sum, the states that retained or quickly reestablished control over their economies, through either statist-authoritarian or market-democratic

[77] International Monetary Fund, *Republic of Belarus*, 16.
[78] OECD Economic Outlook 76 Database, available at www.oecd.org/eco/sources-and-methods; *OECD Economic Surveys, 2001–2002, Russian Federation*, vol. 2002/5 (Paris: OECD, 2002), 44; *Republic of Kazakhstan, Country Assistance Evaluation* (Washington, D.C.: World Bank, 2001), 36; World Bank, *Memorandum*, 2. The WHO Europe European HFA Database, June 2006, has all cases from 1998.
[79] Pradeep Mitra and Nicholas Stern, *Tax Systems in Transition*, (World Bank Research Paper no. 2947) (Washington, D.C.: World Bank, January 2003), 5.

TABLE 5.7
Government effectiveness in transition economies (percentile ranking)[a]

Country	1996	2002
Poland	72.4	72.7
Hungary	69.5	76.1
Russian Federation	20.0	38.8
Kazakhstan	12.4	17.7
Belarus	4.8	11.0

Source: D. Kaufmann, A. Kraay, and M. Mastruzzi, *Governance Matters V: Governance Indicators for 1996–2005,* World Bank (2005), World Governance Indicators Interactive, available at http://info.worldbank.org/governance.

[a] Data represent percentile ranking of country on Government Effectiveness indicator (100% indicates that the country rates higher than any other; 0% indicates that the country rates lower than any other). Government effectiveness measures the quality of public services, the quality of the civil service and the degree of its independence from political pressures, the quality of policy formulation and implementation, and the credibility of the government's commitment to such policies.

means, maintained comparatively high levels of revenue collection and public expenditure.

Government Effectiveness

Last is an indicator of government effectiveness, developed by the World Bank to measure the quality of public services and of the civil service, as well as the quality of policy formulation and implementation, and the credibility of the government's commitment to deliver on its policies. Table 5.7 shows the level of government effectiveness for Poland and Hungary to be quite high, at or above 70 percent in percentile ranking. Rankings for the Russian Federation and Kazakhstan are much lower, although improved from 20 and 12 percent, respectively, in 1996 to almost 39 and 18 percent in 2002. The very low rankings for Belarus probably relate to the indicator's reliance on measures of quality of public services and the civil service, and the degree of civil servants' independence from political pressures, all of which are clearly low. Other evidence, however, indicates that Belarus's government is reasonably effective in its ability to formulate and implement its chosen policies.[80]

Overall, these three measures indicate substantial divergence in the capabilities of the five states to tax, regulate, and govern. Poland and Hungary, and with less consensus Belarus, show strong capacities on all

[80] "Executive Summary", in World Bank, *Memorandum,* n.p.

three measures, whereas Russia and Kazakhstan are consistently much weaker. I show in the conclusion that differences in state capacities combine with different patterns of liberalization to produce distinct types of postcommunist welfare states.

INTERNATIONAL INTERVENTIONS

As in Russia, international institutions were deeply involved in transforming the Polish, Hungarian, and Kazakh welfare states. The World Bank was the major external actor promoting liberalization and retrenchment throughout the postcommunist region. In 1997, Poland and Hungary also began the process of accession to the European Union. The European Union is associated with a European Social Model that, although nowhere codified, is broadly understood to emphasize solidarity, social cohesion, social rights and inclusion, and policy bargaining among the social partners. It contrasts sharply with IFI-promoted welfare state residualism, privatization, and weakening of public responsibility. Accession is sometimes proposed as a major factor shaping development of the East Central European welfare states, drawing them toward European norms and practices.[81] But careful empirical studies generally conclude that the actual influence of the European Union on social policy in the accession states has been modest and somewhat ambiguous, that it has not really challenged the liberal model.[82] I next look briefly at the role of the IFIs in the four cases and then compare EU effects in Poland and Hungary.

In Poland, Hungary, and Kazakhstan during the 1990s, the World Bank sponsored projects across the social sector, in pensions, poverty relief, labor markets, health care, and education.[83] The postcommunist governments in Poland and Hungary worked closely with Bank

[81]   Mitchell A. Orenstein and Martine R. Hass, "Globalization and the Development of Welfare States in Postcommunist Europe" (International Security Program, Belfer Center for Science and International Affairs, JFK School of Government, Harvard University, February 2002).

[82]   This interpretation relies particularly on the studies of Zsuzsa Ferge and Gabor Juhasz, "Accession and Social Policy: The Case of Hungary," *Journal of European Social Policy* 14, no. 3 (2004): 233–51; Caroline De La Porte and Bob Deacon, "Social Policy Influence of the EU and Other Global Actors: The Case of Lithuania," *Policy Studies* 25, no. 2 (2004): 121–37; János Mátyásç Kovacs, "Approaching the EU and Reaching the US? Rival Narratives on Transforming Welfare Regimes in East-Central Europe," *West European Politics* special issue 2, no. 1 (2002): 175–205.

[83]   Lists, costs, descriptions, and reports on the results of these projects for each country are available at www.worldbank.org/Project.

officials, who were directly involved in developing policy designs for major social-sector reform efforts. These policies were subject to bargaining with legislatures and societal constituencies and some failed, but in the end the Bank played a significant role in shaping social policy. The Bank's Operations Evaluation Department rated its performance in both countries as highly satisfactory and sustainable and as having a substantial impact on institutional development, in contrast to its self-assessed failure in Russia. Models of health and education decentralization promoted by global policy networks (see chap. 2) also had a large impact in Poland and Hungary during the early 1990s, and bilateral policy transfers from Europe were important in health-sector reforms.

Of the cases considered here, Kazakhstan was the most heavily IFI-influenced, in the social sector as well as in the broader reform process. According to Olcott's authoritative study, "almost every piece of economic legislation offered during the second half of the 1990s reflected consultation with experts from one or more of the multilateral financial institutions."[84] Bank agendas met few obstacles from Kazakhstan's statist welfare stakeholders; it was symptomatic of the social bureaucracies' weakness that Bank officials complained of frequent change in the government personnel with whom they worked. Virtually every aspect of Kazakhstan's welfare state was adapted to the liberal model with international assistance. A 2001 report recognized the Bank's effectiveness in promoting these reforms, but criticized their preparation and other failures that are familiar from the Russian case: "The strategy did not focus forcefully enough on institutions, protection of the poor or gender issues. Critical analytical work needed for poverty reduction was not undertaken until late in the transition. . . [There was] a lack of country ownership, low implementation capacity on the part of the Government and frequent changes in Government personnel."[85]

For most of the period under review, there was no IFI presence in Belarus. The World Bank did carry out some technical assistance projects in the early postcommunist period, but in the mid-1990s the Bank, IMF, and European Union suspended their programs and withdrew their personnel. By the end of the decade, there was "hardly any Western indus-

[84]   Olcott, *Kazakhstan*, 146.

[85]   World Bank, "Memorandum to the Executive Directors and the President," in *Republic of Kazakhstan: Country Assistance Evaluation* (Washington, D.C.: World Bank, Feb. 20, 2001, Operations Evaluation Dept.), n.p.

trial, economic, or financial activity in Belarus . . . nor . . . much in the way of cultural or intellectual input."[86] The Bank gave abysmally low ratings to its five projects in Belarus.

What of EU influence in Poland and Hungary? Accession states were required to move toward compliance with the *acquis communitaire*, including its social chapter. From 1997, the European Commission drew up annual reports on each candidate state's progress, and its right to accept, delay, or deny membership gave the European Union a potentially powerful source of leverage over accession states. The core of the social *acquis* addressed gender equality, the coordination of social security schemes, health and safety at work, labor law, and work conditions. Programs of technical and other assistance toward compliance were provided. But the effects of this process proved limited for several reasons. First, liberalizing changes in the Polish and Hungarian welfare states were already in place or in process by 1997, and EU monitoring reports endorsed these reforms. Moreover, EU demands for budgetary stringency reinforced pressures for retrenchment and restructuring.[87] Second, EU evaluations focused on a particular and limited set of rights (i.e., gender and work safety), not on broad social rights. Solidaristic policies of social inclusion such as universal access to social insurance were promoted at the rhetorical level, but "there [was] no precise definition of 'high level of employment and social protection' and no legal criteria for enforcing it."[88] A vision connected to the European Social Model could perhaps have been more influential, but, in the event, the liberal vision was clearer and it dominated.

Accession states *were* required to build the legal and institutional framework for social dialog and national tripartite bargaining among labor, government, and business associations. Here the prescriptions were specific and progress was closely monitored, but results were nevertheless limited. This was partly a result of the comparative weakness of labor unions in East Central Europe, but the process was also at fault. The European Union focused on transposing institutions and especially legislation rather than on implementation. Its 2000 Regular Report on Hungary, for example, did criticize policy changes by

[86]   Wieck, "Role of International Organizations in Belarus," 392. The author was an official of the OECD, the only Western organization that had broad access in Belarus during this period.

[87]   Ferge and Juhasz, "Accession and Social Policy."

[88]   La Porte and Deacon, "Social Policy Influence," 124.

the center-right government that debilitated unions, but the final 2003 preaccession reports certified Poland and Hungary for membership while recognizing that their tripartite bodies were not fully functional.[89] In sum, according to one assessment that reflects a broadly held view, "EU influence has been more marginal than might have been expected at every level other than securing an acceptance . . . of the minimum legal requirements of membership."[90]

The EU accession process had significant indirect effects on welfare states by strengthening democratic institutions and policy-making processes in East Central Europe. The consolidation of a democratic society was a core condition for membership. EU influence here strengthened voice and accountability mechanisms and "reinforced the institutions of parliamentary democracy, enabling interest groups to lobby more effectively for continuation of high levels of welfare provision."[91] As Orenstein and Martine Haas point out, the European Union also provided economic opportunities that facilitated the rapid recovery of East Central European economies, thereby supporting maintenance of welfare. Since the December 2000 Nice Treaty, the EU has introduced common social indicators and placed greater emphasis on issues of poverty and social exclusion. Although these measures may have some epistemic influence, they also are not legally binding and have no real authority over social policy.

CONCLUSION: COMPARING WELFARE STATE OUTCOMES

In chapter 1, I set out four measures of welfare state liberalization, based loosely on Esping-Andersen's criteria:[92]
1. the extent of pension system privatization
2. public versus private health-care expenditures
3. the effectiveness of social transfers for poverty relief (as a proxy for proportion of means-tested benefits)
4. structural changes toward efficiency in the health sector.

[89]   Ferge and Juhasz, "Accession and Social Policy," 238.

[90]   La Porte and Deacon, "Social Policy Influence," 134; the quotation refers specifically to Lithuania, but reflects the common view of most of the authors cited in this section.

[91]   Orenstein and Haas, "Globalization," 9; Jan Zielenka, "Challenges of EU Enlargement," *Journal of Democracy* 15, no. 1 (2004): 22–35.

[92]   Recall that Esping-Andersen's three indicators of welfare state liberalism are private-sector share of total pension and health-care expenditures and means-tested benefits as percentage of total social assistance.

Next I provide evidence about each of these measures for the five cases. I then consider the comparative outcomes of different trajectories for welfare provision in the five postcommunist states, including levels and patterns of poverty, access to health and education, and coverage of pension systems. Finally, I integrate the state capacity variable to differentiate the cases into welfare state types.

How Much Liberalization?

Comparative measures of pension system privatization are presented in figure 5.1, based on a simulation of public and private benefits in reformed pension systems for Poland, Hungary, and Kazakhstan by Sarah Brooks. It shows the public-private mix resulting from Poland and Hungary's moderate reforms, with public benefits projected to provide well over half the total in Hungary and about half in Poland. Russia was not included in the simulation because of data inadequacies, although its system will also be mixed. Kazakhstan's system will be completely private; Belarus's (by my projection based on the current system) will be completely public. In sum, the figure shows very distinctive outcomes of pension reform, fitting the pattern of moderate negotiated liberalization in Poland and Hungary, radical reform in Kazakhstan, and stasis in Belarus. Although I have not discussed pension replacement rates here, the replacement rates shown in the figure fit an expected pattern: highest in Hungary, somewhat lower and almost equal in Poland and Belarus, and much lower in Kazakhstan.

The second measure of liberalization, public versus private health expenditure as a percentage of the total, also varies significantly across the cases (see figure 5.2). Although the proportion of private expenditure has increased across all cases since the beginning of transition, in 1998 public spending remained strongly predominant in Hungary, Poland, and Belarus, with higher proportions of private expenditure in Russia and Kazakhstan; these differences increased slightly by 2002. In Russia and Kazakhstan, some estimates indicate that about half of healthcare spending was private.[93] In Kazakhstan, public spending on health care remained under 2 percent of GDP, a decline of more than half from the 1991 level, closer to the average for low-income countries.

[93] The WHO figures for the Russian Federation shown in figure 5.2 are higher than official statistics for public expenditure, as well as survey-based reports on the proportion of public expenditure, apparently because the WHO's definition includes some health insurance funds.

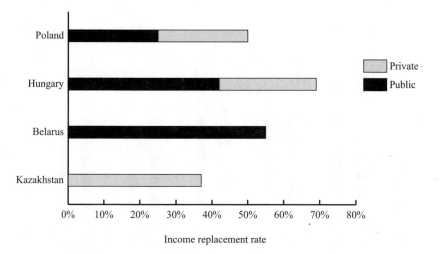

Figure 5.1 Public and private benefits in reformed pension systems (based on a simulation)
Sources: Sarah Brooks, *Social Protection and the Market: The Transformation of Social Security Institutions in Latin America* (Cambridge, UK: Cambridge University Press, forthcoming); data for Belarus from Social Security Administration, *Social Security Programs throughout the World: Europe* (Washington, D.C.: Social Security Administration, 2006).

(By this time Kazakhstan had recovered to more than 90 percent of its 1991 GDP and enjoyed the highest levels of foreign direct investment in the CIS region.)

It is important to note the significant degree of convergence in *total* health expenditure as percentage of GDP for all cases except Kazakhstan. In 2002, total (public and private) health spending in Russia was about 6 percent of GDP, compared with about 7.7 percent in Hungary, 6.6 percent in Belarus, and 3.5 percent in Kazakhstan. The shift in expenditure patterns has meant a decline in public health programs in the low-public-expenditure states. Although core universal indicators of public health provision such as childhood immunizations remain close to 100 percent in all the cases, the costs to public health in terms of adult communicable diseases are high. Keeping in mind the necessary caveats about the lack of demonstrated causation between expenditure and health outcomes, I think it worth noting the comparative rates of tuberculosis in 2002: under 3 per 100,000 in Poland and Hungary, under 10 in Belarus, over 20 in Russia, and almost 30 in Kazakhstan. These rates have decreased from their pretransition levels in Poland and Hungary, but have more than doubled in Russia and Kazakhstan.[94]

[94]   WHO/Europe, European HFA Database, June 2006.

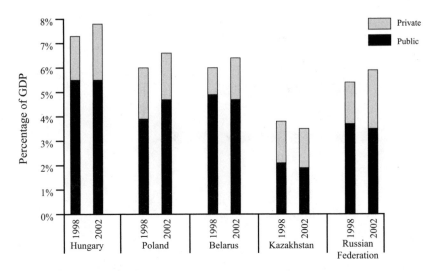

Figure 5.2 Public and private health-care expenditures, 1998 and 2002 (as a percentage of GDP)
Source: WHO/Europe, European Health for All Database, June 2006.

The extent of means-tested social assistance constitutes a third measure of liberalization. As noted in chapter 4, in Russia only about 7 percent of social assistance was means-tested by 2004, partly because of societal pressure for the maintenance of subsidies and privileges. The limited means-tested benefits available were poorly administered. The proportion of means-tested benefits was higher in Poland, Hungary, and Kazakhstan, and it was marginal in Belarus, but comparative data on levels are not available. The World Bank's measure of the relative effectiveness of transfer payments for poverty reduction (i.e., the projected increase in poverty in the absence of all social transfers), serves as a proxy. The measures for Poland, Russia, Kazakhstan, and Belarus are shown in table 5.8 (column 1). The high effectiveness score for Belarus (apparently because of continued broad subsidies) indicates that this is at best an imperfect proxy for means testing. However, the table does reflect Poland's relatively strong programs of means-tested benefits, the weaker effectiveness of Kazakhstan's programs, and Russia's continuing failure to develop targeting.

The fourth measure of liberalization to be considered is structural change toward efficiency in the health sector. Here progress has been

TABLE 5.8
Measures of liberalization, access to social services, and social insurance coverage

Country	(1) Increase in poverty without all social transfers, 2001–2002 (%)	(2) Secondary school enrollment ratio, 1995–1999 (gross)		(3) Pension contributors (% working age pop/labor force)[a]	(4) Average pension (% of per capita income)[a]
		M	F		
Poland	141	99	98	64/68	61.2
Hungary	—	98	99	65/77	33.6
Russian Federation	68	79	85	—/—	18.3
Kazakhstan	100	87 (80)	87	28/38	23.0
Belarus	143	96	93	94/97	31.2

Sources:

1. Asad Alam, *Growth, Poverty, and Inequality: Eastern Europe and the Former Soviet Union* (Washington, D.C.: World Bank, 2005), 21.

2. UNICEF, *State of the World's Children, 2003*, table 4, available at www.unicef.org/sowc03/tables/table4.html; datum of 80 for Kazakstan from Martha Brill Olcott, *Kazakhstan: Unfulfilled Promise* (Washington, D.C.: Carnigie Endowment, 2002), 3–4. World Bank, *2004 World Development Indicators* (Washington, D.C.: World Bank, 2004), 64–86.

[a] For various years.

limited across all cases. Recall that communist social sectors were broadly viewed as being heavily overstaffed and inefficient in international terms. Table 5.9 shows changes in the numbers of doctors and hospitals throughout the transition, with European averages for comparison. Only Kazakhstan, the radical liberalizer, actually succeeded in eliminating a substantial part of its health-sector infrastructure, and even here the density of doctors declined little. In Poland, Hungary, and Russia, the number of institutions declined somewhat, but personnel grew. Belarus remains the largest, with the smallest decrease in the number of beds and largest increase in density of doctors. These numbers indicate that efficiency-oriented reforms have had limited success. Health and education infrastructure and staffing patterns have proven to be the parts of old welfare states that are most resistant to restructuring.

Welfare Provision: Poverty, Access to Health and Education, and Social Security Coverage

Comparisons of poverty levels are complicated by differences in the methods used to calculate national poverty lines. Table 5.1 shows poverty

TABLE 5.9
Measures of structural change in health-care sectors of postcommunist states[a], 1990–2002

	Poland		Hungary		Russian Federation		Kazakhstan		Belarus		EU members (pre-2004)	
	Hosp beds	MDs	Hosp beds	MDs	Hosp Beds	MDs	Hosp Beds	MDs	Hosp Beds	MDs	Hosp Beds	MDs
1990	660	214	983	280	1,306	407	1,367	398	1,323	356	797	304
1994	634	228	930	294	1,196	384	1,214	360	1,246	414	687	319
1998	595	233	808	308	1,110	421	819	353	1,241	443	639	338
2002	557	230	785	319	1,071	426	701	361	1,194	452	593	356

Source: WHO/Europe, European HFA Database, June 2006.

[a] Hospital beds and medical doctors per 100,000.

according to a standardized measure (below $PPP, dollars purchasing-power parity, 4.30 per day) for the five cases for 1998–2002. As the table shows, poverty was higher and more sustained in all three post-Soviet cases, in large part because of their longer recessions, and levels declined significantly everywhere with economic recovery. Across all cases, children, multichild families, and single parents were at highest risk for poverty. Even in Poland and Hungary, poverty among these groups reached 20–30 percent during recession, and they remained the groups most at risk. In both cases, income-tested family benefits that were introduced in the mid-1990s reduced child poverty significantly in real terms and at levels that were high by international standards.[95] In Russia, benefits provided little poverty relief and were poorly targeted, even in comparison to countries at low levels of development, whereas in Kazakhstan income-tested programs proved somewhat effective. It should be noted that poverty was high in Belarus in 1998 and 2000 despite relatively high social expenditures. In all cases, the elderly were relatively protected. Both poverty and inequality remained significantly above their pretransition levels.

Access to health care and education varied markedly across the cases by the end of the decade. Although it is difficult to quantify the levels of exclusion, the evidence presented in chapter 4 for Russia and in this chapter for Kazakhstan indicates that at least 10 percent of Russia's population and more than 20 percent of Kazakhstan's lacked access to necessary health services or treatments. By contrast, in Poland and Hungary health care systems remained inclusive. According to Haggard and Kaufman, in East Central Europe, despite reforms, "principles of universalism were typically maintained de facto if not de jure."[96] Access to primary education remains universal across the cases, but estimates indicate that 15 to 20 percent of secondary school–age children are not enrolled in Russia and Kazakhstan (table 5.8, column 2). Across all five states, unemployment is concentrated among youth ages 15–24 at rates of 15–25 percent, and financial returns to education have risen, driving increased university attendance. At the same time, a proportion of poorer youth are out of school and out of work, contributing to the growth of an underclass that is disconnected from the welfare state.

[95] Forster and Toth, "Child Poverty," 329.
[96] Stephan Haggard and Robert R. Kaufman, "Recrafting Social Contracts: Welfare Reform in Latin America, East Asia, and Central Europe" (draft manuscript, Sept. 15, 2006), chap. 8, 5.

Finally, levels of social security coverage, as indicated by pension contribution rates, varied across the cases. In Belarus, coverage remained nearly universal for the working-age population; in Poland and Hungary it was at nearly 70 and 80 percent for the labor force respectively and two-thirds for the working-age population. In Kazakhstan, coverage levels were much lower, below 40 percent and 30 percent, respectively, numbers that are also seen in other privatized low-wage systems in Latin America, where a substantial number of the working and working-age populations fail or cannot afford to place funds in investment accounts (table 5.8, columns 3–4). The figures in these columns are for various years and are not strictly comparable, but the differences in magnitude they indicate are significant. Note that pension coverage rates even in Poland and Hungary stand significantly below pretransition levels.

Social-Liberal and Informalized Postcommunist Welfare States

The comparisons so far show that all the cases except Belarus have undergone a significant degree of liberalization. At the same time, there are major differences between Poland and Hungary, on the one hand, and Russia and Kazakhstan, on the other, in terms of financing, administration, and coverage of the welfare state; and none conforms well to existing models. In an attempt to capture their fundamental features, I propose two mixed or hybrid models. Poland and Hungary, I designate social-liberal welfare states,[97] combining elements of the liberal and inherited models (see table 1.4). They mix public and private provision, with substantial means testing and insurance markets, but public provision and broad access and coverage continue to predominate. State regulation of social security markets and administration of welfare are relatively effective.

Russia and Kazakhstan mix movement toward liberalization with weak state administrative and taxing capacities to produce an informalized welfare model, characterized both by weak state and market regulation, shadow payments for social services, low social security contribution rates, and substantial limits on access. Within this mix, the Kazakh welfare state is considerably more liberalized than the Russian.

---

[97]   This term was used originally by Mitchell Orenstein to characterize postcommunist East Central European welfare states.

Conclusion

Negotiating Welfare in Democratic and Authoritarian Transitions

The five cases of welfare state reform reviewed in this book show three distinct trajectories and outcomes during the postcommunist decade.

In Poland and Hungary a gradual process of liberalization produced contracted but still relatively extensive and effective welfare states that are characterized by

- moderate welfare effort,
- a preponderance of public over private expenditure in the social sector,
- significant reliance on social security markets (i.e., for pensions and health care),
- limited corruption in the provision of social services, and
- broad, although not universal, access of the population to basic services and coverage by social insurance and state social assistance.

Russia and Kazakhstan followed paths to more radical liberalization and a constricted state role in welfare provision, with the outcome being more extreme in Kazakhstan. Both are characterized by

- relatively low welfare effort,
- a high ratio of private vs. public expenditure in the social sector,
- substantial reliance on poorly regulated social security markets (i.e., for pensions and health care),
- large-scale informality and "spontaneous privatization" in the provision of social services, and

- the exclusion of substantial parts of the population from access to basic services and coverage by social insurance and social assistance.

In Belarus, most of the statist welfare inheritance was preserved, maintaining
- moderate welfare effort,
- very strong predominance of state over private provision,
- virtually no social security markets,
- limited corruption but strong bureaucratic domination of the social sector, and
- nearly universal access of the population to low-quality social services and social insurance.

POLITICS MATTERS: SOCIETAL CONSTITUENCIES, STATIST STAKEHOLDERS, AND WELFARE STATE OUTCOMES

The "politics matters" approach provides considerable insight into the patterns of postcommunist welfare state change. Politics mediates the differing responses of the states to transitional recessions and subsequent economic recoveries. The political balance between the pro- and anti-liberalization actors in governmental, state, and party structures is key to explaining different trajectories and outcomes across the five cases. Where power was concentrated in the hands of liberalizing executives—in Kazakhstan, and in Russia except during the 1994–1999 period—retrenchment and restructuring of the statist welfare systems moved forward. Where executive power was weaker and pro-welfare constituencies exercised some influence through representative political institutions—Poland, Hungary, and to a limited extent Russia—retrenchment and restructuring were moderated or blocked. In sum, the "politics matters" argument travels relatively well, explaining the differences among postcommunist democratic and authoritarian liberalizers, as well as the different policies across time in Russia.[1]

---

[1]   See especially Miguel Glatzer and Dietrich Rueschemeyer, eds., *Globalization and the Future of the Welfare State* (Pittsburgh: University of Pittsburgh Press, 2005), a key study that for the first time uses the "politics matters" framework in a cross-regional analysis of welfare states in middle-income countries. Other representative works focus on the United States and the OECD: Duane Swank, *Global Capital, Political Institutions, and Policy Change in Developed Welfare States* (Cambridge, UK: Cambridge University Press, 2002); Paul Pierson, *Dismantling the Welfare State: Reagan, Thatcher, and the Politics of Retrenchment* (Cambridge, UK: Cambridge University Press, 1994); Evelyne Huber and John D. Stephens, *Development and Crisis of the Welfare State: Parties and Policies in Global Markets* (Chicago: University of Chicago Press, 2001).

Democratic institutions have mattered for welfare state change in Poland and Hungary. My research provides evidence that pro-welfare parties and labor organizations are not, as is sometimes claimed, hollow or uniformly weak across the postcommunist space.[2] True, if the comparison is with continental Europe, as it often is, explicitly or implicitly, then representative institutions do afford less influence on welfare outcomes in East Central Europe. The networks of societal welfare beneficiaries that are characteristically dense in mature welfare states remain much less organized and their influence is far less institutionalized in the new transitional democracies. Finance Ministries prevailed over more solidaristic interests in Polish and Hungarian welfare policymaking during the 1990s, and the significant role of IFIs in shaping programmatic welfare state change there has no parallel in the Western industrial democracies.

But if the comparison is among the postcommunist states, then democratic rights, constraints, and electoral feedback have mattered in decision-making processes. In Poland and Hungary, democratic institutions provided sufficient openings and leverage for societal welfare constituencies to moderate retrenchment and restructuring. Here labor unions and social democratic parties formed alliances and participated regularly in governments. Pressures from these groups, and their direct role in political bargaining, affected welfare outcomes. Unions and parties helped to gain compensation for societal groups that were hurt in transitional recessions, contributing to large expenditure increases in selected social transfer programs, even during the depths of recession. Representative institutions bargained to moderate programmatic change toward privatization and social insurance markets, as shown in the case studies of pension program and health-sector reform. They also pressed to sustain public expenditure and responsibility for welfare provision. Agenda-setting for programmatic change was dominated by government liberalizers, but representative institutions played a significant role both in sustaining compensatory policies during the early to mid-1990s and in maintaining commitments to broad public provision as economies recovered.

---

[2] See, for example, Marc Morje Howard, *The Weakness of Civil Society in Post-Communist Europe* (Cambridge, UK: Cambridge University Press, 2003); Stephen Crowley and David Ost, eds., *Workers after Workers' States: Labor and Politics in Postcommunist Eastern Europe*, (Lanham: Rowman and Littlefield, 2001); Paul Kubicek, "Organized Labor in Postcommunist States: Will the Western Sun Set on It, Too?" *Comparative Politics* 32 (October 1999): 83–102; Steven Levitsky and Lucan Way, "Between a Shock and a Hard Place: The Dynamics of Labor-Backed Adjustment in Poland and Argentina," *Comparative Politics* 30, no. 2 (1998), 171–92.

In Russia, democratic constraints on retrenchment and restructuring proved much weaker than in Poland and Hungary, although somewhat stronger than is usually recognized. Russian society was not dormant in the face of the executive's radical liberalization program. Teachers, women, and others mobilized against threats to educational guarantees and employment rights, and during the mid-1990s Russia's truncated democratic politics provided some limited representation for these societal welfare constituents. Russia's democratic period is distinctive for the dominance of a hard-left, backward-looking coalition of communists, pensioners, and poor and rural strata that mobilized effectively to block liberalization. Although this coalition succeeded mainly in deadlocking reform while real financing fell, it did shape the trajectory of programmatic change and keep in place diminished programs and subsidies that were directed to traditional welfare constituencies during the years of economic decline. Even in the more authoritarian Putin period, when welfare state liberalization did proceed, political resistance and popular protest forced the government to back away from radical cuts in the most broadly distributed housing subsidies and social benefits. Pierson's claim about the difficulty of large, tangible benefit reductions is confirmed here.

At the same time, the Russian case highlights differences in the substance of democracy across postcommunist states. In contrast to Poland and Hungary, even during Russia's relatively democratic period trade unions found few party allies and made only fragmentary and temporary alliances with political parties. Significant public-sector strikes did take place, particularly in education. But although such strikes brought down a government in Poland and at least brought wage increases there and in Hungary, they had little effect in Russia because mobilized public-sector workers lacked influential political allies. In the democratic states, governments compensated societal constituencies for recessionary losses; in Russia, the government responded to recessionary fiscal pressures by cutting expenditures and accumulating pension, benefit, and public-sector wage arrears. The Russian social ministries played little role in defending solidaristic values or the interests of broad societal constituencies. In sum, representative political institutions in Russia had much less bargaining power or capacity to influence policy change or to hold the government accountable.

The Russian case also brings to the fore the importance of statist social-sector elites and welfare stakeholders in states with large inheritances of bureaucratic welfare institutions. During the 1990s, statist stakeholders,

seeking to defend their interests in public expenditure and the centralized administration of social provision, raised major obstacles to welfare
reform in Russia. They became veto actors against the privatization of
welfare assets and introduction of social security markets. As democracy
decayed at the end of the 1990s and political parties were marginalized or lost their representative function, negotiations over retrenchment and liberalization largely moved into the state organization. Statist
stakeholders bargained mainly for their narrow institutional interests in
resource control and role maintenance. In the end the Russian executive was able to proceed with liberalization only by compensating these
interests, partly by assigning them new regulatory roles and partly by
allowing them to retain de facto ownership of parts of the welfare state.
These concessions to elite and bureaucratic interests compromised the
government's control over distribution and access to social services, with
major implications for welfare provision.

In Kazakhstan, a liberalizing executive concentrated power and
dominated throughout the decade, imposing the most rapid and radical liberalization program among the five cases. Legislative and societal
opposition emerged, but was met with intimidation and repression.
Statist stakeholders provided limited demand or supply for the maintenance of old welfare structures. Welfare bureaucracies were marginalized
politically or partially disbanded. Aside from the security forces, presidential power rested on sources outside of the state, mainly economic
elites based in the privatized energy sector. Retrenchment and liberalization proceeded during periods of both economic decline and recovery.
Kazakhstan represents an extreme case of unconstrained welfare state
transformation by an authoritarian government.

Belarus, in contrast, presents a serious challenge to my explanatory framework. Here the economy underwent a sharp and prolonged
decline and the society had no effective rights to representation, yet the
welfare effort and structures were largely retained. While Belarus's economic trajectory is similar to those of Russia and Kazakhstan, in some
respects the Belarussian case resembles Poland and Hungary more than
it does the other post-Soviet cases. What accounts for this outcome? I
have argued that the strength of state-bureaucratic welfare interests in
the executive's coalition is the key factor explaining welfare state continuity here, but my argument is more tentative than in the other cases.
There are a number of alternative factors that should be considered.
First, the much more limited degree of market transformation in Belarus
resulted in weaker pressures for welfare reform than in the other four

cases. This factor was no doubt important, but its weight is difficult to assess; the strength of bureaucratic actors and the continued state domination of the economy were ultimately different aspects of the same process. Second, it has been argued that Belarus's executive sustained welfare provision in order to generate political support and win plebiscitary presidential elections. This argument is premised on the theory that even controlled elections provide some opening for challenge and opposition, that even under authoritarian conditions electoral feedback can constrain welfare state change.[3]

The president's social policies are popular among some strata of Belarus's population, and limited explanatory weight should be ceded to this argument. But the case for popular constraint in Belarus remains weak on three grounds. First, the breadth of welfare state maintenance seems disproportionate to the very narrow democratic opening. Second, unlike in Poland and Hungary, in Belarus welfare provision has not been adapted to respond to societal discontents such as growing poverty and wage arrears. Authorities resisted pressures for reform or re-allocation even when hardships and social discontent became significant in the mid-1990s.[4] Third, Belarus retained the most heavily overstaffed and centrally controlled social sector. As a consequence, levels of welfare effort look much like those in the democratic cases, but the structures of provision and allocation remain stagnant, with almost no efforts at compensation. The statist-bureaucratic claimants, with their predominant interest in keeping old welfare structures and patterns of distribution to established client groups in society, provide a better fit for the outcomes that are evident in Belarus.

A welfare state dominated by bureaucratic stakeholders responds to their interests in centralized controls, quantitative indicators, and rigid curricula and criteria. Established social sector elites and societal beneficiaries of the inherited welfare system also benefit through retention of jobs and streams of income from the state. The broadly inclusive patterns of basic service coverage maintain provision for the poorer strata who are the main losers from liberalization. Still, there are no mechanisms to make welfare responsive to the needs or interests of broader

[3]   Andrew March, "From Leninism to Karimovism: Hegemony, Legitimacy, and Authoritarian Legitimation," *Post-Soviet Affairs* 19, no. 4 (2003): 307–36; Nita Rudra and Stephan Haggard, "Globalization, Democracy, and Effective Welfare Spending in the Developing World," *Comparative Political Studies* 38, no. 9 (2005): 1015–49.

[4]   See Natalia Georgiyevna Prokofyeva, "Poverty Level and Distribution of Income in Belarus" (Xerox, Oct. 22, 2002).

constituencies, or social sector organizations accountable to their memberships or the public. Belarus remains a bureaucratically dominated welfare state, financed and structured mainly in response to statist actors.

This argument draws partly on my close analysis of the Russian case, which reveals the importance of statist elites and stakeholders in the postcommunist defense of the old welfare state. In the communist period as well, I propose, pressure from bureaucratic claimants that were established in the early communist decades at least partly explains the growth and maintenance of welfare states.[5] If European welfare states grew out of the central political processes of democratic bargaining, communist welfare states arguably grew out of the central political processes of administrative planning and allocation to bureaucratic claimants within communist states. These claimants, along with industrial and other ministries, got regular increments to their budgets as long as the communist economies were growing (through the 1960s and 1970s), and then got declining resources when growth slowed (during the 1980s). Their influence and positions varied across postcommunist states. Attention to the influence of statist-bureaucratic actors helps to explain postcommunist welfare outcomes in the authoritarian and semi-authoritarian cases. As veto actors and then elite negotiators in Russia, marginalized in Kazakhstan, and central to the presidential coalition in Belarus, they played a large role in welfare state politics.

THE ROLE OF ECONOMIC FACTORS

The central alternative to the "politics matters" argument stresses the role of economic pressures in forcing welfare state retrenchment and restructuring. My book argues that economics has not been deterministic in the postcommunist cases; states confronting similar economic and fiscal pressures responded differently because politics mediated. Patterns of welfare effort and restructuring varied during both recessions and recoveries in ways that do not correlate with economic pressures. States confronting broadly similar economic downturns, such as Kazakhstan and Belarus, moved in very different directions in terms of welfare state

[5] This thinking constitutes some revision of my arguments in Linda J. Cook, *The Soviet Social Contract and Why It Failed: Welfare Policy and Workers' Politics from Brezhnev to Yeltsin* (Cambridge, Mass.: Harvard University Press, 1993). Although the two arguments are compatible, they identify a different central mechanism for welfare state growth and maintenance.

change. Political deadlock between a liberalizing executive and a hard-left legislative majority blocked restructuring in Russia during an extended period of economic decline and fiscal crisis, whereas changes in political coalitions permitted liberalization as the economy recovered and fiscal pressures eased. Russia and Kazakhstan retained significantly lower levels of welfare effort and public provision than the other cases despite economic recoveries and sustained growth.

At the same time, the intensity of economic and fiscal pressures matters for the comparisons. The East Central European states experienced much briefer and shallower recessions than did the post-Soviet states (see figure 1.1). And although they spent heavily on social transfers even during recessions, their more rapid economic recoveries facilitated the maintenance of higher welfare effort. The deeper and longer recessions in the post-Soviet states, and the more recent recoveries, sustained the downward economic pressure on welfare longer and helps explain the deeper retrenchment and liberalization in Russia and Kazakhstan. In sum, economic decline increased pressures for retrenchment and/or reform in market-conforming directions, while the effect of politics depended on the power relations between winners and losers.

There is also a critical interactive effect between economics and politics across the cases. The briefer and milder recessions in the Poland and Hungary facilitated the maintenance, and in some cases expansion, of societal welfare constituencies such as pensioners and benefit recipients. These groups remained in place after economic recovery as a source of pressure for sustaining welfare programs and public provision broadly, helping to account for maintenance of welfare. In Russia and Kazakhstan, by contrast, the deeper and more prolonged recessions depleted welfare state constituencies. Many benefits eroded because of inflation and economic decline. In Russia especially a significant part of social-sector personnel disappeared into the informal economy, weakening the potential coalitions for formal state welfare provision and making it easier for the state to privatize or abandon public spending. While political institutions facilitated or limited their influence, economics helped shape the constituencies that would be left to bargain politically over welfare after economic recovery.

COMPARATIVE PERSPECTIVES

My book contributes to a newly developing literature that focuses on the relationships among politics, welfare, and the economic pressures associated with globalization in regions beyond the established OECD welfare states. It builds on the pathbreaking study edited by Glatzer and Rueschemeyer on globalization and the future of the welfare state, which uses the "politics matters" framework in a cross-regional analysis of middle-income countries in Latin America, Eastern Europe, and Asia. The results of my research are in broad agreement with their conclusion that the balance of political power within domestic polities shapes welfare outcomes, that "politics makes a decisive difference for the consequences of economic globalization for social policy in a given country."[6] The volume's authors find that, across the cases, where the balance of domestic political power favored welfare constituencies, they were better able to defend claims or negotiate compensation.

Other recent work further extends the study of welfare into little-researched democratizing and authoritarian states, looking at the effects of regime type on welfare state politics. Most agree that democratization can contribute to the maintenance and/or expansion of welfare commitments even in the face of the economic pressures associated with globalization. Joseph Wong's study of health policy during the 1980s and 1990s in South Korea and Taiwan, for example, concludes that the introduction of political competition produced effective incentives for governments to expand health insurance coverage. From the very limited health insurance programs of their authoritarian periods, both states broadened coverage as they democratized and at least partially maintained expanded commitments even when they experienced economic shocks. Rudra and Haggard find that democratic regimes are more likely than others to maintain spending and social commitments under globalizing pressures even in institutionally weak developing-country democracies.[7] Klaus Offe's study of East Central Europe reaches conclusions similar to mine: "Under democratic capitalism in East Central Europe affordability and feasibility assessments will always be mediated through democratic participation."[8]

In their major new study comparing welfare state development in a broad set of middle-income countries in Latin America, East Asia, and Central Europe, Haggard and Kaufman find that in all three regions, "democracy created important new opportunities for contestation over

---

[6]   Glatzer and Rueschemeyer, *Globalization*, 207.

[7]   Joseph Wong, *Healthy Democracies: Welfare Politics in Taiwan and South Korea* (Ithaca: Cornell University Press, 2004). Rudra and Haggard, "Globalization"; the study includes data on fifty-seven developing countries.

[8]   Claus Offe, "The Politics of Social Policy in East European Transitions: Antecedents, Agents, and Agendas of Change," *Social Research* 60, no. 4 (1993): 657.

welfare policy . . . [created] a new politics of welfare reform."[9] They argue that the effects of democracy were, however, systematically conditioned by economic factors and welfare legacies. Where economies are growing, as in East Asia, democracy is associated with the expansion of welfare commitments. Where economic constraints are harsh, as in East Central Europe, democracy limits retrenchment and liberalization. The authors argue that political pressures for welfare state maintenance have been much stronger in Eastern Europe than in Latin America, despite economic and fiscal pressures in both regions, because the universalist communist welfare states created much larger and stronger constituencies and welfare legacies than the more limited and fragmentary welfare structures in Latin America. While Haggard and Kaufman's study places less emphasis on politics in explaining welfare outcomes than I do in this book, it assigns a significant role to democratic politics in limiting welfare state change in East Central Europe.

In a separate study, Rudra and Haggard address the relationship between welfare and both authoritarian and semi-authoritarian regimes. They find that "soft" authoritarian regimes that are subject to some electoral and societal pressures are more likely to maintain welfare expenditures and commitments under globalizing pressures than "hard" authoritarian regimes. Though the politics of benefits reform in Russia does suggest a mechanism for limited electoral accountability in a semi-authoritarian state, overall the admittedly small sample in this book does not confirm Rudra and Haggard's finding. Russia, the most politically competitive of the three, is intermediate in welfare provision. Belarus and Kazakhstan both have highly controlled electoral competition, but Belarus, which makes the greatest welfare effort, is commonly categorized as the most politically repressive. At least for these three cases, the degree of competitiveness within semi-authoritarian regimes does not explain comparative welfare outcomes, and my research suggests the need to look at executive coalitions within semi-authoritarian states. The literature on welfare states under authoritarian and semi-authoritarian conditions remains very limited, even as the number of such regimes grows. Additional research should produce a better understanding of their welfare politics.

In sum, a growing literature extends the study of welfare politics into comparatively little-researched democratizing and authoritarian states,

---

[9]   Stephan Haggard and Robert Kaufman, "Introduction: Towards a Political Economy of Social Policy," *in Recrafting Social Contracts: Welfare Reform in Latin America, East Asia, and Central Europe* (draft manuscript, October 2006), 20.

generally taking issue with economic determinist arguments. These works constitute, as Wong says about his study of Taiwan and South Korea, "A powerful rejoinder to the economic determinism of the globalization thesis."[10] They broadly agree that domestic political factors play a key role in determining welfare outcomes, that the "politics matters" argument extends well beyond the OECD.

STATE CAPACITIES ALSO MATTER: SOCIAL-LIBERAL AND INFORMALIZED POSTCOMMUNIST WELFARE STATES

The effects of state capacity on welfare reform make up the secondary focus of this book. All postcommunist states suffered declines in state capacities. Poland and Hungary, however, managed to substantially rebuild their taxing and administrative capacities as they transitioned to market economies by the late 1990s. These restored capacities were key to their ability to finance public expenditures, to maintain nearly universal social services, and to administer complex liberal welfare models such as means testing. Russia and Kazakhstan, by contrast, suffered a more sustained collapse of their capacities to tax, allocate, and regulate. The levels of informality and corruption in their overall economies remained much higher than in the other cases. In both states, social expenditure patterns shifted spontaneously from public to private, significant parts of society were excluded from access to welfare, and large parts of social sectors were formally or spontaneously privatized.

One of my main conclusions is that liberalization has combined with strong or weak taxing, administrative, and policy-making capacities across these cases to produce distinct welfare state types: a social-liberal type in Poland and Hungary that mixes state and market mechanisms, and a new informalized type in Russia and Kazakhstan in which informal mechanisms, regulated neither by the state nor by markets, affect all welfare state functions (see table 1.4). The combination of liberal restructuring with weak state taxing and regulatory capacities produces this new type.

The social-liberal welfare state mixes elements of statist and market models. The data presented in chapter 5 show that Poland and Hungary largely conform to such a model. A mix of state and private provision

[10]   Wong, *Healthy Democracies*, 172. Rudra and Haggard conclude in a similar vein: "The conventional wisdom that emphasizes the adverse effects of globalization is not particularly robust" ("Globalization," 1038).

is present in health and education services, pensions, and medical insurance. Social services are broadly available, and poverty-targeting of social assistance is substantial. These welfare states are more liberal (i.e., privatized and means-tested) than Esping-Andersen's social democratic model, and they are not underpinned by the effective institutions of tripartite bargaining or social partnership commonly associated with European social democracy. At the same time, the degree of liberalization remains limited. They maintain a predominance of public provision and broad social security coverage. The label "social liberal" is intended to capture this mix.

Overall measures of government effectiveness are relatively high in these welfare states. Legally-mandated social services are broadly accessible, and the poverty-targeting of social assistance is fairly effective. This is not to deny the presence of informal processes in the Polish and Hungarian welfare states. In fact, there is evidence of significant under-the-table payments to health-care personnel, corruption in the social security system, and informal controls over access to social services, particularly in the Polish case.[11] All postcommunist welfare systems in practice mix state, market, and informal mechanisms. But in the informalized cases, informality and the large-scale failure and incapacity of the state to provide mandated benefits or to regulate privatized services is prevalent in all dimensions of welfare provision.

Informalized welfare states have their origins in the extensive infrastructure and overstaffing of the communist-era welfare social sectors. They come from the combination of a large statist inheritance, the collapse of state financing, and weak state control over privatization and regulation of social services. When recessions in these states are prolonged and capacities seriously weakened, developments in social sectors become disconnected from political decision making and are determined by spontaneous and localized processes.

These processes are best illustrated in Russia. There personnel and infrastructure in health and education stayed in place as the state withdrew financing. Social-sector employment became an entrée to informal private income that systematically supplemented that from the state. Large-scale spontaneous privatization of facilities and demands for shadow payments by social-sector elites eroded the state's control over access to social services. De facto income-based limits on access, and the

---

[11]   Conor O'Dwyer, *Runaway State-Building: Patronage Politics and Democratic Development* (Baltimore: Johns Hopkins University Press, 2006).

resulting abstention of low-income strata, became regularized. Private services were legalized but were left largely unregulated, and expenditure shifted rapidly from public toward private. In both health and education, a significant percentage of the population was excluded from basic services that are formally guaranteed by the state. Although Kazakhstan did cut social-sector infrastructure and personnel and processes of "spontaneous privatization" cannot be readily documented there, the rapid decline in state financing and shift toward private expenditure and the evidence of exclusion from access to services (see chap. 5) indicate similar patterns.

Weak taxing and administrative capacities and the presence of large informal economies affect other areas of welfare provision in informalized welfare states. Low social security tax collections (often not due to evasion but to minimal compliance based on understated wages) and low contributions to capitalized pension accounts undermine coverage of social security, excluding workers even in the formal economy or making them eligible only for minimal poverty-level benefits. Social assistance for the eligible poor and unemployed is legally mandated, but payments remain low and fragmentary, and benefits are poorly targeted, accomplishing little poverty relief. Wage and social security laws and other employment-related protections are largely unenforced in the informal sector. These patterns of low tax collection and social security coverage and ineffective social assistance are shown for Russia and Kazakhstan in chapter 5.

Once established, informalization and shadow processes develop their own constituencies among social-sector elites, bureaucracies, and rank-and-file social-sector personnel. Informalized welfare states feature social-sector elites with strong vested interests in parcelized control over access and assets, who resist further reforms or efforts at state regulation. Public-sector salaries remain low, and a recent history of wage arrears and inflation leaves providers distrustful and resistant to reformist initiatives. Tensions may develop, for example, between central social ministries that seek larger regulatory roles and reformist social-sector elites in new formal institutions, but collusion within sectors is more the rule. In sum, powerful constituencies benefit from the informalized system and provide it with a political base among both rank-and-file providers and elite stakeholders.

The shift toward private expenditure and poorly regulated provision of health and educational services accompanied the rapidly growing social stratification in these states. Upper-income strata spent most heavily on privatized health and educational services and eschewed participation in state-sponsored social insurance, disconnecting from the welfare state. Privatized social services developed elite constituencies who favored limitations on the state's financing and provision of welfare. The growing political and economic influence of these elites translated into support for decreased social taxes and other liberalizing policies. Both privatization and informalization gained support against broad, publicly financed state provision of welfare.

INTERNATIONAL INFLUENCES

All the cases considered here (except Belarus) liberalized with direct policy guidance, financial incentives, and pressures from a network of international institutions promoting social insurance markets, privatization, decentralization, and welfare state residualism. Here the World Bank was preeminent, providing a fully articulated liberal model for the transformation of inherited social sectors and intruding deeply into domestic political processes, including the direct involvement of Bank officials in states' policy-planning institutions. The influence of these actors was contingent on domestic political actors and their policy influence.

The IFIs confronted resistance to their interventions. As I showed for Russia, both political and bureaucratic elites opposed Bank-initiated policy changes and protected the flows of resources to their constituents. But IFIs and other institutions that formed part of global social policy networks also connected with reformist political leaders and social-sector professionals, who proved receptive to liberal approaches. The weakness of democratic constraints allowed these technocratic professionals to exercise a great deal of policy influence in some stages of transition. When political constellations favored liberalizing governmental elites, the technocratic professionals were able to shape social policy in Russia, and they had a virtually free hand in Kazakhstan. In East Central Europe, bureaucratic resistance was weaker, but IFI reform agendas had to be negotiated with domestic constituencies. Among the cases considered here, only in Belarus did the government insulate itself from international influences promoting liberalization. In sum, IFI influence was nearly pervasive and not so much weak or strong as conditioned by domestic politics.

The European Union and a European Social Policy might have been expected to have more influence in the accession states, Poland and Hungary. The European Union did indirectly affect welfare provision in these states by rapidly integrating their economies into Western markets, providing the economic underpinnings for recovery, and setting conditions for accession that strengthened democracy and thus democratic bargaining.[12] But in terms of direct influence on programmatic welfare state features, such as universalism of social insurance coverage and income maintenance, the European Union did not present an alternative but largely endorsed liberalizing policies. Nor were effective government-labor bargaining institutions imposed by the European Union. Tripartite bargaining stands at the core of labor's influence on economic, fiscal, and social policy in continental Europe, but the European Union, in its final preaccession reviews of Poland and Hungary, acknowledged that the substance of social partnership had not (yet) been realized.[13] In sum, although there was an expectation that accession would produce a leveling up in social policy, the effects so far have been limited.[14] In terms of the basic programmatic structures of east-central European welfare states, the European Union largely ceded influence to the monetarist organizations.

CONCLUSION

The "politics matters" approach travels relatively well to the postcommunist context. Political institutions and coalitions mattered as postcommunist governments sought to resolve conflicts between old welfare commitments and the demands of market transformation. Economic pressures on inherited welfare states were strongly mediated by domestic factors, especially levels of democratization and the balance between supporters and opponents of welfare reform in state, governmental,

[12] Mitchell Orenstein and Martine Haas, "Globalization and the Future of the Welfare State in Post-Communist East-Central European Countries," in *Globalization and the Future of the Welfare State*, edited by Glatzer and Rueschemeyer, 130–53.

[13] Linda J. Cook, "Globalization and Labor in Eastern Europe and the Former Soviet Union" (draft paper, Watson Institute, Brown University December 2004), citing the 2002 EU report.

[14] John Stephens, "Economic Internationalization and Domestic Compensation: Northwestern Europe in Comparative Perspective," in *Globalization and Future of Welfare States*, edited by Glatzer and Rueschemeyer, 49–74.

and party institutions. While all five postcommunist states retrenched and all except Belarus liberalized, their trajectories of welfare state change varied. Domestic and international promoters of welfare state liberalization proved most effective where representative institutions were weak and executive power strong. Democratic institutions in East Central Europe provided means for societal welfare constituencies to gain compensation and to moderate structural change. Even quite weak democratic institutions in Russia allowed a political coalition to block liberalization for an extended period. Representation of pro-welfare constituencies and coalitions was a key factor in explaining patterns of welfare state change.

At the same time that my research confirms the reach of the "politics matters" approach, it contributes an argument for greater attention to statist-bureaucratic interests in analyzing postcommunist welfare politics. Particularly in the authoritarian and post-authoritarian cases, social-sector elites and bureaucratic stakeholders mattered more than societal constituencies in defending welfare claims, and their place in executive coalitions played an important role in shaping welfare state change. These actors privileged narrow institutional interests in managing public expenditures and administering welfare provision over the broader societal and solidaristic interests that find representation in more democratic polities. Here the politics of welfare became more about elite and statist-institutional interests, though established societal welfare constituencies also benefited from the continuation of social benefits and service provision. Statist-bureaucratic welfare stakeholders are particularly strong in the postcommunist states because of the inheritance of large, centralized welfare systems, but they should also matter for the study of welfare politics in authoritarian and semi-authoritarian states more broadly.

My book also reveals a limitation of the "politics matters" theory for an understanding of developments in contemporary welfare states. Its focus on formal political and economic institutions and policymaking overlooks the processes of corruption and informalization that mattered in the postcommunist context. Especially where states are weak and recessions prolonged, actual developments in social sectors become disconnected from both formal policymaking and market regulation. In these cases, spontaneous and localized processes determine de facto ownership of social-sector institutions and partially control access. Informalization compromises governments' control over distribution of and access to even publicly financed social services, with major implications for welfare provision. Postcommunist states were especially susceptible to such processes because of their extensive inherited social-sector infrastructure and personnel and their sharp economic downturns. However, the growth of informal economies across contemporary states indicates that there may be similar risks in other regions if economic pressures reduce financing of established welfare states.

Index